M-26

Biography of a Revolution

M-26

Biography of a Revolution

by
ROBERT TABER

LYLE STUART · NEW YORK

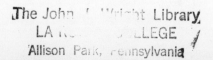

M-26
Biography of a Revolution

At one moment Fidel Castro stands in the wing, bearded, costumed for melodrama, rifle in hand, rehearsing patriotic slogans as he awaits his entrance cue, to outward appearance merely another obscure political adventurer, angrily demanding "liberty or death" and all too evidently on the way to finding the latter.

Then, suddenly, he steps onto the stage of history and springs to full stature, a larger-than-life-sized Cuban hero, cut in the pattern of the Spanish *conquistadores,* defiant, quixotic, crying out for justice and compelling the attention of the world.

Who is he? What does he want? How has he accomplished what he has accomplished? What more will he do?

The revolutionary that I remember from my childhood impressions walked with a .45 pistol in his waistband, and wanted to live on his reputation. He had to be feared. He was capable of killing anyone. He came to the offices of the high functionaries with the air of a man who had to be heard. And in reality, one asked oneself, where was the revolution that these people made? Because there was no revolution, and there were very few revolutionaries.

—FIDEL CASTRO

I

THE NAME of Fidel Castro is known to newspaper readers in Cairo and Khartoum, it is a headline in Pravda; school teachers in Outer Mongolia mention it when they speak of the struggle against "American imperialism," and a million Muscovites turn out to shout the Russian equivalent of *"Cuba sí, Yanquis no!"* and *"Viva Fidel Castro!"* But in the United States, the questions persist, and are evidence of the obfuscation that clouds all aspects of the gathering American Revolution.

There is no novelty in this. The entire history of Cuba is, in American school books, a complicated lie. One must reach the graduate school level to get a glimmering of the truth. Few Americans knew, until well into 1959, that in 1952 a general named Batista seized power in Cuba at pistol point and was recognized by Washington as the legitimate ruler. Even fewer were aware that in 1953 a young attorney named Castro led an assault on a military barracks in Santiago de Cuba and was condemned to serve fifteen years in prison.

The Cuban insurrection of 1956-1958 was popularly regarded in the United States, until its successful conclusion and even for some while afterwards, as an adventure on the operatic scale, a peculiarly Latin-American compound of histrionics, headline hunting, and romantic idealism, sustained not so much by its own virtue as by the blunders of what began to emerge as a brutally stupid and corrupt ruling clique. This was the newspaper view.

Fidel Castro himself was an enigma, a figure of saintly

and slightly sinister presence (Is he a Communist? Will he become a dictator?) passionate, eccentric, capable of exerting great personal magnetism and of attracting a fanatical following but not so surely, in the opinion of "responsible" political analysts, a leader who might direct the destinies of even a small nation—or of a lucrative U.S. economic colony.

The sceptics who chose to view the entire Cuban struggle throughout as a prolonged political skirmish, a noisy tug of war between "in" and "out" parties, judged that he might serve well enough as a cat's-paw for weightier men behind the scenes. Apparently it did not occur to them that there was, in reality, *no one* behind the scenes.

The only significant struggle, amazing in its simplicity, was the drama being enacted under the open sky, plainly visible to anyone who cared to investigate it.

What was in progress that the newspaper accounts and diplomatic reports of the time contrived to conceal? The insurrection that began in early 1957 in the Sierra Maestra mountains of Oriente Province was, however Lilliputian and improbable, the opening campaign of a Cuban civil war and the initial phase of a revolution that is in process, not merely in Cuba, but throughout the western hemisphere.

The fact is that neither Fidel Castro nor the Revolution conform to any stereotype. Both are fresh, new, radical; each has an existence complementary to the other. Fidel* is as much the product of the Cuban Revolution as he is its librettist, stage director, and principal actor.

"We have struck the spark of the Cuban Revolution," he declared in a television interview atop Cuba's highest mountain in April of 1957,† just a few months after his invasion of Oriente Province.

---

* The usage is universal in Cuba; hence: *fidelista, fidelismo,* etc. There seems no reason not to adopt it here.

† Columbia Broadcasting System, Robert Taber and Wendell Hoffman.

At the time he was a hunted fugitive with a price on his head and fewer than one hundred men under his command. Yet he could make his declaration with supreme confidence, knowing that the tinder had already been laid long since, and required only to be kindled by the spark of imagination which he himself was applying.

This is, of course, to reject superficial political interpretations of the Cuban Revolution. "Our movement," says Fidel Castro, "has no relationship with the political past of Cuba."

Who is Fidel Castro? One may anticipate conclusions by declaring at once that he is neither a Communist nor a "tool" of anyone. He describes his political philosophy as "humanism," and might equally well define it as humanitarianism. Whatever else he may be, he is a radical thinker, a pragmatist, supremely a revolutionary: in many ways the prototype of the revolutionaries who even now begin to appear everywhere on the American scene.

He is, and they will be, anti-Yankee and nationalistic to the precise measure that the United States has played, or has seemed to play, the role of exploiter, friend of dictators, employer of gunboat diplomacy, and of what is aptly called, in the modern political slang, "dollar diplomacy."

If the slogans of the Communists are heard in Cuba, and elsewhere in the Americas, increasingly, it is in the absence of better slogans. And if the economic formulae of the Cuban Revolution resemble those of the Russians and the Chinese, that, too, may be a measure of the failure of the theories that support what we like to call "the American way of life," which is not truly *American,* but is only the privileged way of life of a relatively few millions of modern Romans in the United States and in U.S. enclaves abroad.

Who are the Cuban rebels? Fidel Castro Ruz was a young attorney, the third son of a Spanish immigrant who had achieved a modest fortune as a timber merchant and small sugar-cane planter (*colono* is the Cuban term) in the rural municipality of Mayarí, in Oriente Province. Marcelo Fernández was a Cárdenas grocer's son. Abel Santamaría was an accountant. Armando Hart's father was a judge. Frank País was a young schoolmaster in Santiago de Cuba. Camilo Cienfuegos played minor league baseball in Texas. So it goes.

> *Revolution. An instance of great change in affairs, or in some particular thing.* *

We use the word in its full historical sense, to signify the whole of a radical process, the product of long-drawn social, political, and economic developments brought to maturation in a powerful mass movement, expressing the deepest aspirations and most urgent needs of a people, charged with the momentum of their collective experience, articulating their desires, channeling their energies in a common cause, and, once set in motion, irresistible.

Here is the Cuban Revolution. Admittedly it was in this sense not apparent as more than a faint possibility on December 2, 1956, when Fidel, leading an expedition from Mexico, landed at Playa de las Coloradas on the remote southern shore of Oriente with eighty-one reckless followers. Nor had it been apparent when, with the same mad confidence, he led a platoon of clerks and students against a fortress at Santiago, July 24, 1953, in the abortive uprising that gave his *Movimiento Revolucionario 26 de Julio*— MR-26-7—its name. Yet he persisted. And events sustained him.

No doubt the surface phenomena were misleading. On the surface, at least, there was little to distinguish the Castro filibuster of December, 1956, from the hopeless insurrection of July, 1953; nor either of these from scores of other Latin-American political adventures.

* The Oxford Universal Dictionary.

Cuban history, the incredible corruption of Cuban politics, the great wealth at stake, and certain psychological factors—the morbid preoccupation with death, the yearning for eternal glory which are part of the Spanish heritage —all combined to create an atmosphere of conspiracy, adventurism, and make-believe that obscured the deeper struggle. Equally obfuscating were the intricate maneuvers, the endless face-saving devices and graceless compromises of the "out-party" politicos. Post-insurrectionary developments have further complicated the picture.

The Latin-Americans have their idiosyncrasies, like any other people. Their political calendars resemble religious calendars; they are studded with saints' days, the holy days of the martyrs, and this is but part of the *simbolismo* without which no orator expects to hold an audience, no leader to attract followers, no movement to capture the popular imagination.

The founder of a movement invariably establishes a new red-letter day on the calendar, the letter etched in blood, commemorating the day of the heroic martyrdom of Pepe So-and-So, the day of the glorious assault on the citadel of Such-a-Place. Every village in Cuba has its roster of patriotic martyrs; for the most part they were heroic schoolboys, whose obsession seems to have been not so much to *live* gloriously as to *die* gloriously.

Jesús Montané, a studious accountant, relating how he had been on the point of being castrated after the July 26 uprising, remarks: "For us, to die for *la patria* is a satisfaction." And then he adds, as if in afterthought: "Luckily, an officer intervened at that moment."

At an age when schoolboys in the United States are collecting picture cards of baseball players, Cuban boys collect pictures of revolutionary heroes, hurling themselves glory-bound at one or another of the gun-bristling yellow fortresses which were among the principal architectural features of every large and small town on the island.

Cuban youth is brought up on strong doses of history and heroics; the language itself is rhetorical and inflammatory; the universities are political forums in which the boasts and the rhetoric inevitably demand proofs.

Given a history of oppression, such traditions are inevitable. They may even serve some purpose. Yet none of this should be given too much weight in the present context. Countless martyrs have hurled themselves against citadels of tyranny to no effect; countless conspiracies have come to nothing. If the conspiracies and heroics of the Cuban struggle of 1956-1958 came to *something,* it is because there existed a firm social base and an historic necessity.

That Fidel was fully conscious of the social basis upon which his revolutionary career was predicated is beyond question.

His invasion of Oriente Province from Mexico at the end of 1956 was, as previously indicated, not his first assault on the dictatorship, but his second.

The first attempt, in 1953, was a military failure, but it produced certain collateral gains. Fidel, then not yet twenty-seven years old, made an effort to call the country to arms by leading an attack on the second most important military establishment on the island, the Moncada Barracks in Santiago.

During his trial in Santiago in the autumn of 1953, Fidel attributed his failure to accidental factors rather than to lack of popular support. He may have been wrong. Yet the revolutionary manifesto which was the real substance of his nominal defense spelled out clearly his conception of the nature of his support and the basis of his program.

"We had," he declared, "the certainty of being able to count on the people."

The word "people" was carefully defined before the judges in a declamation that had no other intention than to sound a renewed call to rebellion:

By "people" we understand, when we speak of struggle, the great unredeemed mass, those to whom all make promises, and whom all betray; those who long for a country better, more worthy, more just; those who are moved by ancestral desires for justice, having suffered injustice and scorn generation after generation; *those who long for great and wise transformations in the entire order of things,* and who are ready to give in order to achieve when they believe in something or someone, ready to give to the last drop of blood when, above all, they believe sufficiently *in themselves.*

This is surely clear enough. The key phrase is *"transformations in the entire order of things."* But there was more. The rallying cry was specific. It was addressed to:

Seven hundred thousand Cubans without work, who desire to earn their daily bread honestly without having to emigrate in search of livelihood.

Five hundred thousand farm laborers inhabiting miserable shacks, who work four months of the year and starve for the rest of the year, sharing their misery with their children, who have not an inch of land to cultivate, and whose existence inspires compassion in any heart not made of stone.

Four hundred thousand industrial laborers and stevedores whose retirement funds have been embezzled, whose benefits are being taken away, whose homes are wretched quarters, whose salaries pass from the hands of the boss to those of the usurer, whose future is a pay reduction and dismissal, whose life is eternal work and whose only rest is in the tomb.

One hundred thousand small farmers who live and die working on land that is not theirs, looking at it with sadness as Moses did the promised land, to die without possessing it; who, like feudal serfs, have to pay for the use of their parcel of land by giving up a portion of their products; who cannot love it, improve it, beautify it or plant a lemon or an orange tree on it, because they never know when a sheriff will come with the rural guard to evict them from it.

Add to these Cuba's thirty thousand teachers and professors, "so badly treated and poorly paid," twenty thousand small merchants "overwhelmed by debt . . . driven to the auction block by a plague of thieving and venal petty officials"; ten thousand young professionals; doctors, engineers, veterinarians, dentists, pharmacists, journalists "who leave their classrooms with their degrees, filled with hope and eager to enter the struggle, only to find themselves in a dead-end street, all doors closed . . ."

To read the Moncada speech is to become aware of a lively and radical mind at work, seriously grappling with real and not merely semantic problems, concerned with people rather than politics, and providing obvious answers with, as Fidel himself said, "the simple logic of the people."

Feeling himself to be at one with the victims of a decadent political system, Fidel was able to see in Cuba what the politicos were unable or unwilling to recognize as the raw material of a potential mass movement: the landless peasant, the exploited sharecropper, the starving plantation worker, the ill-considered intellectual, the student whose only visible future lay in radical social change.

(Anyone interested in the political future of the Americas need only look about him to see tomorrow's revolutionists. Revolution is already there, existing in social necessity and in the powerful subterranean pressure of the popular will for social justice, mutely seeking expression, lacking only leadership and a symbol to become articulate and urgent. Why so much ingenuous surprise when a corrupt or tyrannical government collapses?)

Revolutionary programs are necessarily tailored to expedience but that need not imply a sacrifice of principle. In 1957, four years after Moncada, Fidel is found describing the Cuban Revolution as "essentially a political struggle," and speaking of such Utopian devices as a provisional government to be nominated by "a special convention made up of the delegates of our various civic organizations: Lions, Rotarians, professional bodies such as the physicians' and engineers' guilds, religious associations, and so forth." *

This has a cosy and comfortable ring; no doubt it was reassuring to those who required reassurance that the Cuban struggle was a "respectable" revolution and was not going to upset any applecarts, other than those of evil-doers, i.e., the dictator and his henchmen.

Moreover, it is true that the Revolution did have broad middle-class support, for the very good reason that—moral issues aside for the moment—the middle classes were being squeezed out of existence by the oppressive forces of military dictatorship and the fiscal policies of an incredibly corrupt and rapacious regime.

Nevertheless, one need only to compare the legislation enacted by the Cuban provisional government in 1959 with the original revolutionary program set forth by Fidel at his trial in 1953 to be impressed with his consistency.

The five revolutionary laws propounded by Fidel at his trial in Santiago, which he said would have been broadcast and implemented immediately, had he been successful, plainly indicate that he was not then thinking in Rotarian terms:

1. Assumption of all legislative, judicial, and executive authority by the Revolution itself, pending elections, subject only to the Constitution of 1940.

2. Land for the landless, through the expropriation of idle lands, and through the transfer of legal title from big owners, renters and landlords to all sharecroppers, tenants and squatters occupying fewer than five caballerias (166⅔ acres)—the former owners to be recompensed by the state.

3. Inauguration of a profit-sharing system under which workers employed by large industrial, commercial, and min-

* Coronet Magazine, February, 1958, Andrew St. George, "A Visit with a Revolutionary."

ing companies would receive thirty per cent of the profits of such enterprises.

4. The establishment of minimum cane production quotas to be assigned to small cane planters supplying a given sugar mill, and the assignment of fifty-five per cent of the proceeds of the crop to the planter, as against forty-five per cent to the mill.

5. Confiscation of all property gained through political malfeasance or in any other illicit manner under all past regimes.

If the foregoing seems prosaic, it is nevertheless necessary to establish, first, that the Cuban Revolution was by no means a manifestation of vaguely idealistic yearnings (the word "idealism" has been much overworked in connection with Cuba), but was directed toward concrete social goals; second, that these goals were, and had every reason to be, the common property of the great "unredeemed" mass of the Cuban people. In other words, that here was the basis of a true, deep-rooted mass movement.

Does the ripeness of the time automatically bring a mass movement into being, or is something more, some catalyst, some agent needed to "strike the spark" of revolution? The Cuban experience suggests that history does, indeed, require a hero.

One sees some of the prescribed qualities for such a hero in the scene recalled by survivors of the yacht *Granma** as, wading through the mangrove marshes of Playa de las Coloradas, under air attack and leading a handful of men to almost certain extinction, Fidel remarks, with a disdainful wave in the direction of the government aircraft: "Look, they are terrified because they know that we have come to destroy them."

* A variation of the familiar American diminutive for grandmother. Reporters, not knowing, or caring, what it meant, originally spelled it "Gramma," and the usage persisted until well into 1959 when someone finally troubled to check.

Herbert L. Matthews, the distinguished correspondent and editorial writer of *The New York Times,* provides this intimate portrait:

A conversation with Fidel Castro is . . . something of a monologue on his part. Words flow like a torrent . . . This much was certain: here was a powerful personality, a powerful physique. Passionate convictions and courage were also obvious enough . . . Standing or sitting, he gets right up close. He cannot bear to sit even two feet from the person he is talking to. His face is inches away; his dark, rich brown eyes are hypnotic in their intensity; one or both hands are on your shoulders or knees and the flow of words comes with such animation and fervor that it is hard to keep one's mind clear to argue or even grasp what he is saying.

Thus the hero. Fidel Castro was, in 1956, the indispensable leader for whom the time was ripe; moreover, he knew it; he was aware of the situation, its requirements, and his own role.

Cuba shook off Spanish colonial rule, after a century of almost continual struggle, at a relatively late date in the evolution of the modern democracies: 1898. The island became a self-governing republic, although by no means an independent one, in 1902.

The Spanish-American War administered the *coup de grace* to a decadent colonial power that had declined past all hope of recovery. The final, supreme effort of the Cuban liberation forces had been in progress for three years; it was rapidly approaching its climax. Revolutionary forces were on the outskirts of Havana, preparing to fight their way into the capital, when the United States, having maintained its traditional neutrality virtually until the end, precipitately intervened.

Thus there is substance to the argument that intervention at this point was, from the Cuban point of view, "a meaningless gesture."

The phrase and the judgment are those of Fidel Castro. Moreover, it is his view that intervention in 1898, however it may have been received at the time, produced positively pernicious results, in preserving the disproportionate wealth and the corrupt institutions of a powerful class of native exploiters, the very merchants and financiers who had *opposed* independence throughout a century of struggle. Given the conditions of 1902, he argues, the modern dictatorship was virtually inevitable.

Colonial Cuba had been a vast plantation and slave market, ruled by and for the benefit of an oligarchy of rich Cubans and Spanish absentee owners. The republican form simply substituted new foreign owners for the displaced Spanish ones, and installed new overseers, a class of scavenging professional politicians whose hire was the loot of a rampant spoils system.

Cuba's first president, Tomas Estrada Palma, was scarcely settled in office before members of his party were involved in a scandal having to do with their efforts to keep him there beyond his legal term. The United States military occupation of 1898-1902 had hardly ended before an open revolt against the Estrada Palma regime brought the troops back again, to remain until 1906. The so-called Negro insurrection brought United States military intervention again in 1912. Charges of election fraud produced another revolt in 1916, against the administration of Mario García Menocal.

The revolt was headed off by a new intervention, in fact if not in name, and after a delay of more than two years, Menocal's hand-picked successor, Dr. Alfredo Zayas, was installed in office, with the aid of the United States. Arriving on the scene in the wake of the financial crash that followed Cuba's "dance of the millions," the great sugar boom of 1918-1920, Zayas inherited a looted and completely empty treasury. Individual Cubans had enriched themselves beyond their wildest dreams by the sale of their land, and in the process had put three-quarters of the nation's sugar industry in the hands of United States investors. But with the collapse of the world sugar market, the country itself was on the brink of economic ruin.

Zaya's successor, General Gerardo Machado y Morales, rode into office in 1925 on a wave of Cuban nationalism, established "a business-like administration, especially devoted to the business classes of Cuba," * sought to prolong his stay in office by re-writing the Constitution, and turned his National Police in business-like fashion to the task of silencing his critics.

Repression only succeeded in driving the opposition underground. The result was the creation of a climate of conspiracy, revolutionary terror, and brutal police counter-terror that all but wrecked the economy, alienated Machado's conservative business backing, and undermined the foreign relations of the regime.

In one of the more forceful applications of the Good Neighbor Policy, President Franklin D. Roosevelt sent a special envoy, Sumner Welles, to seek a solution of the Cuban problem. In the role of conciliator, Welles entered into negotiations with some of the conservative opposition leaders. Three months later, on August 12, 1933, Machado flew into exile. Business-like to the end, he is said to have taken thirty-three suitcases filled with pesos with him.

A wave of anarchy swept the country, hundreds of public and private buildings burned, suspected *machadistas* were shot down in the streets by roving vigilantes, and the hysterical people dipped handkerchiefs in their blood and clamored for more.

The soldiers sulked in their barracks, on the verge of mutiny. The officer corps, divided and fearful, awaited the turn of decisive political developments. Lacking strong sup-

* Leland H. Jenks, in "Our Cuban Colony," Vanguard Press, 1928.

port in any Cuban quarter, the conservative and respectable "government of mediation," which had been formed under the guidance of Sumner Welles proved unequal to the task of governing, or even of restoring public order.

Welles, asking to be recalled from Havana, complained to Washington that the Cuban provisional government came to him, personally, for every decision, great or small.

The situation was made for a strong, ambitious, unscrupulous leader, one who could control the only source of real authority in the country, the Army.

Enter the modern dictator: Fulgencio Batista y Zaldívar, then a sergeant-stenographer in the courts-martial of the Seventh Military District in Havana.

Batista's rise to power and the political and diplomatic interplay of the era are too complex for more than a brief summary here. The essential developments stem from the fact that this obscure Army stenographer, then thirty-two years old, a former railway freight conductor of peasant origin and a professional soldier, was both a shrewd and capable conspirator (a member of the secret society known as the "ABC") and a clever, persuasive army politician, who held in his hand the key to the entire political situation: the non-commissioned officers corps.

The fruit of his efforts, coupled with those of student and civilian conspirators, was the so-called "Sergeants' Revolt" of September 4, 1933.

In a smoothly coordinated coup, the officers were disarmed and relieved of their commands; Batista put himself at the head of the army and placed his troops conditionally at the service of a revolutionary council which, by proclamation, respectfully deposed the short-lived "government of mediation."

Batista and the head of the new *de facto* government, Dr. Ramon Grau San Martín, were denounced equally by Sumner Welles as "extremely dangerous radicals, possibly

Communists." Washington refused to recognize the new regime, which turned immediately, under administrators far more radical than Grau himself ever dreamed of being, to reforming the economy—in ways which worked considerably to the detriment of foreign capital in Cuba.

The new administration inaugurated the eight-hour work day, enacted a minimum wage law, repatriated thousands of Haitian and Jamaican field hands who had been imported to keep sugar plantation labor costs at a minimum, and outlawed the company "script" used by the big sugar corporations during the Machado era to hold half a million Cubans in peonage.

Batista, to whom none of these activities had the slightest appeal, busied himself with his own concern—the consolidation of power. In October his troops laid siege to the big Hotel Nacional in Havana, where some five hundred rebellious army officers had barricaded themselves. The hotel was attacked, and in the course of a day some two hundred officers were killed, most of them after having surrendered.

In the second week of November, the army crushed a powerful counter-revolution, again involving former Machado officers as well as students and other elements. The fighting in Havana lasted for three days before the superior force and organization of the army prevailed.

Shortly thereafter, our special envoy from Washington seems to have had a change of heart with regard to the erstwhile sergeant. Ambassador Welles is found advising the new Army Chief of Staff in December that he appears to be the only man in Cuba capable of governing with a firm hand, and should, in fact, govern.

Within a short while, the same view was impressed on Grau San Martín, the nominal head of the provisional government, and in January Grau sailed off into exile, cheered at the dock on his departure by the Havana populace, but abandoned by his party and obliged by Batista to take a prolonged leave of absence from Cuba and from public life.

There seems to have been no difficulty in obtaining United States diplomatic recognition of Grau's immediate successor, Colonel Carlos Mendieta, first of the provisional or temporary chiefs of state to be installed in office by Batista, as president-maker, during the ensuing seven years.

Batista's role as "enforcer" and manipulator behind the scenes is conceded even by his own public relations agents. During the general strike of March, 1935, involving students, teachers, the professional classes, and some half a million workers (labor on the sugar plantations was *not* involved), the sugar *centrales* had been under martial law. The death penalty had been decreed for strikers and labor agitators—for two months prior to the general strike.

A view of the state of the nation during the Mendieta-Batista stewardship is seen in a contemporary American report* of the experiences of the American Commission to Investigate Labor and Social Conditions in Cuba.

"Batista. . . ," declares the report, "administered a terrible blood purge. Army trucks plunged into every town, and the soldiery fired right and left to terrorize the inhabitants. Every night in the streets of Havana, men were dragged from their homes by soldiers and Batista's police and shot down without trial, without mercy, and left dying in the public highway. Such things are still going on (September, 1935), but the news is suppressed."

History does indeed repeat itself. Testimony taken during the 1959 war crimes trials in Havana, relating to the atrocities of a regime with which the United States maintained cordial relations from the time it seized power by *coup d'état* in 1952 until its collapse on December 31, 1958, and supplied with arms almost until the end, recounts

* Carleton Beals and Clifford Odets, in "Rifle Rule in Cuba," New York, 1935.

details which are scarcely distinguishable from those above. By no coincidence, the author of the massacres of 1935 and those of 1952-1958 was the same: Batista.

Yet if the pages of Cuban history are stained with much blood, marred by all the crimes that can be committed against a people, there is, nevertheless, much of which Cubans can be justly proud.

The blood has been spilled in ceaseless struggle against oppression; corruption and malfeasance stemmed from the abuse of democratic forms, but at least the *forms* existed. It cannot truly be said that the Cuban people passively endured Batista during his years as enforcer and political strong man: they struggled to the best of their means and knowledge to free themselves, and in the end they were successful.

When, in 1952, Batista recaptured by undisguised force the authority that he had formerly held through political skill and duplicity, that was the final straw, the end of patience, the one affront which not even the most conservative of honest Cubans could swallow.

Earlier, making a bid for popular acceptance that comes as a surprise in view of his record, Batista sought and won a legal term as president in 1940, after striking a bargain with the Cuban Communists, for whom he obtained a place on the electoral ballot under the designation of *Partido Socialista Popular*.

When his term expired, Batista got out. There is evidence that he was under pressure from military cohorts to set aside the returns of the 1944 election, in which his hand-picked candidate to succeed him was defeated by Grau San Martín, who had returned from exile and had lost to Batista in the previous election. Batista wisely resisted the temptation.

Now it was his turn to go into exile. Grau's first act was to reorganize the army, so as to curb its political influence.

In other respects, his administration was a disappointment to those who had supported him, in that it failed to carry forward the social program promised by his earlier brief occupancy of the presidential palace.

Grau was succeeded in 1948 by another former ABC revolutionary and a member of his own cabinet, Carlos Prío Socarrás. Of Prío, nothing more need be said at this point than that he had all but completed his term in office when he was abruptly deposed by the Batista coup of March 10, 1952.

The circumstances were simple enough, nor did the coup come entirely unheralded. Some while before, a Miami newspaper, hearing rumors of an impending coup, had obtained from Batista a categorical denial of his intention to seek power in any other manner than by legal election.

Batista had returned to Cuba nearly two years before, after winning a seat in the Senate, *in absentia,* during the mid-term elections of 1950. He presented himself as a presidential candidate in the 1952 elections, scheduled for June, opposing Carlos Hevia, the candidate of the *Auténtico* party of Grau and Prío (*Partido Revolucionario Cubano*) and Dr. Roberto Agramonte, of the *Ortodoxo* party (*Partido del Pueblo Cubano*).

On the first of March, a straw ballot of Cuban electoral sentiment disclosed that Batista was running far behind both Hevia and Agramonte. The latter, representing a party with a militant social and economic reform program, founded by a liberal former *auténtico,* Eduardo Chibás, seemed almost certain to win.

Nine days later, on the night of March 10th, Batista entered the military headquarters at Camp Columbia on the outskirts of Havana—pistol in hand, a cartridge in the chamber, according to his own account—and took control of both the army and the government. The *coup d'état* was conducted with the aid of the same military officers who had supported Batista prior to 1940. The means are not, at the moment, of paramount importance. It is the effects with which we are presently concerned.

Batista's explanation was that he had acted to "preserve the peace," having learned, he said, that Prío had been planning a coup of his own, to retain power. The argument deceived no one. There was some initial resistance in Havana. Troops dispersed the Congress, fired on the palace guard, and seized the University, where the students were preparing to fight in support of the constituted government. In Santiago de Cuba, the officers commanding the strategic Cuartel Moncada refused to surrender their command until some hours after the coup, when it had become clear that the legal president, Prío, had no intention of resisting the usurper. The weakness of the regime had invited destruction; when it came there was nothing to resist it. Had Prío sought support, he might have found it, would surely have found it in the *Ortodoxo* party if not in his own party, and saved the country. Instead, he took political sanctuary in the Mexican Embassy. Three days later, he left the country under a safe conduct pass.

The populace was stunned. There was consternation and bitterness especially in the ranks of the *ortodoxos,* who had been sure of winning the election. However, there was no leadership to form an organized opposition. The only vehement public protest of record in the days immediately following the coup was made by a twenty-six-year-old attorney from Oriente Province, a recent law graduate of the University who had been a congressional candidate on the *Ortodoxo* ticket.

The disappointed candidate filed a brief with the Court of Constitutional Guarantees demanding that the seizure of power by Batista be declared unconstitutional. At the Urgency Court he filed an even stronger brief, demanding that criminal penalties be imposed on the usurper under the existing laws of the Republic for inciting armed insurrection, sedition, interference with an ordained election, and other high crimes, punishable in the aggregate, according to the brief, by "more than one hundred years of imprisonment."

The petition was not a mere legal maneuver, but in substance an ardent appeal to reason and to civic conscience:

If in the face of this series of flagrant crimes, he (Batista) is not punished, how will this court later try any citizen for sedition or contempt against an unlawful regime, product of unpunished treachery? It is understood that it would be absurd, inadmissible, monstrous in the light of the most elemental principles of justice.

I do not prejudge the thought of the court, I only expound the reasons that support my determination to make this complaint.

I resort to logic, I pulse the terrible reality, and the logic tells me that if there exist courts in Cuba, Batista should be punished, and if Batista is not punished, and continues as master of the state, president, prime minister, senator, major general, civil and military chief, executive power and legislative power, owner of lives and lands, then courts do not exist; they have been suppressed.

If that is so, say so as soon as possible, hang up your robes, resign your post; let those who legislate, the very same ones who execute, administer justice; let a corporal sit at once with his bayonet in the august courtroom of the Magistrate. I do not commit any offense by expounding thus with the greatest sincerity and respect; to keep quiet is bad, to resign oneself is tragic, absurd, without logic, without norms, without sense, and without justice.

The document was signed: Fidel Castro Ruz, attorney.

The passion for justice is in essence a cry for order in the universe. No one actually hoped to deflect bullets with legal briefs in Cuba in 1952, nor to persuade an illicit regime to condemn itself. Fidel admitted that his brief was, on the face of it, absurd. Yet it was consistent with his almost naive faith in logic and with the passionate preoccupation with justice which is the persistent theme of all that he has written and said, of all of his actions. The brief, however, calculated, was more than a political appeal. It was sincere, and even necessary.

"If I had failed to follow the course of the law," he said at a later date, "how could I have been justified in doing what I had to do? How would I have been better than the dictator? We had first to appeal to the courts, if only to demonstrate that no courts existed, and then to the law itself, which comes from the people, and is above the courts which are its instruments. It is not I who violated the law, but Batista who attempted to destroy the law by setting himself above both people and law—and so destroyed himself."

The courts refused to act, as it had been obvious that they would.

The way was now open for a direct appeal to the people, a call to arms. Enter: the rebels.

*You could see this . . . That he was to do great things
. . . That he is for great things, not the ordinary thing.*
—REVEREND AMANDO LLORENTE, S.J.

II

JULY 26, 1953: birthday of a revolution.

In Santiago de Cuba, more than six hundred miles east of Havana, the annual carnival was in its closing hours when, with what he called "magnificent coordination," Fidel Castro launched his first military assault against the dictatorship of Fulgencio Batista.

A buzzard's-eye view of Santiago sets the scene: cobbled streets rising sharply and spider-webbing away from a blue-water port, wharves, cranes, warehouses, a railroad yard, a market place, parks, the aimless black dots that are people, just now stirring in the awakening city, the flashing rectangles that are automobiles, the immobile squares of dwellings and commercial buildings. On the outskirts there is a cement plant, a brewery, an oil refinery across Santiago Bay; at the mouth of the beautiful harbor, standing high on a cliff at the edge of the Caribbean, are the crumbling ruins of the ancient Spanish fortress called El Morro.

Such details provide some of the "feel" of the provincial capital; more, they reveal the sweep of the imagination that was able to see this busy, sprawling complex as a battlefield, a military map stripped of all but its essentials—strongpoints, avenues of access and of escape, obstacles to be avoided or surmounted, cover to be utilized by an invading army that was in actuality no more than a platoon of untested volunteers, armed only with shotguns, .22 caliber rifles, and the daring to challenge a regiment of soldiers.

The key to the military map has yet to be seen. It lies in the northwest quarter of the city, on high ground close to a modern highway, flanked by the dazzling white Palace of Justice and a large, new, then almost empty hospital: the high-walled enclosure, the parapets and guard towers, flat-roofed yellow barracks and blockhouses of Cuartel Moncada: huge, imposing, anachronistic, the second most important military establishment on the island of Cuba.

At dawn on the 26th of July, a column of cars entered the city from the East, traveling swiftly with the rising sun along the palmetto-lined highway from Siboney Beach, past San Juan Hill with its great live oaks and iron cannon, past the well-kept lawns and expensive modern homes of Vista Alegre, along the four-lane avenue called Victoriano Garzón, and on toward the sleeping fortress of Moncada.

There were twenty automobiles in all, and in them, one hundred twenty-five armed fighters, two women, a doctor, and Fidel Castro.

Their immediate objective: a little-used gate on the side street called Calle Moncada, guarded only by a few sleepy-eyed sentries; once inside, the vital armory with its store of automatic weapons, ammunition and grenades, the military radio station, and then, one by one, the barracks and administration buildings, defended during the week-long carnival festivities by only five hundred of the normal contingent of twelve hundred troops of the Maceo Regiment.

Fidel Castro says, with considerable understatement, that he attacked Moncada rather than Camp Columbia in Havana because he was "not strong enough" for the latter. There was another reason. He was *sure* of Oriente Province, his own birthplace and cradle of all of the wars of independence, where, he said, even the cocks "crow like buglers sounding reveille," and where, he believed, the people required only arms to be put at once on a war footing.

His purpose was to seize the armory with all speed, exchange the shotguns and light sporting rifles with which his untried revolutionaries were armed for military weapons, broadcast an appeal to the people, and proceed at once to establish a popular militia in support of a revolutionary government, with Santiago as its capital.

A coordinated attack in the city of Bayamo, one hundred miles to the west and north of Santiago, was intended as the essential first step toward establishing advance outposts along the strategic river Cauto, to repel any invasion from the western provinces.

The uprising was not, then, at least not in its conception, a mere suicide attack prompted by psychological and political motives, but an open declaration of war against an illegitimate military regime. Nor was the plan of operations as impractical as it has been made to appear. It came within an ace of succeeding. It may be as well that it did not, for it could have split Oriente off from the rest of the country and plunged Cuba into a bloody civil war for which it was then totally unprepared.

The plan had been in preparation, in its general outlines if not in any detail, for more than a year, financed and manned by revolutionary cells in Havana, in the western-most province of Pinar del Río, and in Santiago itself.

The founders, other than Fidel, were Jesús Montané and Abel Santamaría, both young office workers in Havana; Santamaría's sister Haydée; a young woman attorney, Dr. Melba Hernández; and a forty-five-year-old Havana physician, Dr. Mario Muñoz. They were joined early in 1952 by others: Pedro Miret, an engineer's assistant in the Havana department of public works, a Miami restaurateur, Ernesto Tizol, among the leaders.

Fidel's younger brother, Raúl, then twenty-two years old, was one of the last to join the group, returning from a students' tour of Europe in the summer of 1953.

Taken together, the conspirators represented a fair cross-section of the great mass of politically-conscious younger white collar workers, professionals, students, middle-class intellectuals, who had been abruptly disenfranchised by the Batista coup of 1952.

With the exception of Dr. Muñoz, none of them had yet reached his thirtieth year. For them, the Batista coup represented a sudden stop sign in the path of all of their hopes, their ambitions, their careers. Moreover, it was the ultimate insult.

One recalls a young dentist in Bayamo, in 1957, trying to explain the reasons for his involvement in the revolution, at the risk of his practice, his home, his family, his life, saying, helplessly: "I cannot tell you what it is—only that I cannot accept, I cannot accept."

Their cause was plain enough. When political recourse failed, they turned to military means. Until virtually the eleventh hour, the plan of attack and even the military objective itself remained the secret of Fidel and a few top action leaders.

The assault on Moncada was well timed. The people in the streets, early risers and a few all-night holiday makers, scarcely noticed the motor caravan entering the city. At Moncada, most of the troops not on holiday leave were abed.

The attack was set for precisely 5:15 A.M. The battle plan, like that of any commando action, necessarily left something to chance. For a time, fortune seemed to be with the raiders.

At an intersection ten blocks from the fortress, an army patrol jeep with its mounted .30 caliber machine gun waited impatiently as the column of automobiles rolled by. The rebels were clad in the identical khaki of the Cuban Army, and the encounter was without incident. In nervous parody of the carnival spirit, the insurrectionists saluted their ostensible brothers-in-arms, the four soldiers in the jeep, and received a casual salute in return.

Two blocks from Moncada, the fourth car of the caravan

turned sharply to the right, leading the cars behind it down narrow Calle Moncada, toward the third gate of the fortress, where the five sentries on duty were sleepily awaiting the morning change of the guard.

The three cars which had been in the lead continued up the gentle rise of Avenida Garzón, swung right at a traffic circle, and headed down the broad Avenue of the Liberators. Moncada was a scant two blocks distant, on the east side of the avenue. A block short of the fortress, the third car pulled to the curb before the three-story Palace of Justice, where a squad led by Raúl Castro was to occupy the flat roof, commanding the fort.

The other two cars in the first section, carrying fourteen rebels led by Abel Santamaría, Fidel's second-in-command, headed for the Civil Hospital across the avenue from Moncada, where, under the direction of Dr. Muñoz, they were to prepare to receive casualties. The two women, Haydée Santamaría and Melba Hernández, accompanied the doctor, to serve as nurses.

The first assault car had by now reached Moncada's Gate 3. The driver, Renato Guitart, curbed the car carefully, so as not to block the entrance. Fidel Castro, driving the second car, held back the remainder of the column.

Guitart, Jesús Montané, and Ramiro Valdés scrambled out of the front seat of the "suicide" car and approached the gate. While the sentries eyed them lazily, Valdés abruptly seized the heavy chain hanging across the roadway, and deftly disconnected it. At the same moment, Guitart and Montané cried sharply: "Attention! The General is coming!"

The ruse was successful. Before the sentries could recover from their surprise, pistols were thrust against their bellies, their weapons were snatched from their hands. Inside the gate, the sergeant of the guard moved toward the alarm button in the sentry box. A shot sounded. The sergeant hit the alarm button as he fell, and the heavy clangor of the bell began to signal the opening of the attack.

The assault had not yet failed. There was this instance of success. The gate was taken. Guitart dashed inside and headed for the nearest building, seeking the radio station to broadcast the report that Moncada had fallen and to read a proclamation announcing the purposes of the revolution.

Montané and Valdés herded their prisoners into the nearest barracks inside the gate, expecting Fidel now to lead the rebel motor column into the camp.

Instead, there was a fatal delay. The column had stopped short of a side street intersection forming a "T" with the street that paralleled the fortress wall. From the side street, an army patrol jeep suddenly appeared, screeching to a halt at the intersection, intercepting the motor column. A young lieutenant stepped out of the jeep and advanced on Fidel's car, unholstering his automatic pistol as he came.

(Later, at his trial, Fidel was to call this one of the chief tactical failures of the attack. "The clash with the patrol—totally casual, for twenty seconds earlier or twenty seconds later it would not have been at this point—gave them time to alert the camp. Otherwise it would have fallen into our hands, for the gate was already in our power.")

Blocked by the patrol, Fidel shouted a quick command to one of the youths in the rear seat of his car, Gustavo Arcos: "Take care of the lieutenant!" Then, without waiting, he tried to take the car around the jeep. The automobile bucked violently as he stamped on the accelerator. Arcos, half out of the machine, leveling his rifle at the army officer, was knocked from his feet as the rear door slammed against him. The lieutenant raised his pistol and fired. The slug knocked the boy back again. Then, as he still struggled to rise, a burst from the mounted machine gun on the jeep, ripping through the automobile, caught him full in the body.

The automobile was empty now, except for Arcos, lying half in, half out of it, unconscious and bleeding. The other cars in the column had also been quickly emptied, the rebels scrambling for cover behind the cars or in the doorways of buildings along the street. And now rifle and automatic fire began to come from the walls and turrets of Moncada itself, as the battle was joined.

The Civil Hospital on the other side of the fortress, across the Avenue of the Liberators, had already been occupied, without opposition. Nearby, the Palace of Justice was quickly taken according to plan. On the sidewalk outside, Raúl Castro seized and disarmed a soldier who had been on his way to the fortress. Raúl's second-in-command, Lester Rodríguez, banged at the door of the Palace and was admitted by a blinking, bare-chested sergeant, still buttoning his trousers. The rebels hustled their prisoners through the high-vaulted lobby. As they reached the elevators, the first shots from Moncada were heard.

"*Que pasa?*" asked the bewildered sergeant.

"Batista has fallen; come with us," Raúl answered with authority.

From the third floor they mounted the stairway to the roof, and stood aside for a moment while Raúl shot the lock from the outside door with the sergeant's big nickel-plated revolver. Then, pushing out onto the roof, they rushed to the parapet commanding Moncada to see the battle below.

The scene that presented itself was a shambles. Fidel crouched by the now deserted Army jeep, waving his arms desperately, urging his men forward through Gate 3. The rebels were firing their pitifully inadequate .22 caliber rifles and shotguns from whatever cover they could find—from behind cars, at the corners of houses, from hedges, fences, doorways.

Renato Guitart lay dead at the door of the radio station. Gustavo Arcos, riddled with machine-gun bullets but mirac-

ulously alive, was being carried to a car. Montané and
Valdés were in the barracks nearest the gate, holding their
original five prisoners there, along with some fifty other
soldiers who had been surprised in their sleep.

Fidel appeared briefly in the barracks. More rebels entered the compound, about fifty in all running a gauntlet of
intense automatic fire to reach the first building inside the
gate. A half dozen men dashed up an exterior stairway toward what they thought to be the armory. It proved to be a
barber shop.

The rebels both inside and outside the fortress were now
pinned down by machine-gun and rifle fire from the walls
and from emplacements within the fortress. A .30-caliber
machine gun firing from the parade ground in front of the
main administration building swept Gate 3 and the nearby
buildings where the rebels had taken cover.

From the roof of the Palace of Justice, Raúl's snipers were
able to dominate a concrete emplacement immediately below them, at the southwest corner of the fortress, commanding Gate 3, and they saw at least one soldier there fall beneath their fire. Two soldiers trying to climb a steel ladder
leading to a .50-caliber machine gun atop the two-story
officers' club were likewise killed by snipers atop the Palace.
But Raúl's marksmen were unable to see the sandbagged
machine gun on the parade ground, which continued to
sweep the gate with a deadly fire.

"When I was convinced that all our efforts to take the
fort were useless," relates Fidel, "I commenced to withdraw
our men in groups of eight or ten. The withdrawal was pro-
tected by six snipers who, under the command of Pedro
Miret and Fidel Labrador, heroically blocked the route of
the Army."

The battle had begun at 5:15 A.M. It was 7:00 when the
withdrawal started. Fidel Labrador lost an eye in the subsequent delaying action; Miret was also wounded; Fidel

Castro's secretary, Hildo Flatus, was killed. Nevertheless, the small squad of marksmen managed to hold some five hundred troops at bay for nearly four hours. It was 11 o'clock when the first troops finally ventured through Gate 3.

Meanwhile, runners had been sent to the Palace of Justice and to the Civil Hospital to inform the leaders there of Fidel's decision to abandon the assault. They never arrived.

At the Palace, Raúl Castro, observing for himself the course of the battle, did not await orders. With his squad, he left the roof, descended to the lobby, and was about to leave when a police van drew up outside. There was a heavy pounding on the door. Flinging it open, Raúl snatched an automatic pistol from the hand of an astonished sergeant and informed him that he and his mixed patrol of fifteen soldiers and policemen were under arrest.

The prisoners were quickly disarmed and herded into a small office. Then, in the cavernous lobby, the disheartened rebels discussed their course of future action. For the moment, inside, they were safe. Outside, the shooting seemed to have stopped. The Moncada assailants were fleeing, discarding their uniforms and fading away into the city, or driving off, desperately, in the cars that had brought them there. For the rebels, it was now an enemy city.

The hushed debate in the lobby of the Palace of Justice continued until Lester Rodríguez abruptly reached his own decision. Leaning his shotgun against the wall, he walked slowly out of the door. The street was empty, and he continued on his way, toward his home in the city, without a backward glance.

Raúl Castro watched his second-in-command go. Then he, too, went to the door, started to follow Rodríguez down the street and, changing his mind, turned toward the railroad tracks. His home was in the municipality of Mayarí, far to the north. He set out in that direction, walking along the railroad ties, and was picked up by soldiers the next day at Dos Caminos de San Luís, about forty miles from Santiago.

The men he had left in the Palace got back into the automobile in which they had arrived and, driving through a city which still awaited news of the battle, believing it to have been a mutiny of soldiers at Moncada, they found sanctuary in a private home on the other side of the city.

Others were not so fortunate. At the Civil Hospital, the first word of the withdrawal from Moncada was brought by fleeing rebels seeking shelter. When troops and police finally entered the hospital, they found Abel Santamaría and twenty revolutionaries there, bandaged and in hospital gowns or otherwise disguised as patients, attended by Dr. Muñoz. The two rebel nurses, Haydée Santamaría and Melba Hernández, were in the children's ward, quieting the young patients there.

For a moment, it appeared that the soldiers would be deceived. Then an informer approached them. There was a brief conference. The rebels were routed from their beds, and herded out of the hospital.

Dr. Muñoz was the first of the prisoners to die. A few paces from the hospital, he was thrust roughly ahead of the group. An officer shouted: "Shoot him. He escapes!" There was a burst of submachine-gun fire, and the physician lay in a spreading pool of his own blood.

Elsewhere in the city, the hunt for the fugitives from Moncada was in full cry. Fidel and a part of the rebel assault force fled through the city in automobiles, back to their base of operations on an ostensible chicken farm near Siboney, about ten miles south of the city. Others took their chances in Santiago, finding refuge in the homes of relatives or friends. In some instances, they were saved by complete strangers.

Total rebel casualties at Moncada had come to five dead, four wounded. Army losses totaled twenty-two killed, fifty-seven wounded. Late in the day, an order came from Havana to correct the disparity.

At his subsequent trial, Fidel charged that specific instructions had been delivered by an emissary from the capital, from Batista himself: ten rebel lives for every soldier killed.

Abel Santamaría was one of those who died under torture at Moncada, his eyes gouged out, while in an adjoining cell his sister, Haydée, listened to his shrieks of agony and steadfastly refused to give the information that was sought of her, the betrayal of her comrades.

For reasons still not entirely clear, but presumably to discount any imputation of popular unrest and further to justify the *coup d'état* of 1952, strenuous efforts were made to attach responsibility for the Oriente uprising to former President Prío. Santamaría died stubbornly refusing to collaborate in manufacturing evidence to this effect, and the same fate befell a number of his comrades. Subsequent medical evidence, attested by Dr. Manuel Urrutia Lleó,* then President of the vacation court of Santiago, disclosed that many of those who died had previously been tortured, castrated, and otherwise mutilated.

Troops were combing the countryside in pursuit of Fidel and the others who had escaped the city, and the situation provided an opportunity for the army to dispose of rebel prisoners.

"Before dawn groups of men—already deformed by torture—were removed from the camp (Moncada), their hands tied and their mouths taped," Fidel charged at his trial. "They were taken in automobiles to Siboney, La Maya, Songo, and other places to be killed in solitary fields. Later these deeds were recorded as deaths in combat with the army. This they did during several days, and very few

* Provisional President during the first six months of 1959. Resigned July 17. See Chapter XIII.

prisoners of all those who were arrested survived. Many were forced to dig their own graves."

A small-scale attack on the military *cuartel* at Bayamo, involving only twenty-seven members of the Castro group, had met with the same failure, and the army took similar reprisals in that zone. Two of the participants in the Bayamo attack were found hanged, along the highway from Manzanillo to Bayamo, ten days after the attack. Near Río Cauto, at Barrancas, the bodies of three other insurgents were found at the bottom of a well.

In all, some sixty rebels taken prisoner in the Santiago zone and at least ten captured following the Bayamo attack were killed before the intervention of Monsignor Enrique Pérez Serantes, the archbishop of Santiago, brought an end to the slaughter. The archbishop obtained the promise of Colonel Alberto Del Río Chaviano, commander of the zone of operations, to spare the lives of any fugitives who surrendered, and he went personally into the countryside to accept their surrender.

Twenty of the thirty-eight men who had fled to Siboney with Fidel had surrendered prematurely, and suffered the consequences. Eighteen men followed Fidel into the coastal mountains east of Santiago.

"For a week," he relates, "we occupied the high part of the Cordillera de la Gran Piedra and the army occupied the foothills. We could not descend, and they could not decide to come up after us. It was not then the weapons, but only hunger and thirst that vanquished the last resistance. I had to go on breaking the men into small groups. Some were able to infiltrate through the army lines; others surrendered to Monsignor Pérez Serantes.

"When only two companions remained to me, José Suárez and Oscar Alcalde—all three of us totally exhausted—at dawn on Saturday the first of August a force under the command of Lieutenant (Pedro) Sarría surprised us while we were sleeping. The slaughter of the prisoners had already ceased because of the tremendous reaction it had provoked in the citizens, and this officer, a man of honor, prevented some killers from assassinating us there in the field with our hands tied."

A few similar acts of gallantry relieve a generally gloomy and depressing record of atrocity and cowardice.

Three wounded rebels—Pedro Miret, Fidel Labrador, Luís Crespo—were saved by an army captain who removed them from the military to the civil hospital, literally at pistol point, after soldiers in the former institution had tried to kill them by injecting air and camphor into their veins.

The director of the Colonia Española, a large private clinic, refused to allow an army patrol to take two seriously wounded rebels from that establishment, and was supported by his staff physicians, who said they would die before they would permit any such thing.

Fidel Castro was particularly fortunate in his captor, Lieutenant Sarría. The two men had been classmates at the University of Havana, and Sarría entertained warm memories of Fidel as a popular student leader and president of the FEU, the federation of university students. Before Fidel could identify himself, Sarría warned him in a whisper not to disclose his name, and then ordered him removed to the civil jail in Santiago, the *Vivac*, so saving his life. Later the officer confirmed that he had been under orders to kill Fidel in the field, if possible, and otherwise to bring him to Moncada, where he would have met the fate of many of the other prisoners. A few weeks after Fidel's apprehension, Sarría was dismissed from the army as "unreliable."

From the *Vivac*, Fidel was transferred to the penitentiary at Puerto Boniato, near Santiago, to await trial. Again he was fortunate. The military superintendent of the prison, Lieutenant Jesús Yanes Pelletier, said later that he had been ordered to rid the state of an embarrassment: in a word, poison Fidel or otherwise dispose of him. Pelletier refused, and was also dismissed, after being jailed for several weeks.

The Moncada insurrectionists went to trial in the Palace of Justice on September 21st. Altogether, there were one hundred twenty-two defendants—including many who had had no knowledge whatever of the uprising. Included were a number of supporters and former officials of the ousted Prío government, to whom Batista was still trying to attach responsibility for the plot.

Fidel repudiated the effort in his initial appearance, claiming total responsibility for himself and for the prisoners who had actually participated in the assault—"those young men (who) love the liberty of *la patria* as I do, and fight for it."

He demonstrated that the uprising had been financed entirely by members of the revolutionary movement headed by himself, listing their names and contributions, to the sum of $16,480, and the arms which had been purchased singly or a few at a time from sporting goods shops and from individuals—target rifles, shotguns, pistols, some actual antiques "from the time of Buffalo Bill."

The trial was recessed. When it resumed on the 26th of the month, Fidel was not present. It was announced that he was ill. The refutation came immediately. Melba Hernández, the attorney, stepped forward to present a brief which had been written by Fidel himself, smuggled from his cell at Puerto Boniato, denouncing the plot to silence him, and demanding a hearing.

He had his hearing, finally, on October 16th, ten days after the mass trial of the other defendants had been concluded. The conspiracy of silence persisted. Batista had suspended civil guarantees and imposed an iron censorship on the press at the time of the uprising.

"Even so," Fidel said later, with understandable pride, "they were afraid that my words would cause a riot in the courtroom, and that even my guards would mutiny and turn against them."

Fidel's trial was conducted, not in the Palace of Justice, but in an anteroom of the provincial hospital. More than one hundred soldiers were posted in the corridors, but the only witnesses present in the makeshift courtroom, not attached to the court, were six short-hand reporters. With censorship still in effect, there was no danger that they would publish anything of an inflammatory nature.

Fidel's defense was simplicity itself. The indictment against him charged conspiracy to raise an insurrection and actual rebellion against the constitutional powers of the state. The essence of his argument was that, with the coup of March 10, 1952, the powers of the state had been usurped; hence that the acts cited failed to fit the specifications of the indictment.

In other words, there had been no insurrection against *constitutional* powers, as defined by law, but rather there had been a legitimate struggle to overthrow a usurper, in *support* of the Constitution of 1940, which clearly stated the right of the people to defend themselves against tyranny.

The bulk of his discourse was devoted to other matters; he said that he had no intention to be bound by the narrow legalism of the indictment, and go around and around it, "like a slave turning a millstone."

He claimed, rather, the privilege of outlining the entire history and strategy of the insurrection, from its inception, stating its purposes, which he said were both political and social.

As to the causes of failure, he said he felt that it had been a mistake to divide the unity of his command, by sending some of his best leaders and fighters to the hospital, to the Palace of Justice, and to Bayamo. He blamed the accident at Moncada, the clash with the patrol, and another accident

—the fact that four carloads of rebels had become lost in the city and had never reached the fortress.

Given a few more armed men, he said, or twenty hand grenades, "perhaps we would have saved this honorable court so much bother."

His summation was not a defense but an attack on the regime, citing the crimes committed in its name, denouncing its pretensions of legitimacy, calling on the judges themselves to resign.

The three judges listened for five hours. Then they condemned him to be imprisoned for fifteen years in the military penitentiary on the Isle of Pines.

We come, here, to the real beginning of Fidel Castro's political career. The Oriente uprising had lifted him to national prominence. Even from the military prison on the Isle of Pines, where he was put in isolation because of his "dangerous" influence on the other political prisoners, he was able to make his voice heard.

Despite censorship and the reluctance of the paid press* to oppose the government which subsidized it, Fidel's popularity was such that when former President Grau San Martín appeared at an *Auténtico* party rally in Santiago in 1954, the crowd cheered not Grau but the prisoner, shouting *"Viva Fidel Castro!"* and demanding his release from prison.

The Moncada and Bayamo attacks had greatly accelerated the revolutionary ferment in the country, and efforts were being made to exploit it. From his exile in Miami, former president Prío daily denounced the Batista regime; and the denunciations were materially supported by a flow of clandestine arms into Cuba which only the efficiency of

* Government subsidies to the newspapers ranged from twelve thousand pesos monthly to as much as thirty thousand, and individual journalists received separate stipends.

the Cuban intelligence service kept from being put to use.

The old-line politicians in Cuba, fearful of more radical solutions, or merely seeking a share of the spoils, were pressing for participation in the government. The Batista regime, seeking a "safe" compromise which would legitimize its position, made some steps in this direction by lifting censorship, restoring civil guarantees, and preparing for general elections.

There was increasing pressure from the *Ortodoxo* party and elsewhere for a general amnesty of political prisoners, and the Batista government was not entirely unresponsive. A scandal was produced when Batista's then minister of interior, Ramon Hermida, visited Fidel in prison, even before he had completed the first year of his sentence. Hermida was denounced by his own undersecretary, Rafael Díaz Balart,* for conferring with the author of "the criminal attack against the Army."

Fidel's uncompromising position with regard to collaboration of any sort with an illicit regime was set forth in a letter to a Havana newspaper columnist, Luis Conte Agüero, in March of 1955:

How strange has been the conduct of the regime toward us. They call us assassins in public and gentlemen in private.*** One day an army colonel with his full staff gives us a cigar, offers me a book, and everyone is very courteous. Another day, three cabinet ministers, smiling, affable and respectful, appear. One of them says: "Don't worry, this will pass over. *I* planted many bombs and I used to organize ambushes in the Country Club against Machado. I, too, was once a political prisoner." ***

In order to obtain an amnesty, a prior agreement must be made to respect the regime. The cynics who suggest such a thing assume that after twenty months of imprisonment and

---

* Complicating the picture, Díaz Balart happened to be Fidel's own brother-in-law, a fact which made them no better friends. Fidel was divorced by Díaz Balart's sister, Mirtha, in 1957. They had been married five years.

exile, the people of this island (Isle of Pines) have lost their integrity under the excessive rigor imposed on us.

Comfortably entrenched in their luxurious positions, where they would like to live forever, they are so base as to talk in such terms to those who, a thousand times more honorable than they, are buried in the cells of a penitentiary. The writer has now been sixteen months isolated in a cell, but feels exceptionally strong, strong enough to reply with dignity.***

If we were to believe that a change of circumstances and atmosphere, comprising positive Constitutional guarantees, were to demand a change of attitude in our struggle, we would make that change exclusively as a sign of respect to the interests and wishes of the nation, but never as a cowardly and shameful agreement with the government. And if that agreement is demanded of us in order to gain our freedom, we say point-blank: no.

There was continued pressure for an amnesty. Grau San Martín had opposed Batista in the nominal "elections" of November, 1954, and had withdrawn at the eleventh hour, charging election fraud. Batista's inauguration for a four-year term in February of 1955 changed nothing. There was continuing clamor on all sides for a peaceful political solution, and—perhaps to gain time—Batista finally agreed to a so-called "Civic Dialogue" in which representatives of all of the political factions were to present their various formulae. Each contained the same inescapable conclusion: nothing could be settled without new and genuinely free, honest elections.

No such solution was acceptable to Batista. He was, however, at length maneuvered into agreeing to an amnesty, and in May the necessary legislation was approved by the Congress and signed.

Fidel was released from prison on May 15th, 1955, with his brother Raúl, who had been sentenced to thirteen years' imprisonment, and all of the other participants of the Oriente uprising still alive, who had not already been

freed. The liberated prisoners were met on the Isle of Pines
by Haydée Santamaría and Melba Hernández, who had
been released some while earlier. It was one of the rare
occasions when the indomitable Haydée was seen to weep.

In Havana the heroes of Moncada were greeted by the
national committee of the *Ortodoxo* party and the officers
and virtually the entire membership of the students' federation (FEU) of the University of Havana. The celebration
lasted until dawn.

Fidel refused all inducements of political party position
as well as several lucrative commercial offers, saying that
he had no wish to trade on his prestige in any such manner.
He had stubbornly refused to collaborate with Batista, nor
was he willing to lend his name to those who were willing
to compromise.

In July he flew into exile. Within six months, he had
established the firm base of his *Movimiento Revolucionario
26 de Julio*, with chapters in half a dozen American cities.
Cuban exiles seeking him out in Mexico were organized
into para-military units. A large ranch was leased in the
federal district, and the training of an expeditionary force
began, under the supervision of a Cuban-born veteran of
the Spanish Civil War, General Alberto Bayo, a noted
authority on guerrilla warfare, and the author of several
books on the subject.

Cuban conservatives were still seeking a peaceful political
solution. Fidel would have none of it. In December of 1955
he wrote:

The political business of opposition is fully discredited and
decadent. First they demanded a neutral government and immediate general elections. Then they stopped at demanding only
general elections in 1956. They are no longer talking about a
particular year. They will end by taking off their last fig leaf
and accepting *any* arrangement with the dictator.

The intransigence of the *fidelistas* and the rapidly growing strength and appeal of the exile movement alarmed both the Batista government and the conservative leaders of the Cuban opposition. The former sent intelligence agents to harass the exiles: as a result of their efforts Fidel was twice arrested, and on several occasions the police raided *fidelista* arms caches and confiscated weapons and supplies which had been acquired at great pains and expense.

The old-line politicians were seemingly even more in fear of the revolutionary threat that was growing in Mexico than of the continuance of the dictatorship, and Fidel made his quarrel with them as well as with the regime, writing:

The names of those who impede the task of liberating their country should be recorded in the same place of infamy and shame as the names of those who oppress it.

It is to be recalled that Fidel had been, in 1952, a congressional candidate of the *Ortodoxo* party, making his political debut on the strength of his popularity as FEU leader at the University of Havana, and on the working-class following he had acquired as a young attorney with the reputation of being ready to defend the poor, in evictions and cases of political persecution, without regard for fees.

Now he made a clean break with all formal political alignments, proclaiming the *Movimiento 26* as a revolutionary movement that retained the best of the *ortodoxo* program "without sugar barons, without stock-market speculators, without magnates of industry and commerce, without lawyers for big interests, without provincial *caciques,* without small-time politicians of any kind."

Rather, he declared, the *Movimiento 26* was "the revolutionary movement of the humble, the hope of redemption of the Cuban working class, the hope of land for the peasants who live like pariahs in the country that their grandfathers liberated, the hope of bread for the hungry and justice for the forgotten."

Despite the efforts that were being made to disrupt the movement and to prevent any overt military move against the Batista government, Fidel made no secret of his intention to land an expeditionary force in Cuba. He had hoped to return to the island on the anniversary of the Moncada attack—July 26. Interference from the Mexican authorities made this impossible. Innumerable difficulties retarded the plans for the invasion. Fidel refused to be deterred by obstacles, nor would he follow the dictates of caution. On November 15th, he gave formal warning of his imminent departure for Cuba, declaring: "We shall be heroes or martyrs in 1956." Only six weeks were left of the waning year.

A sea-going motor cruiser had been purchased and hidden in the Tuxpan River, in the state of Veracruz. Preparations for the invasion were finally complete. On the night of November 25, accompanied by his brother and eighty other followers, Fidel sailed from Mexico, bound for Oriente.

No panic, no fear, but, yes, perhaps nervousness . . .
—Dr. Fernando Sánchez Amaya

III

THE SHIP made slow progress at first, because of a combination of circumstances: the weather, engine trouble, the fact that she was heavily overladen with fuel, stores, men, munitions.

She was plainly a pleasure craft: the converted yacht *Granma*, a twin-engine motor cruiser, sixty-four feet in length, sturdy but old, designed neither for work nor for war.

On the first day out, the wind began to rise. Whitecaps danced on the choppy waters of the Gulf. The captain complained that he could not apply full power; the clutch kept slipping. The blow intensified, and the *Granma* began to ship water as she lurched heavily into each successive trough.

The pump failed. The eighty-two men aboard, their stomachs lurching, too, with the pitch and roll of the vessel, were forced to bail water with buckets, kitchen utensils, mess kits, whatever they could find for the purpose.

Gasoline fumes added to their queasiness. The yacht was carrying two thousand gallons of fuel, twice normal capacity. In the cabin, in the hold, even in the bilge space there were arms and supplies: rifles, machine guns, wooden boxes of ammunition, canteens, compasses, maps, uniforms, canned goods.

Throughout the storm and afterward Fidel remained in the bow of the cruiser, visibly straining forward, leaving his post only to go to the cabin to confer with the captain, or to listen to news broadcasts on the ship's radio.

For a short while, seeing the misty lights of Tuxpan fade in the distance, the expeditionaries had sung the Cuban national anthem and the marching song of the *Movimiento Revolutionarío 26 de Julio*—*"Adelante cubanos!"* Later they had become hungry, and thirsty, the stores aboard being strictly rationed. Still later, they were seasick.

The *Granma*, wallowing along, low in the water, moved slowly through the Straits of Yucatan, into the incredible blue of the Caribbean. At times, in the Straits, the men would sight a Mexican shrimper lying close in to the distant shore, and on such occasions they would hasten to cover or flatten themselves against the deck, keeping their heads down until the danger had been passed.

Once they saw an airplane or a helicopter, too remote to identify, a small, buzzing black fly against the bright sky. Most of the time the sea was as empty as the sky.

At night there were the stars. The men, after much talk through the long, incandescent day, would lie on the deck staring up into space, feeling the rise and fall of the ship beneath them, and silence would descend on them, like a blanket. It was a short voyage, in time, but long for waiting. It seemed to go on forever.

On the sixth day of the voyage from Tuxpan, the 30th of November, the radio brought news from Cuba. There had been a revolutionary uprising in Santiago. Crushed. The men were silent. Fidel returned to the bow of the *Granma* to resume his watch, touching one or another of the group as he passed, saying—"Don't worry. We will avenge them," or words to that effect. He was grave, but confident, as always.

At four o'clock on the afternoon of the seventh day, the ship turned toward land. The *Granma* had been paralleling the southern coast of Cuba for more than six hundred miles, avoiding the shipping lanes as she moved slowly eastward through the Caribbean. Now the course was north by northeast, toward the land mass of Oriente Province, which resembles the flattened tail of a great dolphin, then due east toward Cape Cruz, which is the extreme tip of the dolphin's lower tail fin.

The land at this end of the island is wild; it is a country of coastal swampland, saw grass, mangroves, thickets, tangled lowland jungle merging into scrub pine and thick brush marked by great juts of naked rock as the coastal strip gives way to wooded foothills that in turn rise to the purple mass of mountains called the Sierra Maestra.

On the upper edge of the dolphin's tail fin there is the busy port of Niquero, and still farther north, in the Gulf of Guacanayabo, the larger port city of Manzanillo. In the Niquero area, a scattering of tiny villages, *pueblecitos, caseríos* consisting of a few earthen-floored dwellings; here and there a clearing in which stands a single, lonely *bohío,* the thatched hut of some solitary charcoal burner.

The point of disembarkation lay between Cabo Cruz and Niquero, near the tiny fishing village of Belic. From here the map indicates two possible routes of march—north to Niquero and Manzanillo, or due east, into the deep-thicketed sanctuary and high bastion of the Sierra Maestra.

On the *Granma*, civilian clothes were exchanged for olive-gray combat uniforms, with the red shoulder patch and black "26" of the movement. Anti-tank rifles were brought up from the hold and uncrated, cleaned, oiled, put in operating order. Crates of small arms and boxes of ammunition were pried open. Fidel distributed the weapons to each man personally, as he tried to do everything personally, laying heavy hands on the shoulders of the men, peering into their faces with bright, intense eyes, talking, instructing, encouraging, advising, reading their minds and answering the unspoken questions.

What if we meet a patrol?

"Hold your fire until you receive the command; do as I do."

And when we come to the garrisons?

"We will not fight unless it is necessary. Our fight is not against the soldiers. A soldier is a man. We do not kill him needlessly. If we attack, we let them know, first, that we are there. We lay down enough fire to show them our force, to show them that they cannot escape. We give them the chance to surrender, and perhaps to join us. It is their arms that we want, not their lives."

How will we live if we must go into the mountains?

"The people. The people will feed us. The people will be our supply line, our watchdogs, our eyes and ears, and the troops of our army. They know who we are and why we fight, and they will fight at our side. If we can find the arms to give them, who can doubt that ten thousand *guajiros* of the Sierra will join us? The soldiers themselves will join us."

What if I am wounded and cannot walk?

"We will carry you. The country people will hide you. We are all brothers."

And if I die?

"Had you been afraid of that, you would not be here, for we are neither mercenaries nor adventurers, but men who fight for an idea, which you know well, and we do not speak of dying, but of living and fighting and winning."

Unit commanders are given their orders. The men are assembled in the order of disembarkation. Fidel is in the bow with his headquarters group, his *"estado mayor."* Raúl Castro is a captain, in command of a platoon. He looks very young, but is a veteran of Moncada, dependable and serious. Juan Almeida, another Moncada veteran, dark-skinned, tough, cheerful, is also a platoon commander. One of most serious and capable of the men to be trained in Mexico is the Argentine, Ernesto "Che" Guevara. But he is a physician, and for the time being, he heads the medical corps, which also includes a young medical intern from Havana, Faustino Pérez.

Final instructions aboard the *Granma,* final conferences, talk, jokes, thoughtful silence. Waiting.

With darkness the wind began to rise and the waves to kick up, causing the cruiser to pitch and toss. A low-lying mist clung to the shoreline, or to what should have been the shore, and where there should have been faintly twinkling lights to guide the *Granma* to a landing, there was nothing; only, perhaps, a darker darkness, suggesting the mass of land ahead.

The mate, Roberto Roque, climbed to the moisture-slick roof of the cabin, clinging to the radio antenna, to try to find something on which to take a bearing. The ship pitched forward, into a trough. A shout, a splash. Roque was overboard. "Man overboard!" The *Granma* plunged on ahead, then slowed, stopped, swung about. The engines were silenced. Cautious calling. No answer to be heard above the wind and the slapping of the waves on the side of the ship. "Turn on the light." The searchlight cut into the blackness of the night and then died away. With the engines stilled there was no generator, and no power. But something had been seen, flashing palely in the black water. A face, upturned, appealing. By a miracle, Roque was found and hauled aboard, half dead. Three quarters of an hour lost. This was only the prelude to disaster.

Soon the mist began to lift, and the expeditionaries were able to see, very faintly, the outline of the shore. The engines were throttled down to slow speed, then cut entirely. The *Granma* glided slowly forward under its own momentum; the keel grated on sand, bumped, stopped. Silence. The men spoke in whispers. Up forward there was a struggle with the dory, packed to the gunwales with boxes of ammunition and heavy weapons. Another accident. The small boat swung over the side, dipped precariously, slipped into the water bow foremost—and sank below the surface with a gurgle.

In a motion picture, such incidents can provide comic relief. Here they are no joke, but part of the conspiracy of all inanimate objects and of nature itself to obstruct, resist, delay; they are nerve wracking, maddening. The men struggle and sweat, all too acutely conscious of the danger that may be waiting on shore, the danger that may be approaching from behind.

The small boat was lost. Finally the men began to splash into the water, one at a time, so heavily burdened that some of them slipped and went under immediately, to be hauled up, gasping, by their comrades. Before, they had talked in stage whispers. Now the order was to speak not at all, and only an occasional splash indicated the course of their progress toward shore.

The place: Playa de las Coloradas, better called a swamp than a beach. The time: dawn of December 2nd. The *Granma* had grounded on a narrow key of sand and clay extending from a thick, watery forest of mangroves, with their spiny high-looping octopus roots that reach out into the tidal lagoons and, capturing leaves and silt in their tentacles, slowly, inexorably work their natural reclamation project, accepting what the tide brings and turning it to use, gradually taking possession of the sea.

There was no boat, no beach, no bridge; nothing to do but wade ashore. Chest deep, Indian file, rifles and packs and equipment held overhead, the expeditionaries began to fight their way to solid ground.

Dr. Fernando Sánchez Amaya gives this account of the landing:

We throw ourselves into the mud and are entangled in the branches of the mangroves and tripped by the roots concealed beneath the surface of the muddy water. If we support ourselves by the branches, so as not to fall, the thorns stick into us, sharp as razors, and every sort of obstacle cuts our hands and faces, but we push on without rest. Finally, at Fidel's order, exhausted, we abandon everything that is not essential—clothing, cooking utensils, blankets—taking only what is needed for combat. In a matter of three hours, we have advanced some three or four hundred meters. We begin to feel firmer footing, thicker clumps of grass, more open spaces. Finally, we are past the mangroves. It is in these moments that we hear at our backs, in the direction of the coast which we have just left, a shot, followed by others.

The *Granma* had been sighted during daylight, while still far off shore, by a peasant in the Cabo Cruz area. The information had been duly passed along to the coast guard. The first shots came from a naval frigate which had been seeking, and now had found, the *Granma*—abandoned.

The sound of the shelling increased in tempo. A bomb burst. An army airplane appeared, then another, skimming so low that they seemed almost to touch the tops of the mangroves. The planes methodically began to comb the landing area, raking the swamp with machine-gun and automatic cannon fire, gradually working their way inland toward the area where the expeditionaries, scattering, lay hidden in the thicket.

"No panic, no fear, but, yes, perhaps *nervousness*," says Sánchez Amaya in his diary, describing the sensations of the quarry.

It had been discovered that eight men were missing.

Ragged, wet, exhausted, covered with mud, the scarecrow column moved out at double time, toward higher ground, stumbling, falling, lost in the thicket. Far behind, the bombs continued to burst.

They soon became used to the airplanes, which continued to patrol. Sometimes the aircraft, almost touching the treetops, flew so close that they could see the pilots. Once or twice during the next few days they heard the sound of strafing, but it was never directed at them. The government planes were strafing the *bohíos* of the country people, perhaps believing them to be occupied by rebels, and the people were fleeing into the hills.

Their contacts with the people were few. In one place a *campesino* gave them honey to eat, and most of the men became ill. Another *campesino* led them to a reunion with the eight men who had been lost. Sometimes the *campesinos* would hide in the woods when the rebels approached, scattering like chickens, abandoning their homes. The rebels would take food, if there was any to spare, and would leave money behind in payment.

On other occasions the people would stand their ground, timidly, the men in front, behind them the barefoot women, the children holding to their mothers' skirts, and Fidel would explain who he was and why he had come.

He had the utter confidence of the born proselytizer. He could have been a missionary in a country church. If he cut an incongruous figure, in ragged shirt, scraggly week-old beard, muddy boots, he was unaware of it, nor did the country people seem to notice. At first they were frightened by the sight of the weapons. Then they would become more assured, and interested, listening to Fidel arguing, haranguing, persuading, explaining, his white teeth glinting in his sun-blackened, scratched face, his chin lifted in a gesture of oratorical passion.

He liked to use a Socratic method of argument to explain things, and would ask many questions, sometimes putting both hands on a man's shoulders to hold him, peering into his face while he talked, as if to compel him to think by sheer force of will.

"What is your name, *compay?*" Such a name.

"What is your work?" A woodcutter.

"How much do you earn, *compay?*"

"Some sixty centavos a day, that doesn't come to me for nothing, *caballero,* and I have the woman and six little ones, all wishing to eat."

"Then listen, *compay*. This is why we are fighting. *Mira,* we have come a long way, and we have seen no schools, no hospitals; we have seen only hundreds of starving children, and in the cities, of which you know, men are enriching themselves while you are hungry. It is for this that we have come, to change everything, and to free the land."

If the words seemed strange, coming from a tattered fugitive, they were no more unusual to the country people than any new thing that came their way, in a remote country where all new things were strange. As for Fidel, he seemed unconscious of danger. His movements were unhurried; it was only his speech that was furious.

It was true that there was little food in the countryside. The expeditionaries accepted a portion of what there was, a few yams, a bit of pork, beans and rice, or whatever could be spared, and made a point of paying for it with cash. They made a point, also, of courtesy, and asked for reassurance that they had not imposed, knowing the impression their weapons and numbers made.

"*Qué va!* What a question." But the peasants were pleased to be asked, and would say that it was the other uniformed ones, the soldiers of the army, of whom one must beware.

The expeditionaries had been traveling by night. Shortly after dawn of the fifth day, they made their way across a broad valley near a place called Alegría de Pío and camped in a stand of trees on a rise in the midst of canefields and brush-covered range land.

During the morning they slept under the trees. There was open country ahead, and Fidel decided to wait until the sun had begun to sink before pushing on. A chicken was to be cooked; there was rice, and also some canned goods, bought in a little *bodega* in the area by Faustino Pérez, who had been out on a foraging expedition. Meantime, the men chewed sugar cane. A few wrote letters, hoping to be able to entrust them to some *campesino* to mail. Some of the men had their boots off and the medicos, Pérez and "Che," were attending to their blisters and cuts.

Sánchez says that he had divided his last cigaret with a comrade and was disposing himself to smoke his half of it when he was startled by the sound of a shot. His first thought was—an accident. Several seconds of dead silence followed. Then the illusion was abruptly shattered. A roar of intense automatic fire came from the front and slightly to the left of the woods. For a moment there was utter confusion. No guards had been posted; or, if there had been sentries, they had been cut down by the first bursts of fire.

The rebels were taken completely by surprise, and for the first few minutes they were in such a state of disorder that an aggressive army force could have massacred the entire group. It was not immediately clear where the fire was coming from. Some of the men thought that, by mistake, they were being fired upon by members of their own group outside of the wood. The cooler heads, those who had had some previous military experience, quickly regained control.

Juan Almeida, whose unit was disposed to the left of Sánchez, sent a scout to investigate. The scout returned in a moment with the news that there were khaki uniforms beyond the trees—some three to four hundred soldiers surrounding the wood on three sides.

The expeditionaries began to return the fire. Some of the unit commanders put their men to work building parapets of stones and earth. Other units began a disorderly retreat. Fidel's headquarters unit had been at Sánchez' right. Juan Almeida, crawling across from the left to get orders from Fidel, returned in a few minutes with the report that he was no longer there. The headquarters group was pulling back toward the only remaining exit, the canefields at the far end of the copse.

Almeida gave the order to his platoon to get out while it was still possible. Bullets were clipping the twigs above the heads of the rebels and skipping about them on the ground, sending up little geysers of dust.

The intense fire began to take its toll. A man near Sánchez suddenly dropped his rifle, the tendons of his wrist severed by a ball. Guevara's adjutant pitched forward on his face, a bullet in his chest. Another man ran past, toward the soldiers, shouting *"Adelante!"* and Sánchez Amaya relates, in his diary, "The blood was spurting from his throat so that I wondered that he was able to speak at all."

Soldiers began to infiltrate the wood, and the retreat turned into a rout.

Almeida, seeking safety in the canefields with his platoon, sent a scout to find Fidel. The scout was never seen again. Killed or captured. Three members of Almeida's platoon came in from the left flank, all wounded. The platoon continued to retreat through the cane, which the army now had set afire on both sides. Aircraft appeared on the horizon and came buzzing down, called in by an army field transmitter. Fragmentation grenades began to burst in the field. Almeida, still seeking Fidel, came upon Guevara, his shirt red with blood from a wound in his neck, preparing to make a suicidal last stand there in the cane. He dragged the Argentine off bodily, ignoring his protests.

The rebel force had been fragmented into groups of two or three men.

Sánchez Amaya writes:

At times I found myself alone, cane crackling on all sides, to my left, to my right, behind; shots whistling in all directions. It is impossible to tell whether the man immediately ahead, invisible in the cane, is friend or enemy, but I proceed, my finger tensely on the trigger, expecting that at any moment the soldiers will stumble over me and machine-gun me.

Then, ahead, I distinguish some of our uniforms. I join them, the same men who entered the canefield with me. We come out on a path, cross it, pass into another canefield. The planes have been flying very low, but are not firing, probably fearing to hit one of their own men, so mixed are we. There is only one of us wounded, and I take off my shirt to make a bandage for the wounded one, who is losing much blood, but comports himself bravely. All of us have a terrible thirst, and there are only three canteens. We agree to save the water for the wounded man. I consult my watch. It is exactly 5:55 P.M. We have been fighting for two hours. Still heard, intermittently in the distance, are shots and isolated bursts of automatic fire.

In isolated small groups and individually, the shattered expeditionary force emerges from the fight, disoriented, totally dispersed by the pursuing army. Behind lie the burning canefields, and the survivors realize in agony that there are wounded men in the path of the flames, lying unable to move, helplessly awaiting death.

The sun has set, and from hiding places in the outer darkness, the surviving rebels watch the glow of the fire and listen to the sporadic detonations of cartridges set off by the heat of the burning cane.

Fidel Castro was among the survivors. For a week he lived on sugar cane, skulking through the brush at night, hiding by day, with two of his command, Universo Sánchez, the grizzled, worried chief of his personal guard, and the medico, Faustino Pérez.

Raúl Castro, emerging from the burning canefields at Alegría de Pío with another small group, also survived the battle, and his experience was similar.

Juan Almeida, "Che" Guevara, and three other men, traveling at night and depending on the Argentine's slight knowledge of celestial navigation to guide them, went astray, and after six days came again to the sea—this time on the southern coast of the peninsula, east of Cabo Cruz. In a native shack, they found Camilo Cienfuegos and two of his original unit.

Fourteen of the expeditionaries who had fled from Alegría de Pío were surrounded by army troops near the north coast, as they wandered, hopelessly lost. They made the mistake of surrendering, and were shot on the spot.

Sánchez Amaya and six other men, also lost, found themselves a week after the battle on the coast where they had landed. Three of the group decided to go their separate way, and a day later, the fate of the fourteen overtook them. They surrendered to the notorious chief of naval intelligence, Lieutenant Julio Laurent, and were butchered as soon as they had handed over their weapons.

In some instances, informers led the military forces to their quarry. In Havana, the government had announced that the entire Castro expedition had been wiped out. The repression forces seem to have done their best to justify the statement.

The survivors were the toughest and wiliest of the expedition—or the most fortunate. Sánchez Amaya was one of four men who eventually made their way to Havana, at the other end of the island. His account of his escape is anticlimactic, to say the least. After hiding for some weeks in the jungle, drinking water from vines "and spitting out the bugs," he obtained civilian clothing by sending a countryman to Niquero for them, rode in a farmer's truck to Bayamo, and simply boarded a bus for the capital.

The odyssey of those who remained in the hills resembles a practical course of instruction in jungle warfare survival, taken from a military manual. The survivors subsisted on broiled snake, sugar cane, edible cactus, prickly pears, an occasional tortoise. For a time, Guevara, who suffered from asthma, managed to obtain a supply of drinking water for his men by siphoning the moisture from porous rocks with the breathing apparatus which he was obliged to use when ill.

On December 19th, the small group headed by Almeida

and "Che" at last located Fidel, who had previously been joined by his brother and what remained of Raúl's platoon.

There still exists some difference of opinion as to the original plan of operations, prior to the *Granma* landing. Had all gone well the expedition would have been met by rebel sympathizers with trucks at Belic. From there the expedition would have proceeded north by road to Niquero and Manzanillo, and thence, skirting the Sierra, across island to Bayamo, Palma Soriano, and on to Santiago, attacking one army stronghold after another.

Lest such a plan seem wildly optimistic for an invasion force of fewer than one hundred men, one must recall that the landing at Playa de las Coloradas had been timed to coincide with uprisings in the cities of Oriente. Thus there was actually some reason to hope that the invaders would find the way paved for them.

The Oriente population had long been anticipating the invasion; there was even the remote possibility of swinging elements of the Cuban Army to the side of the revolution, and in consideration of this possibility as well as for other reasons, Fidel had given orders that, *if* any army *cuartel* were to be assaulted, the soldiers were to be given every opportunity to surrender.

In imagination, at least, Fidel could see himself marching on Santiago, enlisting a revolutionary army en route, gathering men and arms, as an avalanche that begins in a trickle of sliding earth and pebbles becomes a thundering, irresistible force, sweeping all before it.

This, at least, was the brighter picture. At the same time, it is clear that he was prepared to improvise. Nearby was the deep, trackless sanctuary of the Sierra Maestra, a refuge and a fortress within which a few dozen men could hold off an army forever, if need be.

It is significant that the revolutionaries had been trained in mountain guerrilla tactics by a noted authority in that field, significant also that the rifles brought to Cuba by the invaders were expensive, long-range weapons mounted with eight-power telescopic sights—weapons for a mountain campaign, not for close-in fighting.

It is still not known precisely how many of the expeditionaries were killed at Alegría de Pío, how many later, after surrender or capture. Twenty-two survived as prisoners to face trial in Santiago. A few escaped to the cities. In the end, only a dozen of the original force of eighty-two were left to carry on the campaign in the Sierra Maestra.

On Christmas Day, led by *guajiro* guides enlisted by a widely known and respected Oriente landowner, Crescencio Pérez, the survivors began their ascent into the mountains.

More than 100 miles away in Santiago de Cuba, some followers of Castro did shoot up the town in a faint echo of the promised national uprising. But by and large the Cuban people ignored the whole affair.

—*Time*, December 17, 1956

IV

THE WRITER dimly recalls the reports of the Castro landing in Oriente that were received in New York soon afterward as having consisted of a few paragraphs of "wire copy" on the teletype machines of the international news agencies. There was also some mention of a brief-lived uprising in Santiago de Cuba on November 30th, two days before the landing. Neither event made much of an impression outside of Cuba. The feeling seemed to be that insurrections in the Caribbean were not very interesting.

The "affair" in Santiago was actually set in motion on November 27th, when a cable arrived from Mexico City, bearing the name of a non-existent book shop and the message: "Work requested out of print." Roughly translated it meant: *Granma out of Mexico.*

The message passed through several hands before reaching those of Frank País,* the M-26 "coordinator" in Santiago and chief of the small underground action groups of the movement throughout the island. País—twenty-three years old, the son of a Baptist minister and himself a former schoolmaster—set out to visit his eleven district action chiefs in the city.

Telegrams were sent to centers of underground resistance elsewhere on the island, confirming previously laid plans of action and indicating an effective date, November 30th. Hopefully, the *Granma* was expected to touch shore in

---

* Francisco Isaac País García. Christian names are often anglicized in Cuba, and the family name of the mother, appended to the surname in the Spanish fashion, is often dropped in common usage.

Oriente at dawn of that day, or so País calculated the probable arrival time.

Plans for the Santiago underground had been drawn up by País in collaboration with his chief lieutenant, a twenty-four-year-old University of Oriente student named José Tey, and several veterans of the Moncada assault, among them Lester Rodríguez and Haydée Santamaría.

Presumably the plan had Fidel Castro's personal approval. Twice during the summer of 1956, País, as coordinator of action for all 26th of July groups in Cuba, had made the long trip to Mexico to confer with Fidel, after touring the island extensively and talking with underground leaders. His own appraisal was that the Cuban underground, however ready and even eager it proclaimed itself to be, was by no means prepared for any really ambitious undertaking.

For urgent political and practical reasons of his own, possibly influenced also by the fact that he had signed a pact in July with FEU President José Antonio Echevarría in which he was promised strong, coordinated support, Fidel overruled País.

The Santiago underground went into action at dawn of November 30th. A headquarters was established in a large, old-fashioned apartment in the center of town, on a hill commanding a wide view of the city. A successful arms raid was carried out on a sporting goods store on the Plaza Dolores. A number of automobiles were requisitioned. Fighters in olive drab, wearing the red-and-black armbands of the 26th of July, began to move toward their assignment areas.

At seven o'clock, attacks were launched simultaneously against the headquarters of the Maritime Police, occupying a corner of the Customs Building in the dock area, and the National Police in their fortified yellow brick headquarters on Intendente Hill, overlooking the docks and the bay on one side and the city on the other.

Thirteen youths in three cars were committed to the assault on the Maritime Police. A diversion was created by half of the assault force on one side of the building. Then the other half of the force, led by a prosperous warehouse owner's son named Jorge Sotús, stormed into the building from the other side and captured some fifteen cowering police officers. Two bodies lay on the floor. There were several wounded. Sotús ordered the prisoners to lie flat on the strip of concrete pavement outside of the building, and his men began to carry rifles and bandoliers of ammunition to their waiting "supply car."

Nearby, the National Police offered stiffer resistance. From weapons emplacements and rifle apertures in the two-story yellow building they maintained a steady fire which held an assault platoon of thirty rebels at a distance. The rebel second-in-command, Otto Perellada, was killed by a bullet as he tried to climb to the roof of the building. The rebels succeeded in setting the headquarters afire with Molotov cocktails hurled through the windows, and the fire burned brightly as the battle continued. But that was the outside limit of their success.

The key to the military situation in Santiago was, as it had been three years earlier, the Maceo Regiment in Cuartel Moncada, with heavy weapons and, by 1956, two thousand troops.

Another direct assault on the fortress, after Fidel's own failure, was clearly impractical. However, País had reasoned that, if the fortress could not be taken by storm, it might yet be contained.

Plans had been worked out accordingly. An 81-millimeter mortar and fifty-six shells were obtained, at great cost and risk. The precise firing range and angle of the mortar were determined, and a location for it was found near a public high school five blocks northeast of and overlooking the barracks, from which the mortar could fire to best effect.

A .30-caliber tripod machine gun was provided to cover the mortar from a nearby rooftop. Ambush points were checked off on a map after a careful survey of the Moncada district, to seal off the streets leading from the fortress.

The plans were excellent insofar as they went, but they failed to take into account an element of chance, and of necessity they banked too heavily on the reliability of untried fighters, boys, the great majority of them, without experience or discipline.

The attempt to seal off the fortress failed.

Lester Rodríguez was picked up by a roving army patrol, on simple suspicion, while on the way to the mortar post. Frank País' younger brother, Josue, and two other members of the mortar squad were arrested at the same time.

When they failed to make an appearance, the rebels who had delivered the mortar to the school simply abandoned it. Lester Rodríguez had been the only man who knew how to operate it; he had had no time to train anyone else, and now the weapon was useless.

Several of the action leaders and many of the men who had been assigned to ambuscades around Moncada failed to report for duty. Those who arrived on time, perceiving their weakness and the hopelessness of the situation, wandered in confusion for a while from post to post, and then discreetly withdrew.

When the fighting began in the city, there was nothing to hinder the truckloads of soldiers that promptly began to roar out of the fortress. No bursting mortar shells spread terror and confusion on the base, no snipers pinned down cowering soldiers, no rebel ambushes delayed the speeding trucks.

The arrival of army reinforcements at the burning police headquarters brought the police themselves into the street, and the rebels there, attacked on two sides, began a disorganized retreat. The group leader, José Tey, was killed by a burst of machine-gun fire as he crouched on the pavement. Another rebel fell dead at the top of the picturesque street of stairs called Padre Pico. Tey's adjutant was already dead, and the rebels were left leaderless, to shift for themselves.

For a time the rebel machine-gun squad which had been assigned to protect the mortar toured the city with the machine gun in an automobile, firing on stray soldiers and occasional jeep patrols. But there was no concerted resistance, and no possibility of successfully opposing a trained regiment of vastly superior numbers.

A group of insurgents from the Moncada area gathered at the high school, and with some students, members of the 26th militia, prepared to defend themselves there.

Troops arriving in trucks in front of the high school went about their business in brisk, military fashion, setting up a mortar and two machine guns facing the entrance. An officer called through a megaphone for the surrender of the insurrectionists. The rebels replied with a few defiant pistol shots.

The troops, apparently under orders to avoid unnecessary bloodshed at the school, fired extravagantly at the building but made no attempt to take it. Fighter planes buzzed the area but found no targets. The soldiers could have been expected to try to surround the school, but instead they remained in front, leaving an exit open to the insurgents at the rear. There were no casualties. Within an hour, the rebels had all gone, fleeing across the athletic yard in back of the school and over an eight-foot wall to safety.

At noon Frank País reluctantly gave the order to abandon the apartment which had been occupied as a command post. The Santiago uprising was over.

Elsewhere there had been no sign of insurrection, except in Holguín, where an action squad tried to seize a warehouse to obtain dynamite, and failed. The Santiago fighters had been alone in their battle. The other cities were quiet. The *Granma* was still far away at sea, churning slowly east through the Caribbean.

It is questionable, in retrospect, whether it would have made any difference had the *Granma* arrived on schedule. The unfortunate fact is that the underground groups on the island were, as País had believed, far from ready for a large-scale, coordinated action. The signal for a general insurrection timed to coincide with the landing of the *Granma* should have put in motion plans that had been in preparation for many months. In fact, it did no such thing. When the morning of November 30 failed to bring news of a successful landing in Oriente, the underground leaders outside of Santiago seem to have decided simply to await developments. Perhaps nothing would have happened in any event.

It would be pointless to seek to assign responsibility for the failure. Inadequate liaison, uncertain channels of communication, and the inexperience and indecision of youthful leaders were perhaps equally to blame. Only in Santiago was there any determined attempt to carry out orders, and here the task force, although relatively strong and brilliantly directed, proved hopelessly inadequate to the assignment. One must pay tribute to the courage of the participants by acknowledging that it was a formidable assignment: the capture of Cuba's second largest city, with a population of one hundred thousand and a garrison of two thousand soldiers, by fewer than three hundred youngsters, most of them not yet out of their teens, and only a third of them armed.*

It is, in fact, a matter for speculation whether Fidel had really anticipated success, or had merely required a di-

* In fact, only eighty-six members of the País organization actually took part. Casualties were surprisingly few; only three rebels were killed, although reprisals raised the toll considerably.

versionary action. In view of his indomitable optimism
under all circumstances, one must suppose that he took the
sanguine view, but was prepared to improvise, if necessary.
Later he sent a bitter rebuke to Echevarría, the young FEU
leader in Havana, reproaching him for having failed to act.
Yet it is difficult to see what he could have expected.

The Cuban underground was, in 1956, an unknown
quantity at best, compounded of diverse, unstable, and often
incompatible elements—romantic schoolboys living a fan-
tasy life, with little comprehension, until taught by experience, of the risks they ran; political ward heelers whose
services and following were often for sale; young idealists
with a yearning to "do something" and no clear idea of
what was to be done; older men with proud but perhaps
hazy recollections of the revolutionary escapades of their
own youth; adventurers of every sort.

Increasingly there were the embittered victims or relatives
of victims of police methods and the police state.

Conspiracy was in the air and the wildest rumors passed
unchallenged. One recalls the "story" (for once the newspaper term is used literally) filed by an American reporter
who wrote of having visited the flickering campfires of a
"rebel chieftain" identified as one Lauro Blanco, who was
said to have been preparing to march on Havana with a
thousand armed men, to overthrow the dictator. The only
Lauro Blanco even slightly known to Havana at the time
proved to be a petty gangster of small political pretensions
who might possibly have raised a "rebel army" of a dozen
men, his male relatives included. He had no need to march
on Havana, being already there.

It would be a serious distortion of fact, however, to suggest that there was no real opposition to the Cuban dictatorship other than that of Fidel Castro and his followers, before
the *Granma* landing, or even after it. On the other hand, it
is fairly safe to assert that there was no *effective* opposition,

even including that of the 26th of July cells, until the various revolutionary groups had been coordinated under the leadership of the *fidelista* movement, and given a firm base in the Sierra Maestra.

One is constrained to pass over the formal political parties in opposition. They might just possibly have accomplished something had they acted in time, before Batista was able to consolidate his power, but they failed to act.

The parties were fragmented, and irretrievably discredited. Their failure is found in their disunity, their weakness, their intramural rivalries, in the jealousies and personal ambitions and venality of the politicos, and in the skill with which the Batista regime used the means at its disposal— bribery, intimidation, murder, diplomacy, and *a careful adherence to the outward semblance of constitutional procedure,** to render all legal opposition impotent.

Party members who believed in the possibility of a purely political solution, or who found it convenient so to believe, were converted, willy-nilly, into collaborators, used by Batista to create the illusion of a "loyal opposition" to shore up the democratic pretensions of the dictatorship. Honest men either became active revolutionaries, or lapsed into inaction and despondency.

Of active opposition groups, aside from the *Movimiento 26,* the most effective were the revolutionary directorate of the university students' federation in Havana, before the regime shut down the university as a breeding ground of insurrection, and a Revolutionary Directorate (DR) which, although an outgrowth of the FEU, extended its membership to a broad spectrum of insurgent youth off the campus.

Among the earlier influences contributing to the haphazard growth of the underground was a so-called National-

---

* The Constitution of 1940 provided for the suspension of civil guarantees, censorship, and similar "emergency" measures invoked by Batista with the aid of a rubber-stamp Congress. The courts, too, were packed.

ist Revolutionary Movement (MNR) headed by Dr. Rafael García Bárcenas, the instigator of a plot to capture Camp Columbia in April of 1953, with the connivance of dissident military officers.

Bárcenas went to prison on the Isle of Pines, with a number of officers who had been involved in the plot. When he was released, with the amnesty of 1955, the MNR was dissolved. Nevertheless, its influence continued to be felt, in the leadership of such outstanding tacticians of the *fidelista* movement as Dr. Armando Hart, who had studied under Bárcenas when the latter was a professor of philosophy and social studies at the University of Havana, and who later, as a young attorney, made a brilliant defense of the professor at his trial. Frank País was briefly a member of the MNR, at the age of seventeen, before forming his own Revolutionary Action Movement in Santiago, which he merged with the 26th in 1956.

In early April of that year, in Havana, a military conspiracy inspired by a civilian group called the *Montecristi* was aborted with the arrest of several high-ranking army officers, among them Colonel Ramón Barquín, a former military attaché to the Cuban Embassy in Washington and Cuba representative on the Inter-American Defense Board.

In the same month, on April 29th, a group of seventy-six youths under one Reynold García raided the "Margot" mine near the port city of Matanzas, an hour's drive from Havana, seized six trucks and fifteen hundred pounds of dynamite, and proceeded to attack the military garrison at Matanzas, the Cuartel Goicuría.

According to one of the surviving raiders, Arnaldo Ramos Lechuga, the primary purpose of the assault was to disrupt the so-called "Civic Dialogue" then in progress.

However, again according to Ramos Lechuga, some two hundred unarmed volunteers assembled from various parts of the island were standing by in the park opposite the

Matanzas provincial government building and, had the assault been successful, these men would have been armed to defend the city against the army reinforcements which presumably would have been dispatched from Havana. This, at least, was the plan.

As it presently developed, there was no need for army reinforcements. The rebels were poorly armed; one hundred twenty-four grenades which they had obtained from a Miami gun-runner proved to be charged with, not gunpowder, but cement.*

On arriving at the *cuartel,* the insurrectionists found an even more deadly surprise awaiting them. The army had been apprised of the plot, and the commandant, Colonel Pilar García, had his men posted on the parapets, ready for action. The raiders came under a hail of fire as soon as they reached the fortress. The lead truck penetrated the compound, and was literally shot to pieces there. The second truck somehow backed out and limped away, its front tires punctured by bullets; the third remained jammed in the entrance. Those of the rebels who were still able to do so fled in confusion through the streets of the city, some in their vehicles, others on foot.

A sequel to the Goicuría attack appeared in a subsequent issue of *Life* magazine. A photograph taken shortly after the attack showed the bodies of ten rebels lying in a row inside the Goicuría compound. Another picture, exposed some hours after the first, revealed *eleven* bodies in the same row where before there had been only ten.

The discrepancy was explained by yet another photograph, this one made surreptitiously by a Cuban newsman. It showed a soldier, at the foot of an exterior stairway, in the act of shooting a captured rebel in the back as he ascended the stairs.

---

* A similar substitution was discovered in bazooka rockets bought by Prío supporters in the United States.

Witnesses later declared that the prisoner, identified as Julio García Rodríguez, had been captured, taken to Havana for questioning, then returned to Goicuría, and shot.

The murder of this and other prisoners, taken alive in Matanzas, was protested before the Supreme Court by the *Ortodoxo* party, represented by its president, Raúl Chibás, and two eminent attorneys, Dr. Francisco Carone and Dr. Pelayo Cuervo Navarro, a former senator. Confronted with the documentary evidence of the *Life* photographs and the names of eye-witnesses who were prepared to testify to the murder of the prisoners, the Supreme Tribunal relegated the case to the Matanzas district court, which quietly tabled it.

Some of the survivors of the Matanzas assault went into exile in Mexico. Others were tracked down and killed. Two of them were slain in Havana after taking refuge in the Haitian Embassy.

Their murder followed the assassination of Colonel Antonio Blanco Rico, chief of the dreaded military intelligence service known for its initials as the "SIM" (*Servicio de Inteligencia Militar*). Blanco Rico was shot to death by four members of the FEU in the early morning hours of October 28th as he was leaving the second-floor premises of Havana's Montmartre night club with a group of friends.

Two days later, Batista's chief of police, Colonel Rafael Salas Cañizares, tried to force his way into the Haitian Embassy in search of some political refugees suspected of having taken part in the Blanco Rico assassination, and was himself shot and mortally wounded. A squad of police led by a brother of the Colonel returned to the Embassy, forced an entrance, and killed ten young Cubans there with submachine-gun fire. Among the slain were two of the Goicuría survivors.

A wiser or a stronger government might have retarded the revolutionary process by dealing with it more discreetly. As one thoughtful member of the underground asked: "Why kill these boys? It only helps us. Every *rebelde* killed has a hundred friends and relatives who can no longer be reconciled with Batista under any circumstance, but must join us."

Instead of seeking to neutralize the revolution by employing moderate means, the Batista regime contributed to it by meeting terrorism with a murderous counter-terrorism that defeated its own ends.

The excesses that followed the attack on Moncada in 1953 were not immediately repeated after the Santiago uprising of 1956, the reason being, probably, that Colonel Chaviano, who had been largely responsible for the 1953 massacre, was no longer in command. He had been transferred to Camagüey and replaced, in the fall of 1956, by the more moderate and intelligent General Martín Díaz Tamayo.

Where Chaviano had ruled Santiago like a feudal baron, controlling the illicit lotteries and the red light districts as sources of personal income (it is said that he once kicked to death a madame who had tried to cheat him of three hundred pesos) and giving his troops free rein in what was, to all effect, a city under military occupation, Díaz Tamayo turned out to be, in the phrase of the Santiagüeros, "a decent enough fellow."

However, it was clear that Díaz Tamayo did not completely control the situation. He admitted as much to a delegation of citizens when, returning to Santiago from an interview with Batista following the November 30th uprising, he was informed that four young boys had been found murdered on the outskirts of the city during his absence. Their bodies showed evidence of torture.

Díaz Tamayo deplored the murders, but indicated that he was not always able to prevent such excesses. The reason was partly political. Although the military commanders could, if they chose, use their power to extort tribute in one form or another from the city, Santiago was, and continued to be, the fief of one of Batista's strongest allies and personal friends, an old-style *"cacique"* and Cuban senator named Rolando Masferrer.

It would be an understatement to say that Masferrer was to Oriente what Capone had been to Chicago. Having the support of the government and working in close collaboration with the military commanders, he was considerably more.

His personal "army" of an estimated two thousand men wore army uniforms when it suited their purpose, or his, rode in the khaki-colored short-wave radio patrol cars known as *"micro-ondas"* and in times of crisis formed a rabid vigilante force that worked closely with the military in suppressing disorders and eliminating the more troublesome rebel leaders.

The chiefs of the *masferrista* "militia" were gangsters, who divided the province into districts for more efficient exploitation. Where the military might exercise a certain caution, the *masferristas* had no need, and did not stop at robbing even the priesthood. Their principal sources of income, necessarily shared with the army chiefs, were gambling, prostitution, and extortion.

Masferrer received his due portion of all of this, and the files that he left behind when he abruptly fled the country disclose the nature of the power which he exercised. The records show that he engaged in an extensive blackmail of his own associates, against whom he painstakingly assembled evidence of the murders which he, more often than they, found profitable or necessary.

His legitimate sources of income were also considerable; they included some of the largest plantation holdings in the country. He maintained a small hotel and a cafe as a headquarters for his followers in Santiago, and his newspapers,

Libertad * in Santiago and *Tiempo* in Havana, were the only uncensored journals in Cuba.

Of the thousands of political murders† that occurred during the seven years of the Batista dictatorship, a high percentage must be attributed to Masferrer, who remains at the top of the "wanted" list as a fugitive from Cuban justice.

Chaviano had worked closely with Masferrer. Díaz Tamayo, whatever his relationship with Batista, did not; nor did he remain long in Santiago. He was transferred back to Havana in early December, and Chaviano was recalled from Camagüey.

Reprisals and repression quickly followed. Civil liberties had been suspended throughout Oriente and squads of soldiers patrolled the city streets. The jails were soon filled. More than one hundred youths were held for trial in connection with the November uprising. Suspects against whom it was difficult to obtain evidence were simply shot in the streets, if they ventured from home. Several were removed from hospitals and murdered. With all youth suspect, it was dangerous for young men to go out alone, and it became not uncommon to see blushing high school boys being escorted to and from their classes by their mothers. At least ten young men were killed in Santiago during December alone.

The situation was possibly even worse in Holguín, Oriente's second city, on the western edge of the province. The commander of the military garrison at Holguín was a former aide to Chaviano, a Colonel Fermin Cowley. Like Chaviano, Cowley subscribed to the principle of fighting fire with fire, and he applied the policy to his 7th military district with a vengeance.

* The cafe and hotel were also named "Libertad," the supreme irony, to anyone who knew Masferrer.

† Some 20,000, according to the estimate of the revolutionary government.

The result was "Batista's Christmas Gift" of 1956: the bodies of twenty-nine men and boys left littering the countryside or hanging from trees over the Yule holiday of that year.

Although the Holguín underground had failed to produce a general uprising in response to the call to arms on November 30th, the M-26 leaders had inadvisedly let it be known that strong clandestine forces in the area were prepared to support Fidel's invasion from Mexico.

On the day after Christmas, the bodies of five members of the movement in Holguín were found on the grounds of the city cemetery, some ten miles out of town. During the course of the day, ten more bodies were discovered in the surrounding countryside, in ditches, on highways and country roads, hanging from trees. Subsequently fourteen more corpses were found at greater distances, some as far away as Banes, Batista's birthplace, and on the property of the United Fruit Sugar Company at Preston, on the north coast.

In some cases, the bodies found nearest to Holguín were those of strangers to the city; it was not until news of the massacre had swept the district that families from nearby towns and villages came to Holguín to claim the corpses of the victims.

All had been picked up by flying squads of soldiers and police on the afternoon and evening of Christmas Day. Some of the bodies were pocked with machine-gun bullets, others with ice-pick wounds. Each corpse, including the hanged, bore the Cowley "trade mark," a bullet wound at the nape of the neck.

The underground struck back, to the limited extent of its ability. In Santiago, the action squads organized by Frank País took grim reprisals. Soldiers and police informers were shot down on the streets.

Saboteurs spread fire through the canefields across the island. In Havana, members of the 26th and the FEU distributed pamphlets denouncing the government, and the more timid of the American tourists fled to quieter playgrounds as nightly bomb explosions underscored the revolutionary protest.

"The public does not know who is doing the bombing," wrote Herbert Matthews in *The New York Times*, "for the police have thus far caught only one small group in Havana and none elsewhere. As a desperate measure of counterterrorism, therefore, the police kill someone virtually every time a bomb is exploded in Havana, riddle his body with bullets, put a bomb in his hand, and call the press photographers to come and take photographs. This macabre procedure is sardonically called by *Habaneros* 'Batista's classified advertisement.' "

The same sort of "advertising" continued at the eastern end of the island. On the afternoon of January 2nd, 1957, a high school boy named William Soler was seized by soldiers on a busy shopping street in Santiago, dragged into a khaki-colored *micro-onda,* and driven away.

William Soler's body was one of four corpses to be found in the city the following night, dumped in an empty lot. His body bore mute witness to the reason for his slaying. He had been tortured far beyond the point where it would have been discreet to allow him to live. Medical testimony recorded after an autopsy declared that he had been under torture for twenty-four hours prior to his death. He had been fourteen years old.

The murder was one too many. The city was gripped in a wave of indignation. Work came to a standstill. Amusements were abandoned. Tension grew.

Where the organized resistance heretofore had depended on the efforts of avowed revolutionists, young men and women whose motives, however elevated, were subject to question if only on the grounds of their inexperience and passion, it now began to engage their elders. The first public manifestation of the change came on the morning of January 4th, two days after the murder of William Soler.

At ten o'clock in the morning, some forty women dressed in black left the Church of Dolores on the plaza of that name and moved in slow procession, praying in unison and fingering their rosaries, down Calle Aguilera, through the shopping district. At their head marched the mother of William Soler, and with her the mothers of other youths slain by police and soldiers during the year's-end wave of repression in the city. Over their heads they carried a large white banner with the black inscription: *Cesen los asesinatos de nuestros hijos.* (Stop the murder of our sons.)

As they moved on past the park and through the shopping district, other women joined them. There were two hundred by the time they had passed the first block, then eight hundred, then a thousand. At every step more women left the shops to join the procession, pressing slowly forward through the narrow, cobbled street. A few policemen stood by, helpless, at the intersections. Men watched from the doorways and many wept with shame as the women passed by, the only sound their murmured litany and the funereal tapping of their heels.

At one intersection, a jeepload of soldiers suddenly appeared, training a machine gun on the procession, blocking the way. The women waited, silently. The demonstration continued to grow until it overflowed into nearby streets, blocking all traffic.

When the soldiers tried to break up the manifestation, pushing their way into the dense crowd, the women simply opened aisles for them to pass through, and then closed ranks again. The mothers refused to be provoked into any overt act of physical resistance, but stood in quiet dignity until the soldiers gave up their futile efforts and, shamefaced, turned away. Then the women began, still silently, to disperse. Part of the procession continued on to the city hall and to the offices of several newspapers to leave petitions, demanding an end of the terror and the restoration of civil law. Then these women, too, went quietly home.

The mothers' protest march in Santiago had significance because it was the first public act to signal the beginning of organized civic resistance on a broad and effective scale in Cuba, under the aegis of the *fidelista* movement. In Oriente, the basis for a coalition of civic groups working in collaboration with the active revolutionary units had already been prepared by influential professional, business, and social leaders. The medical profession in particular played an outstanding role, supported by courageous, intelligent, and influential women, without whose participation little could have been accomplished.

The agency through which the community lent support to both the urban underground and the active fighting units in the mountains was the *Resistencia Cívica*—in effect, the civil arm of the 26th of July movement, charged with fundraising, the collection, storage and transportation of military provisions, and similar logistical and economic activities. Such aid had heretofore been provided on an informal, individual basis. Now it became the business of a large and powerful organization.

By the end of January, the president of what remained of the splintered *Ortodoxo* party, Raúl Chibás, had conferred with País in Santiago and returned to Havana to establish a similar, but more elaborate structure of civic resistance.

The Lions Club, the Rotarians, the various professional and cultural societies were brought into a coalition of *Instituciones Cívicas*—in effect, the civic conscience of the capital, seeking to curb, by public protest and by legal means, the excesses of the Batista regime.

The Havana branch of the *Resistencia Cívica* drew its members from the same organizations which comprised the *Instituciones Cívicas,* and from the influential banking and business classes. But, as in Santiago, it was essentially a clandestine organization—an arm of the *Movimiento 26,* and Chibás, with the assistance of Armando Hart, then action leader in Havana, took pains to form it on the cellular lines of the old revolutionary ABC organization, so that no ordinary member of it knew more than ten others, and no chief knew more than ten cell leaders.

At both ends of the island, the *Resistencia* exerted a wide and powerful influence in the upper strata of Cuban business and society. The spacious suburban home of a wealthy broker, Ignacio Mendoza, became a headquarters of underground groups in the capital, known as "the club on First Avenue." It was only one of a number of such "clubs."

In Santiago, the private laboratory and pleasant home of Dr. Angel Santos Buch, a prominent physician, served a similar purpose, being used as a way station for rebel couriers and important fugitives, on their way to or from the Sierra. Similar underground stations were established in each city, throughout the island, and slowly, almost reluctantly, the business and prosperous professional classes began to turn their considerable means and influence into revolutionary channels.

Fidel Castro, the rebel leader of Cuba's youth, is alive and fighting hard and successfully in the rugged, almost impenetrable fastnesses of the Sierra Maestra.
—HERBERT L. MATTHEWS in *The New York Times,*
February 24, 1957

V

THE BATISTA GOVERNMENT managed during the first months of 1957 to convey the impression that despite continued unrest in the cities there was no insurrectionary force, actually under arms in the country, that could be considered worthy of the name.

It was given out, first, that Fidel and his entire expedition had been killed or captured; later, with more truth, that the rebels in Oriente Province had been reduced to a mere handful of fugitives, of no importance, scarcely worth the trouble of pursuing. At one point, Batista gave it as his personal opinion that Fidel had never landed in Cuba, but was still in Mexico, hiding.

Despite such distortions of palace propaganda, and in spite of censorship, it was impossible to conceal for long the fact that the army had committed three thousand troops to the Sierra Maestra. The reason, too, quickly became apparent—to the soldiers if not to the public. Fidel was in the process of rebuilding his shattered force, and the army itself was providing him, reluctantly and at some cost in military manpower and prestige, with weapons and supplies.

The rebels had their first successful skirmish at a place called La Plata, in the foothills of the Sierra. The rebel objective was a small *cuartel,* one of the numerous advanced outposts with which the army had ringed the mountains in pursuance of what was thought of as essentially a police action, to exterminate the survivors of the *Granma* and any *campesinos* who might have joined them. No aggressive action was expected of the fugitives.

Suddenly, the quarry turned hunter. On January 17th, a dozen of Fidel's guerrillas infiltrated the La Plata area under cover of darkness and launched a silent, lightning attack, holding their fire until they were actually in among the soldiers. It was their first experience of commando fighting under field conditions, where the stakes were life or death, but they acquitted themselves well. Eleven soldiers were killed by the raiders, almost before they had become aware of their danger.

Their rifles armed an equal number of *guajiro* volunteers in the rebel column. The ammunition and supplies taken from La Plata provided the means for more ambitious and far-ranging operations. At least four such raids were conducted during January, as the rebel force began to find its strength in the guerrilla tactics taught in Mexico by General Bayo.

Army forces entering the mountains in pursuit of the rebels found nothing, or else, when they least expected it, they found themselves suddenly under fire, being picked off by the telescopic rifles of Fidel's snipers, high in the hills above them, invisible in the dense sub-tropical forest.

The *guajiros* contributed generously of what there was to spare of food, in a hungry country, and became, as Fidel had predicted, the supply line as well as the eyes and ears of the revolutionary army. Soon, strong and willing couriers and supply carriers began to pass through the army lines to Bayamo, Manzanillo, and Santiago, and to return, along precipitous mountain footpaths where no mule could travel, laden with heavy burlap sacks of canned goods, dried codfish, rice and beans, blankets, hammocks, new uniforms, boots, and squares of plastic table covering or shower curtains that served as shelter from the rain during the wet nights in the Sierra.

The supplies were provided by the underground in the towns, for the most part from the contributions of the

Resistencia Cívica. The soldiers had not yet learned to be suspicious of women, and many of the automatic pistols and heavy bandoliers of rifle cartridges that moved into the mountains came part of the way, through army roadblocks, in stout canvas pockets concealed beneath the billowing skirts of smiling schoolgirls.

To the people of the Sierra, reared in a feudal tradition, Fidel and his followers were a revelation. They had been accustomed to the tyranny of a *Guardia Rural* recruited from the most shiftless and brutal of their own kind—*guajiros* who found it more pleasant and profitable to administer rude justice with a rifle butt than to work on the land. In addition to the rural guard, there was a scattering of small traders and a few more prosperous farmers whose position brought them certain privileges—for example, a license from the nearest military post to carry a pistol—and whose relationship with the military authorities tended to make them, in effect, intelligence agents of the regime. There were also a few bandits, *campesinos* who, like the rural guard, found it easier in a lawless mountain country to prey upon their neighbors than to scratch the soil for a living.

The rebels, coming into the mountains, were prompt to promulgate a revolutionary code of justice, and to enforce it with rigorous impartiality. The death penalty was imposed for murder, rape, and informing, throughout the wide "free territory" administered by Fidel. Malefactors were tried in summary courts-martial, and shot against the nearest tree.

The *fidelistas* scrupulously paid for supplies with cash. The *guajiros* who joined the rebel force, or who were killed or forced to become fugitives because they had aided Fidel, were provided for from the rebel store of cash and supplies.

The youths of the Sierra who could not be accepted as volunteers in the regular force, because of a lack of military weapons, were organized into para-military groups of *escopeteros*—shotgun bearers—employed to help enforce the revolutionary law, and sometimes to lay ambushes along the roads of access to the "free territory." Others formed a counter-intelligence corps to guard against infiltration by government agents, and to keep the rebels informed of the movements of the army.

"We always know where the soldiers are," Fidel told the first journalists to visit him in the Sierra, "but they never know where we are. We can come and go as we like, moving through their lines, but they can never find us unless we wish them to, and then it is only on our terms."

What was gradually emerging was the classic pattern of guerrilla warfare seen in other backward areas of the world in the modern era, in Algeria, in Viet-Nam—slow, shadowy, erosive, virtually impossible to stamp out, because it gives the professional soldier nothing with which to come to grips and leaves him to deal with an increasingly hostile civil population that passively resists him and with which he can find no fault, while knowing, none the less, that it is the source of his phantom enemy's sustenance, intelligence, and manpower.

As the campaign progressed, Fidel began to bring underground leaders from the towns into the Sierra to consult on political and tactical questions, and to receive instructions concerning such matters as sabotage, fund-raising, and the smuggling of arms from outside of the island.

Faustino Pérez had been sent to Havana, where, in consultation with Frank País, he reorganized the action units of the capital under Aldo Vera, a leader of the 26th of July labor section.

The effect of these efforts, and of developments in the Sierra, was to encourage the members of the movement in the towns, and to spur them to greater activity. Yet there was much still to be done. To the great mass of Cuban people, Fidel Castro remained more myth than man. Virtually nothing of his campaign was heard outside of Oriente, except by committed revolutionaries and members of the *Resistencia*.

Batista retained his hold on the urban workers, especially in the capital, by virtue of his control of the Confederation of Cuban Workers (CTC), by tremendous work-creating public projects, and through the notorious system of government sinecures known as *botellas*.*

In the middle classes, to be a *fidelista* was more a political tendency than a commitment to action. Censorship and the vigilance of the military intelligence service and the police made it dangerous and difficult to create any liaison between one small oppositionist group and another, or even to know what was going on outside of one's own immediate circle of acquaintanceship.

Lacking an effective means of communication with the people, the movement found it difficult to provide them with a program, or to direct their dissatisfaction with the regime toward revolutionary ends.

As to the effect of the insurrection in Oriente on the world outside of Cuba, it was non-existent. Skirmishes were fought, raids were carried out; the Cuban Army retaliated by bombing the Sierra, more to terrorize the *guajiros* and keep them from cooperating with the rebels than from any real hope of actually inflicting casualties on Fidel's elusive force. For a time, the government tried to apply a scorched-earth policy by evacuating the people from entire districts. In short, all of the conditions of civil war applied, over a wide area. The world took no notice.

* Literally, bottles. A form of political patronage involving the payment of small stipends to thousands of persons on the government payrolls who actually held no post and performed no services. The original intention was to make a provision for the widows of government servants and other worthy indigents, but the system under Batista was greatly abused for political ends.

Some of the facts filtered through censorship, to be reported, tersely, in the American press. Newspaper editors found little interest in the situation, and the public remained largely ignorant of it. Official Washington was apprised of more of the facts, through diplomatic and consular channels. The revolutionary movement had its active sympathizers among United States diplomatic personnel stationed in Cuba, and such individuals exerted what influence they possessed.

Nothing seemed to make any serious impression on the U. S. policy makers, who continued to support the regime, tacitly in Washington and explicitly, with a considerable show of cordiality, on the ambassadorial level in Havana.

In an effort to break through the curtain of censorship and misrepresentation raised by the Havana government, Fidel sent a courier, René Rodríguez, to Havana during the first week of February, with instructions to bring a foreign correspondent into the Sierra, to learn at first hand the nature and scope of the Cuban struggle. The results far exceeded expectations.

Rodríguez, on reaching Havana, contacted Javier Pazos, the twenty-two-year-old son of Felipe Pazos, former president of the national bank in the Prío administration, and an internationally known banker and economist.

The problem was discussed with Pazos, senior, and he agreed to make a contact. The choice of a journalistic outlet was a fortunate one. Pazos conferred with the Havana representative of the conservative and influential *New York Times,* and learned that Herbert L. Matthews, a member of the *Times* editorial board and one of its most distinguished correspondents, a noted authority on Latin-American affairs, was expected to arrive in the capital within a few days.

On Matthews' arrival, a series of conferences was held, first with the elder Pazos, then with his son, Javier, René

Rodríguez, and Faustino Pérez. It was agreed that the gray-haired *Times* correspondent would make the hazardous and physically demanding journey into the Sierra.

Matthews left by automobile on the afternoon of February 15th, accompanied by his wife, Faustino Pérez, Javier Pazos, and a young woman member of the movement, Lillian Mesa—to all appearances a group of tourists on holiday, driving down the central highway to Bayamo, thence to Manzanillo. Once within striking distance of the Sierra, the "tourists" separated. Mrs. Matthews was lodged in a private home in the countryside. The *Times* correspondent, dressed in rough country clothes and more or less "disguised" as an American planter, continued with several guides by jeep and finally on foot into the mountains.

Thirty-six hours after leaving Havana, just before daylight on the 17th, he found himself in a woodland grove in the Sierra, where, he wrote later:

. . . the dripping leaves and boughs, the dense vegetation, the mud underfoot, the moonlight, all gave the impression of a tropical forest, more like Brazil than Cuba.

With the dawn, he met Fidel, who came striding into the grove from the place where he had been encamped, some distance away. Matthews' impression of the revolutionary leader was a vivid one:

Taking him, as one would at first, by physique and personality, here was quite a man—a powerful six-footer, olive-skinned, full-faced, with a scraggly beard.*** The personality of the man is overpowering. It was easy to see that his men adored him, and also to see why he has caught the imagination of the youth of Cuba all over the island. Here was an educated, dedicated fanatic, a man of ideals, of courage, and of remarkable qualities of leadership.

The *Times* reporter's interview with Fidel, conducted in whispers because they were in an area heavily infiltrated by army troops, lasted for three hours. It more than satisfied

Matthews' expectations, and he lost no time in hurrying back to the States to get his impressions into print.

He related in the *Times*:

We ploughed our way back through the muddy undergrowth in broad daylight, but always keeping under cover. The scout went like a homing pigeon through woods and across fields straight to a farmer's house on the edge of the Sierra. There we hid in a back room while someone borrowed a horse and went for the jeep, which had been under cover all night.

There was one road block to get through, with an army guard so suspicious that our hearts sank, but he let us through.

After that, washed, shaved, and looking again like an American tourist, with my wife as "camouflage," we had no trouble driving back through the road blocks to safety, and then on to Havana. So far as anyone knew, we had been away fishing for the weekend, and no one bothered us as we took the plane to New York.

A week later, *The New York Times* began to tell the world, in a sensational series of front-page articles under Matthews' by-line, the dramatic truth about Cuba:

Fidel Castro, the rebel leader of Cuba's youth, is alive and fighting hard and successfully in the rugged, almost impenetrable fastnesses of the Sierra Maestra, at the southern tip of the island.

President Fulgencio Batista has the cream of his army about the area, but the army men are fighting a thus-far losing battle to destroy the most dangerous enemy General Batista has faced in a long and adventurous career as Cuban leader and dictator.

Matthews devoted three long articles to exploring the entire political, military, and economic situation of the island, taking care to underline conditions that had kept the information from the public until now:

This is the first *sure* news that Fidel Castro is still alive and still in Cuba. No one connected with the outside world, let alone the press, has seen Señor Castro except this writer. No one in Havana, not even the United States Embassy with all its resources for getting information, will know until this report is published that Fidel Castro is really in the Sierra Maestra. This account, among other things, will break the tightest censorship in the history of the Cuban Republic.

Ironically, the Havana government had chosen just this time to *lift* the censorship which had been imposed on the Cuban press. It is difficult to understand why. The first of the Matthews articles appeared in the *Times* on February 24th, a Sunday. Before the day was out, the Cuban underground was busily producing photostatic copies for distribution in Cuba, and was working on a translation. The second installment of the series appeared on Monday, and the third and final chapter on Tuesday. The government must have known of the articles.

Yet, on the same day, February 27, the decree of censorship that had prevented the press from reproducing the articles was rescinded, three days before it need have been,* and in no more time than was required for translation and typesetting, Cuban newspapers brought out the story, or summaries of it, making it the "lead" article in virtually every journal on the island.

The arrogance of the government had led it into some remarkable blunders, and none more damaging than this. It is just possible that Batista, blinded by his own cynicism, failed to realize what echoes of dynamic idealism the ringing prose of the *Times* correspondent would evoke in Cuba, or what encouragement his disclosures would lend to an opposition that was, as yet, uncoordinated, almost unformed, and, to the extent that it *was* organized, fighting in the dark.

* Censorship had been imposed under emergency decree, made possible by a series of temporary suspensions of constitutional guarantees. Guarantees could be suspended, legally, for no more than forty-five days at a time, and the last such suspension had been on January 15th. Thus, censorship in this instance was lifted before the automatic restoration of guarantees, on March 1, would have required.

Fidel was alive. That in itself meant much. Incredibly, he was fighting a successful guerrilla campaign, the very existence of which had been no more than a whispered rumor to most Cubans.

Matthews went on to describe a formidable movement of opposition to Batista that had been developing, known only by hearsay to perhaps the majority of the people on the island outside of Oriente, a revolutionary movement that called itself both socialistic and nationalistic, comprised of the social elements which the *Times* correspondent described as the best in Cuban life—"the unspoiled youth, the honest businessman, the politician of integrity, the patriotic army officer."

These elements, Matthews said, were supporting a program which, although vague, amounted to "a new deal for Cuba."

The old, corrupt order in Cuba is being threatened for the first time since the Cuban Republic was proclaimed early in the century. An internal struggle is now taking place that is more than an effort by the outs to get in and enjoy the enormous spoils of office that have been the reward of political victory. This is the real and deeply significant meaning of what is happening in Cuba today, and it explains the gravity of the menace to the military dictatorship of President Fulgencio Batista.

The rebels fighting in the mountains, wrote Matthews, were backed by thousands of Cubans who were "heart and soul" with Fidel Castro. The reporter's own feeling, he said, was that the revolutionary leader was invincible in his mountain retreat.

With any luck, the *Times* man concluded, Batista could hang on until the expiration of his term in February of 1959, but he had lost the younger generation in Cuba, and, "from the look of things," he had no hope of suppressing the revolution.

The reaction of the Havana government, when it finally awoke to the damage that was being done, was an angry, blanket denial of the Matthews report. The Cuban minister of defense, Santiago Verdeja Neyra, declared in a cable to the *New York Herald Tribune* that the "interview and adventures described by Correspondent Matthews can be considered a chapter in a fantastic novel."

The defense minister asserted that Matthews had *not* interviewed the "pro-Communist insurgent, Fidel Castro," and remarked that it was strange that Matthews had not taken pains to produce a photograph of himself with Castro, if he had actually had the opportunity. *The New York Times* promptly published such a photograph. The Havana government responded with the assertion that the photograph obviously could not have been made in the Sierra Maestra, since the vegetation shown was not typical of that found in the Sierra. The commanding officer in the Oriente zone of operations, General Martín Díaz Tamayo, contributed to the debate by declaring that it would have been impossible for anyone to penetrate the army lines which had been thrown about the section in which Fidel was operating. Hence, said the General, there was no doubt whatever that it was "an imaginary interview."

Within six weeks, an American radio-television reporter and a cameraman were in the Sierra with the rebels,* and in May the fruit of their effort, a half-hour documentary film containing an interview with Fidel atop Pico Turquino ("We have struck the spark of the revolution. The last battle will be fought in the capital . . .") established beyond question the veracity of Matthews' report.

Díaz Tamayo's boast that no one could penetrate the army lines was effectively given the lie, and other reporters, following, continued to demonstrate its hollowness. The

---

* Taber and Wendell Hoffman, Columbia Broadcasting System, "Rebels of the Sierra Maestra."

army, for its part, continued vainly to declare that all was well. On March 1st, the chief of the military press service announced that the situation in the Sierra Maestra was "practically normal," and that the troops in the Sierra were, in fact, about to embark on a program of home and school construction for the benefit of the poverty-stricken *guajiros*. As to the rebels, the army spokesman said they had been reduced to about twenty as a result of the January raid on La Plata, in which, he asserted, the army had killed forty rebels and captured twelve. The remaining insurgents, he said, had scattered in groups of two and three, and were desperately trying to escape the army dragnet.

On the same date, a published report from Oriente told of clashes between rebel and army forces during the preceding several days in no fewer than seven separate areas in the foothills of the Sierra. It was also reported that the army was using artillery against Fidel's forces, and that the military intelligence service (SIM) was being strengthened by an additional two hundred men, at the request of the army chief of staff, General Francisco Tabernilla.

A short while later, it was further disclosed that the army was air-lifting twelve hundred troops into the Oriente zone of operations, to reinforce the soldiers already there.

It was difficult to see the need, in view of the declarations of the government. The fact was that the government was trying desperately to do two things at once—to stamp out the insurrection and at the same time to persuade the public that it had already done so. It failed in both efforts.

Civil guarantees, suspended on January 15th for a forty-five-day period, were automatically restored on March 1st. On March 2nd, Batista imposed another forty-five-day suspension, attributing his action to continuing acts of terrorism throughout the island, and the need to protect the vital sugar harvest.

On March 7th, General Tabernilla declared that Fidel Castro's forces had been "completely overcome."

On March 10th, denouncing Castro as "an agent of the Soviet Union," Batista announced that the rebels in the Sierra Maestra had now been reduced to scarcely a dozen.

Tabernilla's announcement coincided with a report from the United States Embassy in Havana, which, after keeping the matter quiet for some weeks, disclosed that three youths, the dependents of United States naval personnel stationed at Guantánamo Bay, had vanished from the base on February 17th.

The youths were identified as Charles Ryan, Victor Buehlman, and Michael Garvey. There was speculation that they had joined the rebels in the Sierra Maestra. This was indeed the case, although the fact was not fully verified until the latter part of March, when photographs of the boys in uniform and photostatic copies of the oaths that they had signed, and of a letter which they had written to President Eisenhower, were made available to *The New York Times*.

The three young Americans were among a group of fifty-eight armed and uniformed recruits who went into the Sierra to reinforce Fidel in mid-March, and although the government had greatly exaggerated the difficulties that the rebels were having in the mountains, it must be admitted that the reinforcements and the arms they carried provided a badly needed transfusion of strength.

Supplies and uniforms for the recruits were provided by the *Resistencia Cívica* in Santiago. Their weapons came from an arms pool that had been organized by Frank País, who had been stockpiling arms sent from all over the island to be forwarded to Fidel, at his express request. Some of the weapons came from the U. S. naval base at Guantánamo Bay, where a large and active 26th of July underground was flourishing.

The rebel reinforcements were assembled, a few men at a

time, on a rice farm outside of Manzanillo. On the night of March 14th, they climbed into two stolen trucks and drove into the foothills. The empty trucks were abandoned, and the new rebel unit, commanded by Jorge Sotús, one of the outstanding fighters of the November uprising in Santiago, began the long march into the mountains, to join Fidel.

In Havana the sensation produced by the Matthews report was having its effect not only on the government and the populace, but on revolutionary factions which may be considered to have been, to varying degrees, *rivals* of the 26th of July organization, notwithstanding the fact that some of them were also collaborators.

Included were several separate action groups within or related to the university students' federation, one of these being the revolutionary directorate headed by José Antonio Echevarría, who had signed a pact of unity with Fidel in Mexico the preceding summer. Also included were a number of agents, followers, or former partisans of the deposed president Prío.

Prío had been pouring money into arms for various revolutionary groups in Cuba almost from the beginning of his exile. In all, he is said to have spent five million dollars for the purpose over a period of slightly less than seven years. The estimate is probably conservative. Through ill fortune, bad management, and the efficiency of the Batista intelligence service, most of the arms that arrived from Mexico and the United States were seized almost as soon as they had reached Cuba.

Among the beneficiaries of Prío's largesse was a Spanish refugee named Martin Labandero, a former Loyalist officer who had fought against Franco during the civil war in Spain. During the summer of 1956, Labandero organized a group of more than one hundred youthful insurgents, most of them university students active in the FEU, and proceeded to lay plans to assassinate Batista. Reportedly, Prío himself was to come to Havana, entering the country by a clandestine route, to be on hand when Labandero's students attacked the presidential palace. Presumably the former president would again have been installed in office, had the plot succeeded.

Needless to say, it failed. An informer alerted the authorities to the preparations that were being made; and, shortly before the attack was to have been launched, police and SIM agents raided the headquarters of the conspirators in a garage in the Jesús del Monte section of the capital, seized their arsenal, and arrested a third of the plotters.

Labandero escaped, only to be arrested the following October in connection with a plot to blow up the Línea tunnel linking the suburb of Vedado on the outskirts of Havana with Marianao. Members of the group stormed the Príncipe prison and actually succeeded in freeing their leader, but he broke a leg while fleeing down the steep hill from the prison, was re-captured, and soon afterwards was shot.

Command of what remained of the Labandero group fell to Carlos Gutiérrez Menoyo, also a veteran of the civil war in Spain, later a fighter in the French underground, and then a sergeant with U.S. forces in Europe during the second world war. Like Labandero, Gutiérrez Menoyo was for a time committed to Prío. The nature of the liaison is not important. In any event, a certain disenchantment had occurred, perhaps related to the remarkable regularity with which arms sent by Prío's agents were being seized by the authorities. Menoyo decided to break with Prío, and act independently.

The same decision had been reached by a Havana bus company official and former *priísta* senator named Menelao Mora.

The two combined their forces, amounting, in all, to about two hundred fifty men.

On February 25th, Menoyo, having decided that the

group needed an operational headquarters for imminent action, sent an agent, Luis Goicochea, to rent an apartment. Goicochea and his wife leased the top floor of a three-story building on 21st Street, in the Vedado section. Another member of the group rented the bottom floor. On March 9th, some fifty men moved into the two apartments, arriving a few at a time, during the night.

Menoyo revealed his plan. It was, in essence, the same plan originally conceived by Labandero (quite possibly, in fact, by Prío, who knew the presidential palace, and the habits of Cuban presidents, as well as anyone). The revolutionaries were to storm the palace, assassinate Batista, and—?

In the minds of most of the conspirators that was enough. It was to be a suicide attack. One sees, in the imagination of the participants, the dramatic climactic scene: the bloodied, dying dictator, the cheering populace, the solemn proclamation from a balcony of the palace, and the slow Hollywood fade-out.

José Antonio Echevarría and the leader of another FEU group, Faure Chaumont, were invited to participate. Some of the members of the 26th of July movement were also brought in, but as individuals and not as representatives of the movement. Fidel had not been consulted. He said later that, if he had wanted Batista assassinated, he could easily enough have found a less costly method. He preferred to fight in his own way, and said he viewed terrorism as at best a dangerous and unreliable expedient.

Echevarría was to lead a group of students in four automobiles to the broadcasting station of Radio Reloj in Vedado, seize the station, and broadcast the announcement that the presidential palace had fallen and that Batista was dead. Volunteers were to be asked to assemble at the university, where they would be given arms with which to carry out further instructions.

It was agreed that Menoyo himself would lead the first wave of the assault on the presidential palace, commanding a group of fifty armed fighters, who would storm the entrance and seek out Batista in his office on the second floor of the building. Faure Chaumont was named second in command.

A *priísta* named Ignacio González was to lead the second wave, consisting of one hundred fifty to two hundred men, members of what was to become Prío's *Organizacion Auténtica*. González' men were to ring the palace square and to occupy the rooftops of the buildings commanding the palace, to hold off the army reinforcements that might be expected to come to the aid of the palace guard.

The tentative date of the assault was March 12th. An informant who had access to the palace was to telephone the conspirators' headquarters in Vedado if Batista were in his office. If the call came before three o'clock in the afternoon, the plans for the attack would be put in motion immediately. If not, the attack would be postponed until the following day.

For three days before the action was to occur, the forty-odd men who were to comprise the first wave of the assault force were confined to the building on 21st Street. Smoking was curtailed, so as not to arouse the suspicions of the neighbors. Conversation was conducted in whispers. The only party to the conspiracy permitted to leave the building was Luis Goicochea. Goicochea, a thirty-three-year-old native of Matanzas, employed as a bookkeeper in a Havana dry goods store while studying civil service administration and political science at the University, was to have the questionable privilege of riding in the first assault car with Gutiérrez Menoyo. While waiting, he busied himself with small errands—the purchase of groceries, a few at a time, from different stores in the neighborhood, final meetings with the liaison officers of the other groups that were to take part in the attack on the palace.

March 12th came and went. There was no telephone call. It came the following morning, shortly after eleven o'clock. The information was that the president was in the palace. He planned to have lunch there, and would be back in his second-floor office after the luncheon hour—three o'clock.

In the building on 21st Street, Goicochea and a companion laid out food for those who might wish to eat something before leaving. No one touched it. The conspirators waited, nervously.

At three o'clock, they began to file from the building, ignoring the stares of the few passers-by on the street as they entered the three vehicles at the curb, an inconspicuous blue Buick sedan, a faded red panel truck with black fenders and the words "Fast Delivery" painted on the sides, a red-and-cream-colored Ford. Goicochea entered the blue sedan, with Gutiérrez Menoyo. Chaumont rode in the Ford.

All were wearing open-necked sports shirts and slacks, to distinguish them from the people in the palace, where coats and ties were customarily worn. All carried heavy .45-caliber automatic pistols tucked in the waistbands of their trousers, beneath their shirts. There were other weapons in the cars.

The three vehicles moved away from the curb, and turned toward the city proper, maintaining a distance of about twelve yards between them. Once the blue sedan became separated from the other vehicles, and had to circle a block to rejoin the caravan. Otherwise there was no problem. En route, at the appointed corner, Ignacio González was waiting. He lifted his hand as the caravan passed, to signal that all was well.

Havana, April 22 (AP)—President Fulgencio Batista laughed when told that his political opponents called him a "dictator." "Yes, I've often heard that," he said, "but I think that the only dictatorship around here is that which my beloved wife and four sons exert upon me."

VI

"RADIO RELOJ reporting . . . Radio Reloj reporting . . . At this moment, armed civilians are attacking the presidential palace! Radio Reloj reporting—President Batista has been struck down by bullets in the presidential palace!"

The time: 3:25 P.M. The date: March 13, 1957.

The radio announcement, preceded by the clatter of a telegraph key and delivered in the dramatic, bulletin style of Havana's familiar news-and-time channel,* carried a note of urgency that sent a shiver of apprehension through the capital. Traffic slowed on the broad Malecón as drivers, hearing it, reached to turn up the volume of their automobile radios. An unaccustomed ripple of excitement interrupted the drowsy afternoon routine of banks and business offices, halted the chatter in bars and cafes along the Prado, quickened the pulse of police precinct commanders and aging army staff officers at Camp Columbia.

The voice of another announcer cut in, reporting that General Francisco Tabernilla, the chief of staff, had been relieved of his command and was under arrest, along with other high-ranking officers of the regime. The announcer introduced a third speaker. The voice that was heard after a moment's hesitation, beginning a formal proclamation, was that of José Antonio Echevarría, president of the FEU and head of its revolutionary directory: "People of Havana! The Revolution is in progress. The presidential palace has been taken by our forces, and the dictator has been executed in his den . . ."

* Radio Reloj, i.e., "Radio Clock."

The voice was abruptly cut off, as a switch was thrown in the radio transmitting plant.

A moment later, a fusillade of pistol shots smashed the central control panel in the Radio Center building in Vedado and the three students who had seized the Radio Reloj studio hurried out of the building, pushing one of the announcers ahead of them.

Other armed students had been standing guard in the lobby and outside of the entrance. Now all of them entered two automobiles that had been standing at the curb. The announcer,* apparently a hostage, was pushed away and told to continue walking down the street.

The two cars sped away, heading in the direction of the University, even as sirens began to sound and the first of the police vehicles that were already converging on the area came into sight. An automobile was intercepted. There was a roar of automatic fire. The students scattered, on foot. One of them was left behind: Echevarría.†

The FEU leader had kept his part of the pact signed with Fidel Castro, eight months before, in Mexico. For him the revolution was over. He lay dead in the gutter, his dark eyes closed, his boyish face a ghastly white, thin lips compressed in a half-smile half-grimace of pain, blood seeping slowly from under the thick, wavy chestnut hair.

The report of Batista's death had been false, based on expectation and not on certain knowledge. He was alive. But

---

* The announcer was Floreal Chaumont, a brother of Faure Chaumont, one of the leaders of the conspiracy. While not actually a party to the plot, Floreal had known something of it, and it was thought best to get him out of the building before police arrived. He went into hiding, two months later took refuge in the El Salvador Embassy, and left the country under a safe conduct.

† The two students who seized Radio Reloj with Echevarría were José Westbrook, propaganda secretary of the FEU, and Fructuoso Rodríguez, for a time secretary-general of the offshoot organization which assumed the name of Directorio Revolucionario. Both survived the events of March 13th only to be killed by police a week later.

he had come close to death and was not yet out of danger. The attack on the palace was in progress.

The assault, simple and suicidal, as one reporter called it, had a single purpose: assassination. There had been some talk of forcing Batista to telephone General Tabernilla and order the chief of staff to surrender the Camp Columbia garrison. But to whom? The idea was absurd. Batista would probably have refused to make that small concession to his reputation as a fighter. Had he done so, no military commander would have paid him the slightest heed, under the circumstances. It is doubtful that the idea was discussed at all seriously.

Echevarría's students were prepared to occupy the University, and some arms had been stockpiled with which to make a stand there. According to Faure Chaumont, the rebel coalition was prepared to fight for control of the city itself. In the light of later developments, one must dismiss the statement as the rhetoric of revolutionary enthusiasm. The Camp Columbia garrison had crushed far more serious uprisings in the past with little difficulty, and there is nothing to indicate that this one would have presented any great problem.

Of the palace assailants of March 13th, only four succeeded in penetrating to Batista's second-floor offices, and only one of these survived the revolution to tell about it: Luis Goicochea, the thirty-three-year-old civil administration student from Matanzas. The account that follows is largely based on his experience.

The blue sedan in which Goicochea and Carlos Gutiérrez Menoyo rode, with two other men, reached the Colon Street entrance of the palace at precisely 3:22 P.M., a few minutes before Echevarría burst into the radio station in Vedado to keep his appointment with death.

The car drew up behind an army jeep parked across the

street from the palace. There was a policeman posted on each corner.

Without waiting for the men with him or the two vehicles following, the action leader, Menoyo, stepped from the sedan, swung quickly about with a submachine gun in his hands, and fired a short burst at the policeman on the west corner of the palace, at the junction of Zuluata and Colon. Without pausing to take note of the effect of his shots, he put his head down and charged toward the black iron gate of the palace, firing as he ran. Goicochea and the two men with him followed at his heels, also firing.

For reasons never explained, only three or four soldiers were at the gate, where normally there would have been a dozen. All fell before the first wave of the assault, and the assailants burst through the gate to find only dead or dying men in their immediate path.

Inside, there was a delay. A few soldiers on the ground floor of the palace had taken shelter behind the stone columns of the interior courtyard, and they began to fire rifles. A moment later, a machine gun on the other side of the courtyard opened fire.

The men in Faure Chaumont's car and the nearly thirty rebels in the red "Fast Delivery" truck had also run into trouble. A passing bus had cut in between the first car to reach the palace and the two vehicles following, forcing the second car and the truck to halt short of the palace gate, near the corner of Colon and Monserrate.

Menoyo's first burst had alerted the palace guard throughout the area, and now Chaumont's car and the truck filled with men came under direct fire from several directions. A .30-caliber machine gun emplaced high in the Church of Santo Angel on the corner opened up. Simultaneously, the rifles and automatic weapons of soldiers on the roof and upper floors of the palace began to speak.

The men climbing out of the panel truck were scattered by what Chaumont describes, in his account of the attack, as a "rain of bullets." A few of the rebels fled across the broad lawns and through the hedges and sculptured catalpa trees of the Parque Presidente Zayas, bullets singing about their heads and flinging up pebbles from the gravel walks beneath their feet. The majority chose the short and suicidal path taken by Gutiérrez Menoyo. About half of the entire force, a score or so of determined youths, gained entrance to the palace. Few of these came out alive.

Gutiérrez Menoyo and the three men with him—Goicochea, José Castellanos, and Luis Almeida—had paused inside the gate. Now, with Menelao Mora, Chaumont, and seven or eight others at their heels, they ran up the white marble steps from the guardroom on their left, stopping only to destroy the palace telephone switchboard with a grenade. The machine gun in the patio had already been put out of action and there were no immediate obstacles to the second floor.

At the top of the stairs, they turned east along the narrow hallway past a row of closed office doors, heading for the southeast corner of the palace. Goicochea remembers having seen a woman who stepped from one of the offices, screamed "Don't shoot!" and abruptly vanished, as though by magic.

Something halted the group at the end of the corridor. The rebels retraced their steps, seeking a route that would lead them to Batista's offices on the other side of the building. A locked door at the end of the west hallway barred their progress. One of the men put a submachine-gun burst through the door, then shot off the lock and kicked the door open. Beyond was a gleaming, white-tiled kitchen, then a spacious dining hall and an unpolished mahogany table forty feet long, bare except for two demitasse cups at its farther end, in the President's place. Three frightened servants wearing the gray-blue palace livery were huddled in a corner. Goicochea says that his first impulse was to shoot them. They were the first "enemies" he had met, and he was understandably excited. Menoyo restrained him. The mess attendants, pale with fear, said that the President had just taken his after-luncheon coffee and had retired. They did not know where he had gone. The attendants were searched for weapons and left cowering in the corner, crouched on their heels.

Goicochea leaped up on the long table and ran three-quarters of its length, looking through the windows to see what was happening outside. He jumped off, ran to a window, thrust his carbine through the slats, and fired at a police car below on the street. Then he leaped back on the table and off on the other side, and ran to join three of his comrades as they entered the ceremonial Hall of Mirrors leading to the north end of the building. The others in the group had gone in another direction: Goicochea does not remember where, or why.

The four insurgents ran the length of the great Hall of Mirrors, and phantom warriors ran crazily beside them, while others, disheveled, wild, menacing, appeared to charge toward them: their own images, reflected in the glittering mirrors that paneled the empty, echoing hall.

Beyond the Hall of Mirrors there was a small anteroom and swinging, opaque glass-and-wood doors that opened onto the first office of the presidential executive suite. Outside of the palace the crash and rattle of furious gunfire could be heard. From inside the office came the sound of excited voices.

Goicochea was on the right of the swinging doors. Gutiérrez Menoyo, José Castellanos, and Luis Gómez Wangüemert were on the left, close to the wall. Gutiérrez Menoyo shouted, "Come out with your hands up!" There was a moment of stunned silence, then a salvo of pistol shots, the bullets shattering the opaque glass panels of the swinging doors.

Menoyo waited for a moment. Then he cautiously reached out and tossed a grenade into the office, through the broken glass. It failed to explode. The grenades were of Brazilian manufacture, old and defective. The second failed, and the third. The fourth exploded with a shattering concussion. Instantly the rebels burst through the swinging doors, firing bursts from their automatic weapons to right and left.

Goicochea, entering behind the others, saw two men lying dead on the tile floor. He did not recognize either of them.

The conspirators had been provided with a detailed floor map of the palace, indicating a secret passage leading from Batista's offices to his residential quarters on the floor above. No such passage could be found.

To reach the third floor was beginning to seem impossible. Machine-gun and rifle fire was coming from the third floor balcony walk ringing the interior courtyard; the troops up there were directing their aim at anything that moved on the lower floors or in the courtyard itself. The four men in the presidential office suite had little ammunition left, and the sound of the shooting above warned them that their time was rapidly running out. Yet they were reluctant to withdraw without making some final effort to accomplish their mission.

Stepping outside onto the second floor balcony walk, José Castellanos tried to hurl a grenade to the balcony above, judging by the uproar immediately over his head that it would fall close to the machine gun that was dominating the courtyard. The grenade hit the balcony railing and fell back. The four rebels leaped to cover behind a pillar as it exploded six feet from them. No one was hurt.

They hastened back through the Hall of Mirrors and,

peering through the closed French doors that gave onto an
outside balcony overlooking the mall of the Avenida de las
Misiones park, they saw a swarm of police cars and three or
four policemen on foot. The police, weapons in hand, were
cautiously advancing toward the palace. Goicochea and
Gómez Wangüemert fired in their direction, but the range
was too great, and the trees in the park sheltered the men
on the ground. Menoyo's "grease gun" had jammed. Castellanos had almost exhausted his ammunition.

It was time to retreat. They had expected reinforcements
from the second wave of the assault force by this time. None
had appeared. The four men now made their way back
through the dining room, passing the servants still crouched
in a corner, through the kitchen, and back to the south corridor.

There was a sign over a door that said "Telegraph Office"
and a telephone was ringing inside. They entered the
small office and found Luis Almeida there. Wangüemert
picked up the phone, listened for a moment, and said: "Yes,
it is true. The palace has fallen. Batista is dead. We are
free!" He hung up.

José Machado and another man, whose name Goicochea
has forgotten, appeared in the corridor. The rebels, now
seven in all, prepared to descend to the ground floor. To do
so, it was necessary to cross an open landing on the stairway
by which they had ascended. The machine gun on the upper
balcony at the north end of the building was still firing
sporadically across the courtyard, sweeping the landing and
everything in sight.

Castellanos was first to go. He stepped squarely out onto
the landing, loosed a submachine-gun burst in the direction
from which the fire was coming, and was cut down instantly as he fired. Menoyo, infuriated, leaped onto the
landing, and he, too, was instantly hit. He staggered back a

few paces and fell dead at the feet of his comrades. The others ran the gauntlet successfully, one at a time. Now there were only five.

Goicochea was the last to reach the guardroom below. The marble stairs and the tile floor were slick with blood and the guardroom and the patio littered with dead. There was no one alive but Goicochea and his four companions. Chaumont and a few others had escaped, but this was not to be discovered until later.

There was no indication that Ignacio González' men had ever reached the palace. The first wave had been entirely unsupported. Some of the conspirators had succeeded in placing a machine gun on the roof of the Sevilla-Biltmore Hotel overlooking the palace, but it never got into action.

Troops arriving in front of the palace completely dominated the park, pouring thousands of rounds into the buildings facing it and the rows of automobiles parked around it, acting, perhaps, under the impression that the palace was under attack from outside. An American tourist who put his head out of a hotel window was shot down by an armored-car gunner before he could withdraw it. The plate glass of the museum directly opposite the palace was smashed and its handsome black marble facing was pocked with holes from .50-caliber machine-gun bullets.

As yet, however, no troops had even attempted to approach the south side of the palace, where the rebels had breached the gate. The five men still in the building, leaving the way they had come, found no immediate obstacle before them as they moved through the gate and along the curving walls of the semi-circular entrance on Calle Colon.

At the curb were the vehicles in which they had arrived, riddled with bullet holes, and in the sun-baked street lay the bloody corpses of eight or ten youths who had died trying to reach the palace. Beyond, in the Parque Presidente Zayas, other bodies lay sprawled in attitudes of interrupted flight.

Nothing moved, in the street or in the park. Above them, the survivors could hear the heavy staccato of a machine gun and the sporadic boom of rifles, although no targets were to be seen. In the intervals of firing, there was no other sound. A heavy stillness seemed to hold the entire city, the afternoon air was shimmering and glassy, the eyes of the five survivors ached in the glare of the sun, their ears rang, and they moved on leaden limbs, like sleepwalkers.

Wangüemert was the first to make the inevitable decision. He ran heavily across the street and into the park. Juan Pedro Carbó and José Machado followed. Goicochea, too, started across the street. He heard a muffled shout behind him and, turning his head as the guns above again started to chatter, saw Almeida still at the palace entrance—his last sight of him on earth.

He ran on, faster now, moving diagonally left through the park. Nearing the broad ornamental pool at its center, he saw Wangüemert, running ahead of him, stagger and fall in mid-stride as he came under the sights of the machine-gunners in the palace.

Goicochea plunged headlong into the bushes and rolled against the foot-high rim of the pool, pressing close to it as bits of cement chipped off by the machine-gun bullets showered down on him. Lying there, he could see the bodies of ten or fifteen fallen comrades scattered on the green grass, now reddened with their blood. The walks of the park, he says, resembled "rivers of blood." The firing continued. For a time—it could have been several minutes—he fell into a reverie, seeing in his mind's eye the hectic events of the afternoon, in vivid sequence, "like a war movie."

He does not know how long he remained there, but only that, at the first lull in the shooting, he again became a fighting machine, instantly up and off, zigzagging through bushes and flower beds and among the trees, then out of the park and in full flight across the avenue and on at top speed into Calle Villegas at the nearest intersection.

A man thrust his head through the doorway of a tavern on the corner of Villegas and said in a stage whisper, "Quick! In here!"

Reacting by pure reflex, Goicochea bared his teeth and shouted, "Get inside or I'll kill you!" He had raised his carbine in a menacing gesture, becoming aware for the first time as he did so that it was still gripped tightly in his sweaty hands, in the position of attack. The stranger hastily withdrew.

Panting, Goicochea slowed his pace to a walk, and continued swiftly up Calle Villegas. As he walked he began to take account of his condition. His clothing had been perforated by fragments of the grenade that had exploded near him in the palace; the rents in the cloth resembled large, ragged mothholes. His trousers were pierced in no fewer than ten places by bullet holes. His brown-and-white-checked sports shirt, wet with sweat and blood, was plastered to his body. He discovered that he was bleeding from a flesh wound in his right forearm, although he could not remember having been hit, and felt no pain.

He was entering the old section of the city. At this hour— it was now past five o'clock—the narrow street would normally have been filled with cars and hurrying pedestrians, homeward bound from the shops and offices. But there was nothing, no one. The shops were closed, the street empty.

Goicochea's problem was to dispose of his carbine and bandolier of cartridges, and to find a change of clothing. At Number 13 Villegas, next to a shuttered bicycle shop, he saw an open door and the stairway of an apartment. A man and a woman were coming down the stairs. The woman, seeing the armed and bloody apparition approaching, gasped and exclaimed, "Don't shoot!"

"No tenga miedo, señora," the fugitive replied, politely. Brushing past the couple, he dropped his weapon and bandolier behind the door, and continued deliberately on his way.

He was not yet out of danger. Approaching the next intersection, he was startled by the blast and whine of a sudden rifle shot from the roof of a building across the street. He scurried to the opposite sidewalk and hastened on.

Halfway up the next block he saw a policeman strolling from a corner cafe. The policeman glanced casually in his direction, then, without seeming to see him, continued across the street and out of sight.

Goicochea crossed the street again—he was still on Villegas—and entered the same cafe. He ordered coffee, gulped it down, and hurried out again, turning the corner in the opposite direction from that taken by the policeman.

In the middle of the block he encountered a woman (he recalls that she was young and pretty, with red hair) lounging in the doorway of an apartment building. With the briefest of explanations, he asked her for a change of clothing. The girl replied, seriously and courteously, that she lived with her mother and had nothing that a man could wear.

Goicochea retraced his steps to Calle Villegas and took serious thought, for the first time, of where he must go. The only close refuge possible was the dry goods shop in which he had worked as a bookkeeper, and he now realized that he had been walking toward it, unconsciously, all the while. There were six more intersections to cross, and in the distance he could still hear the roll and thunder of gunfire.

He walked the remaining six and a half blocks without meeting anyone, and reached the shop. It was open. A few men and women were standing outside, talking in low voices. They eyed him curiously as he entered, but said nothing.

An hour later, wearing a new shirt, a pair of new green slacks, and a gray summer sports jacket, his face washed and his wound bandaged, Goicochea was driven by the son of one of the shop-owners to the apartment of a girl acquaintance in Vedado. At the end of the week, he moved to another apartment, and after a month in hiding, he was taken to his father's farm in the province of Matanzas, near the village of Perico. By year's end he was fighting in the mountains of Las Villas Province with the guerrillas of the "Second National Front Escambray," led by Eloy Gutiérrez Menoyo, a brother of the leader of the palace assault.

A bronze plaque in the anteroom of the executive office suite in the palace, placed there since the Revolution, reads:

On March 13th of 1957, a group of Cuban fighters reached this point with the intention of executing the tyrant Batista, in order to re-conquer lost liberties. Remain constant to this heroic gesture, so that injustice and oppression may never again return to Cuba.

At the bottom of the plaque, in smaller letters, is the line:

Directorio Revolucionario 13 de Marzo.

Practically speaking, the date marks the founding of the Revolutionary Directory (DR) as a fighting organization distinct from the small, loosely knit *directorio revolucionario* of the FEU, headed by Echevarría.

It was a costly initiation. First reports placed the death toll at thirty-three; the final "official" figure was forty, including five members of the palace guard slain in the attack. That total does not, however, begin to take into account the many conspirators and suspected revolutionaries who were hunted down and killed by the police *after* the palace assault, numbering some seventy-five to eighty victims in all, according to the estimates of the various revolutionary organizations.

It has not been possible to verify the number. Scores of bodies, buried in unmarked graves in cemeteries, in the cellars of police stations, and even in the parade ground at

Camp Columbia, have been exhumed since the overthrow of Batista. In most cases, the circumstances of their death and their very identity remains unknown.

Among the unquestionable instances of reprisal slayings, evident at the time, were the murders of three youths whose deaths were reported in the Havana newspapers of March 14. Two of them had been hanged, the third shot to death. Popular report, later sustained by the testimony of witnesses who had seen the youths being arrested, said that they had met their death at the hands of the notorious captain of police, Esteban Ventura.

Far more shocking than even the murder of the three youths, to a people almost inured to the casual killing of students, was the assassination of Dr. Pelayo Cuervo Navarro, a respected former Cuban senator and leader of the *Ortodoxo* party, whose body, pierced by eight bullets, was found in the early morning hours of March 14th at the edge of a little lake in the fashionable Country Club suburb of the capital.

Dr. Cuervo's wife heard the news of his death on the radio and went to identify his corpse. She was able to shed little light on his murder, other than to say that he had spent the night away from his home in Marianao, anticipating, with an apprehension all too well founded, that there would be reprisals for the attack on the palace. She said that police had been to the house during the night to search for her husband. They had found her alone with her ailing infant granddaughter.

The police had also called at the home of Dr. Vidal Morales, a prominent attorney and, like Dr. Cuervo himself, a former revolutionary of the Machado era. Not finding the man they were seeking, the police took Morales.

He relates that he was held incommunicado in the dread Bureau of Investigation headquarters in Havana for four days and subjected to numerous indignities, not the worst of which was to be forced to drink water from a toilet. He did not learn of the death of his friend until after his own release.

Cuervo was found, at length, in a home in the suburb of La Sierra, the residence of José Aguirre Oteiza, a financier with sugar interests in Oriente. Dr. Cuervo himself answered the door, and was informed that he was under arrest. He was seen to enter one of the three automobiles that had drawn up in front of the house. Some hours later his body was discovered at the edge of the Country Club Lake.

Post-revolutionary investigation has disclosed the names of the assassins, and of those who directed them. The evidence produced leaves no room for doubt that the order for Dr. Cuervo's murder came directly from the presidential palace, from Batista himself. The agents who transmitted the order were Colonel Orlando Piedra, then chief of the dreaded Bureau of Investigation, and his deputy, Lieutenant Colonel Mariano Faget. The actual killer was the head of the Bureau's narcotics squad, Sergeant Rafael Gutiérrez.

It speaks volumes for the character of Batista's police enforcers to learn that one of the men who accompanied Gutiérrez on his mission was not a policeman but a notorious informer, assassin, and narcotics addict, employed by the Bureau for just such tasks.

Cuervo was driven to the edge of the lake and ordered from the automobile which he had entered at the house in La Sierra. The driver later testified that Sergeant Gutiérrez, submachine gun in hand, asked the elderly political leader to give him the names of the persons who had provided the arms for the assault on the palace. The question was a mere formality. When the older man replied that he knew nothing of any arms, Gutiérrez shot him down without another word.

A short while later the police radio, broadcasting the names of persons killed during the disorders of the day,

announced that the body of an unidentified man had been
found at the edge of the *laguito del Country Club*. The dead
man was, of course, Pelayo Cuervo Navarro.

The question of interest is not who killed Pelayo Cuervo,
but why? The answer is evident in the victim's personal
character, reputation, and political position. The *Ortodoxo*
leader had been a fearless voice of political conscience in
Cuba. His public denunciations of the dictatorship, in a
series of CMQ radio broadcasts and elsewhere, had tended
to arouse Cuban conservatives whose natural inclination
might otherwise have been to let sleeping dogs lie and to
pursue the course of least resistance. And he was on the
point of saying, and doing, much more.

It will be recalled that Cuervo had been one of the attorneys in a court action brought against the military authorities responsible for the murder of prisoners following
the abortive attack on the Cuartel Goicuría in Matanzas
in 1956.

About a year before his assassination he had filed another
suit, a citizen's action to block a proposed increase in the
rates of the American-owned Cuban Telephone Company,
adding fuel to a scandal that had reached directly into the
presidential palace,* involving both Batista and his minister
of communications.

For some years prior to this, Cuervo had been pressing
a suit against Grau San Martín, alleging that Grau, as
President, had looted the public treasury of upwards of one
hundred million pesos. And shortly before he was murdered,
the *Ortodoxo* leader had announced that he was finally
ready to start similar litigation against Batista himself. He
had further declared that he was in possession of ample
evidence to support the allegations that he intended to make.

In the light of what is known of the Batista regime, there

* The rate increase was granted on the day of the palace attack, within
a few hours after it occurred.

seems to be little doubt that such declarations could easily have sealed his death warrant, even had he not already been considered a serious threat to the political stability and continued illicit revenues of the regime.

Dr. Cuervo had been arrested some fifteen times between March 10, 1952, when Batista seized control of the government, and March 13, 1957, when the attorney was murdered. In some instances, his detention lasted for only a few hours; on four occasions he was held for periods ranging from a week to a month, without any specific charge being filed against him. His three sons were all active opponents of the regime, associated with Sánchez Arango's Triple A organization, and there is no doubt that the father, too, was involved to some degree. However, it is extremely doubtful that he had any part in, or was even aware of, the plot to assassinate Batista.

According to his widow, the *Ortodoxo* leader spent the morning prior to the palace assault in his law office. He returned to his residence in Marianao in the mid-afternoon, and there, hearing on the radio that the palace had been attacked, he decided that it might be wise to go into hiding, in view of the government's established practice of taking reprisals among prominent oppositionists for such incidents. It is unfortunate that he did not find a better hiding place.

Various published reports on Cuervo's assassination have referred to a slip of paper supposedly found in the pocket of the slain student leader, Echevarría, bearing the notation —"Pelayo Cuervo Navarro. *Presidente*."

The inference drawn is that Dr. Cuervo had been thought of as a candidate for provisional president in the event of Batista's death and the overthrow of the regime.

In actuality, it is highly unlikely that any such notation was found. Echevarría would certainly not have been in any position to name a provisional president. Nor would he have been likely, embarking on a virtual suicide mission, to have carried such incriminating evidence in his pocket.

Perhaps Batista actually believed that Dr. Cuervo *had* been involved. The more reasonable conclusion, however, is that the dictator simply chose this occasion, when the capital was in a state of emergency, and passions were running high, to remove a particularly uncomfortable thorn in his side.

In so doing, he may also have thought to take the opportunity to strike fear into the hearts of other prominent oppositionists, lest they be emboldened by the manifestation of popular unrest to raise new outcries against the regime.

If so, the effort backfired. Some fifty *Ortodoxo* leaders, headed by Raúl Chibás and Roberto Agramonte, promptly signed their names to a statement asserting that Pelayo Cuervo had been vilely assassinated by the Batista dictatorship and reaffirming a pledge to combat, by whatever means, the sinister regime which was staining Cuba with the blood of martyrs.

The bloodshed continued. It could scarcely have been otherwise. Batista had gone too far to draw back now.

On April 20th, five automobiles carrying a score of uniformed and plain-clothes policemen led by Captain Ventura drew up in front of an eight-story, chocolate-brown apartment building at Humboldt 7, a few doors off the Malecón and not far from the Hotel Nacional in Vedado. Policemen were posted around the building. Ventura led a squad directly to Apartment 201.

There were four youths in the apartment, all members of the *Directorio Revolucionario,* all important fugitives. Two of them, José Machado and Juan Pedro Carbó, had taken part in the attack on the palace. Six months earlier they had participated in the execution of the SIM chief, Colonel Antonio Blanco Rico. The other two were Fructuoso

Rodríguez, secretary-general of the *Directorio,* and José Westbrook Rosales, the twenty-year-old propaganda secretary of the DR, both survivors of the March 13th raid on Radio Reloj.

As the police entered the building, Machado and Carbó fled down an airshaft—in effect, a narrow, interior courtyard—to the floor below, reached an open window, and leaped fifty feet to the concrete pavement of an alley at the side of the apartment house. Machine-gunners who had been posted at the alley entrance killed them both as they lay there helpless, Machado already apparently lifeless from the fall, Carbó with both legs broken, weakly raising his hands in sign of surrender.

Rodríguez had also reached the floor below. He fled down the hallway, was caught at the stairway landing, thrust roughly against the wall, and shot before the astonished eyes of a woman tenant who witnessed the struggle from the peep-hole of her apartment door, only a few feet away.

José Westbrook had taken refuge in the apartment next door to the DR hideout. Fearing to bring harm to the occupants, he surrendered without a struggle, was led to the elevator landing, out of sight of tenants in the hallway, and there he, too, was shot.

One can only wonder at the policy which sanctioned such senseless slaughter. The fact that the Cuban law provided no death penalty, even for homicide, may have been a factor in provoking police and SIM agents who found themselves the prime targets of revolutionary terrorism to adopt methods which they certainly viewed as no more than fighting fire with fire. Yet it is clear enough that no better result of such methods could have been expected than an intensification of the bitterness already felt by a people whose sons were dying in what *they,* for their part, saw as a battle against tyranny. Each murder could only produce another martyr, and new recruits for the revolution.

Commenting editorially on the slaughter in Humboldt 7, *The New York Times* declared:

Whether any particular reader . . . is or is not acquainted with the difficulties of Cuba today, he must surely have had a shock on seeing a front-page story in the Sunday edition headlined: "Police in Havana Kill 4 Students." Most people will wonder at a situation where the police hunt down university students like the most dangerous type of criminals. They could also wonder why these students did not surrender when they saw themselves trapped.

The answer to these questions is that Cuba has a harsh military dictatorship which the youth of the island—the university students included—oppose. It has always been the tradition of Cuban students to fight and die for liberty. They did so against the Spaniards; they did so against the brutal dictatorship of President Gerardo Machado twenty-five and thirty years ago; they are doing so now against the dictatorship of General Fulgencio Batista.

Students like the four who were killed in Havana on Saturday are almost all well-bred, devoted, high-minded boys who—whether one agrees with them or not—fight and die for their ideal of freedom. The main reason they are nowadays shooting it out with the police or taking refuge in foreign embassies rather than surrender is that they know from previous experience that if arrested they will at the very least be beaten up, and may be tortured abominably.

This form of counter-terrorism is not bringing internal peace to Cuba. On the contrary, it is exacerbating an already embittered atmosphere . . .

In the same editorial, the *Times* added:

To keep denying that Fidel Castro, the young rebel leader, is in the Sierra Maestra, is bound to prove a boomerang. The truth is that Fidel Castro is still in the Sierra and apparently stronger than ever. In any circumstances, it is really useless to persuade Americans that all is well in Cuba today.

Batista laughed, two days after the Humboldt 7 incident, when an Associated Press correspondent told him in an interview that his "political opponents" called him a dictator.

"Yes, I've heard that," AP quoted him, "but I think the only dictatorship around here is that which my beloved wife and four sons exert on me."

In the same frolicsome vein, the General admitted that he kept a pistol in his desk drawer, and then produced a cap pistol with which he fired a few harmless shots.

"I would like to know," the AP report quoted Batista, "how I could be a dictator. Everywhere I go, people embrace me, and I know the people are happy and with me. There has never been a military man in my Cabinet. There are no restrictions on freedom of speech, freedom of press, freedom of religion. There are no concentration camps in this country. The Congress can override any legislation I might veto, or refuse to pass what I want passed. There is no libel law in Cuba. Everybody says what they want. Is this what dictatorship means?"

Sixteen rebels were killed in the battle, an announcement said. Army headquarters added that Government troops had suffered no casualties and were pressing their pursuit of the insurgents.

—*The New York Times,* May 29, 1957

VII

NEWSPAPER pictures of Batista made immediately after the abortive attempt on his life show him wearing an assured grin, his hands clasped overhead in the triumphant gesture of a veteran boxer who has won yet another in a long series of ring victories. No doubt he felt that way.

The meaning of defeat, too, is seen in the stark photographs of the losers, sprawled broken and blood-spattered on the pavement.

Yet this is not to say that the frustration of the assault on the presidential palace was actually a triumph for Batista, except in the sense that he had survived another crisis and emerged alive.

Nor can it be considered, in the long view, a serious setback to the forces of revolution. On the contrary, from the revolutionists' viewpoint, it may have been for the best.

One can easily imagine what success would have meant. At worst, a slaughter of opposition elements by the army, a mad scramble for power within the Cuban military establishment, and a succession of military juntas, prolonging the revolution indefinitely. And at best, perhaps, restoration of the political circumstances of the pre-Batista era— i.e., renewal of the very conditions that had created Batista in the first place.

In the latter instance, what would there have been to suggest any alternative to another slow, weary turn of the political wheel, moving again inevitably toward corruption, crisis, and *coup d'état?*

In failure, the assault on the palace still served, as *The*

New York Times observed, to cast "a lurid light on a dark and unhappy situation." In this respect, the sacrifice was not in vain.

But this is not the significant aspect. What was important, in the long view, was the effect the failure had on the revolutionary cadres themselves.

It is here that we come to the heart of the matter, the reasons that made the frustrated assassination attempt not merely another bloody chapter in a long history of bloodshed and frustration, but a turning point, a critical juncture in the Cuban Revolution.

In terms of what one might call intramural revolutionary politics, the plot to assassinate Batista had been, among other things, an acknowledgment of the strong lead which the *Movimiento 26* had seized, by the bold and quixotic filibuster in Oriente, with its powerful appeal to the romantic imagination.

As noted in an earlier chapter, the various insurgent groups in rivalry with the *fidelistas* had felt the need to "do something" if only as a matter of saving face. That there were also strong political and economic motivations on the part of some of those concerned is seen in the following leaf from a reporter's notebook,* dated March 2, 1957:

With regard to Batista's opposition, the U.S. Embassy in Havana feels that the oppositionists are divided among themselves principally by fear of the political demands that Fidel Castro might make, were he to emerge as the hero of a popular revolution. They don't want him on their team; they feel that he's too young, fiery, militaristic, anti-Yanqui; in their opinion, a potential dictator worse than the present one.

In this connection, my source in the Embassy agrees with Cuban contacts that Prío's people here in Havana probably do have a big cache of arms and are sitting on it, not so much for revolutionary purposes, as to use in exploiting the chaos that would be attendant on a popular uprising sparked by Fidel

* Taber, CBS.

Castro. That is, if Batista were to fall, the arms would be used in the resulting race to beat Fidel to the presidential palace.

The spring of 1957 found Fidel's position little changed from what it had been at the end of January, except that he now ranged over a wider expanse than before, and was more secure within the confines of his chosen zone of operations.

With the arrival of fifty-eight volunteers led into the mountains by Jorge Sotús in mid-March, he was able to muster perhaps one hundred forty lightly armed men; that is to say, the number for whom he was able to provide weapons. The heaviest arms possessed by the rebels were a few submachine guns and a single, antiquated light machine gun.

The terrain compensated for much that was lacking. The maze of mountains and valleys, the steep ascents and sudden precipices, the heavy cover of sub-tropical forest and brush favored the hit-and-run tactics of a guerrilla campaign.

The rebels were hardened by the life they lived. They had gained experience during the first months of their struggle for survival. They had the stoicism of fanatics and the will to fight.

The government troops, for their part, had little heart for challenging an invisible enemy and, indeed, little incentive to seek death in the mountains, far from barracks, bars, and brothels. They were not an army, but a constabulary, untrained and unfit for such a campaign.

In consequence, Fidel was able to engage the army or to avoid it as he chose. He could not be forced to fight except on his own terms. It was useless to pursue him, impossible to defend from sudden, devastating attack the numerous small outposts which the army had scattered through the foothills. On the other hand, the rebels could not yet safely venture onto the plain.

To the journalist marching through the Sierra with the

fidelista rebels during this early period, it seemed to be not so much a military campaign as a long, toilsome expedition through an interminable wilderness, a hiatus during which time stood still, and one's only preoccupation was with immediate necessities: rest from endless hours of climbing and slipping along muddy mountain footpaths, food to provide energy for yet another day or night of tramping through wet brush and bramble, shelter from the soaking spring rain.

The army was abandoning its fruitless campaign in the mountains and falling back on a strategy of confinement that was soon to prove equally futile. Government troops made only occasional forays into the Sierra, and rare encounters with army patrols scarcely broke the rhythm of the rebels' spartan existence.

Fidel was secure, but he did not yet have the means of posing a serious military threat outside of the Sierra. The army could accomplish nothing by entering, in whatever force. The situation was, in a word, static.

It nevertheless held promise. The *fidelistas* had not only an impregnable citadel, but a scattered rural population within it to sustain them, and sufficient military potency, even as a small guerrilla force, to keep several thousand soldiers engaged, creating a drain on the Cuban treasury and a continuing embarrassment to the Batista regime. Above all, the Sierra held the potential of future development.

The tangled political jungle of the Cuban underground offered less apparent promise, yet here, too, a potential existed, sufficient to justify the conclusions submitted in a report to the news directors of the Columbia Broadcasting System on April 1, 1957:

The revolution which Herbert Matthews sees in progress in Cuba does indeed exist, in the sense that a great many Cubans are at work in one way or another, gnawing away at the foundations of the existing government. The Batista regime will owe its downfall in large measure to the self-contradictory policy of denying the existence of any real opposition, while at the same time clandestinely employing the most brutal and unintelligent methods—and men—to suppress it. The very corruption of the regime is enough to insure its eventual overthrow.

At the moment, the anti-Batista forces lack two important elements of success: (a) a generally acceptable leader, (b) a mutually agreed-upon program. There is no real collaboration among these forces. Each bides its time, hoping to exploit the recklessness of the other. The opposition groups contain a number of diverse elements with totally opposed philosophies.

In view of the circumstances outlined, it would seem that the outlook for a popular, general uprising is remote. The revolutionaries are intelligent enough to see that. They say their hope is to keep the spark alive, to keep the country in a state of emergency which will undermine the government by damaging its economic and diplomatic arrangements, so as to create a climate in which the Batista regime must ultimately strangle and collapse of its own weight.

The underground is disorganized, inefficient; in the half-boast, half-apology of some of its members, it is made up of "a lot of amateurs." Yet the Batista regime, too, is confused, disorganized, inefficient, and, what is more, frightened.

Thus, although the government has the great advantage of being *in,* and solidly entrenched, time works against it. Fidel Castro serves a vital purpose in keeping the insurrection alive, in the public press and in the minds of the people. The same applies to the underground which exists outside of the Sierra Maestra. Each time the government captures or kills a young rebel courier, or jails or murders an elder statesman, or spends another five thousand dollars for information leading to the discovery of another arms cache, there is another newspaper headline, and another hundred Cubans enlisted on the side of the rebels.

Sooner or later, economic support, diplomatic support, must be withdrawn from Batista. The funds to subsidize public works will dwindle. Popular clamor will interfere with the free flow of graft. Police terrorism will reach an excess which will demand reforms even within the police state. The agents of that state will begin to look out for their own skins and investment. And the end will be at hand.

Although the end was still far off in April of 1957, the events of March had brought it appreciably nearer. The failure of the assault on the presidential palace left the underground groups which had participated in the attack rudderless and demoralized. Influential and wealthy Cubans who had, in a manner of speaking, placed their bets on one or another of these groups, now looked reluctantly toward Oriente.

Slowly but surely, the effect of the failure in Havana was to integrate the various unsuccessful insurgent factions under the leadership of the only force in Cuba that, unique in its possession of a positive program and a firm military base from which to implement it, seemed capable of producing a genuine revolution—the *Movimiento 26*.

As it happened, something of immediate material use was also salvaged from the fiasco in Havana: arms, heretofore withheld from the rebels in Oriente, and desperately needed by Fidel.

The arms in question had been held in readiness for the attack on the palace, in trucks which were to have sped to the scene, to support the planned "second wave" under Ignacio González—the wave which had failed to materialize because those responsible for the delivery of the weapons had failed to give the necessary orders. The reason for this grave lapse—later denounced in bitter terms by the *Directorio Revolucionario*—remains a mystery.

In any event, a portion of these same weapons was surrendered to the *Movimiento 26* in Havana, and soon afterwards the arms were dispatched to Oriente. It is this shipment which formed the basis for the following prediction:

Within a very short time, the rebel band headed by Fidel Castro, which invaded Cuba in December and has since grown considerably in strength, will take the offensive in Cuba's eastern province of Oriente, outside of the mountain range called Sierra Maestra.

For some months now, the Batista dictatorship in Havana has been denying the existence of any potent rebel force in the mountains. Failing in all attempts to crush Castro's force, the Cuban army has endeavored through the various organs of government propaganda to convey the impression that Castro's mountain guerrillas are figments of subversive imagination. But, as one who has just emerged from the Sierra Maestra after three weeks with Fidel Castro, this reporter can assert with confidence that, if fiction is being written, it is in the presidential palace in Havana.

The foregoing passage is a quotation from a report written for radio broadcast to the United States in early May of 1957, six weeks after the abortive assault on the presidential palace in Havana. The dispatch continued, in part:

The government recently announced that it was withdrawing the bulk of its military force of some three thousand men from the Sierra, because no problem existed there. The fact is that the government has withdrawn its troops at least in part to defend the towns which lie on the plain outside of the Sierra. City garrisons are being reinforced in fear of imminent attack. And despite the disparity which exists in the relative strength of the opposing forces, the fear is justified.

Cuban army morale is at low ebb; the revolutionary spirit is running high in Oriente. In a mountainous area of some five thousand square miles, the people are ready to support the rebels against whatever force may be dispatched from the capital. When I parted from Fidel Castro a few days ago, he was on his way to receive a shipment of arms—heavy machine guns and bazookas. On my way out of the mountains, I met twenty-eight volunteers, on their way into the Sierra to help put those weapons to use. In the first village I reached, I spoke with a dozen men who told me: "We pray that Fidel will come here. If he came today, the entire village would rise as one man to join him in his march on the capital of Oriente."

Obviously there is no intention, in quoting the above report, to suggest that Fidel was even remotely thinking of marching on Santiago, at the time the dispatch was written. The day of such a march was still far off, as he was well aware.

It was true, however, that he was planning to take the military initiative, if only in a limited sense; true also that all depended on an anticipated shipment of arms—the weapons sent from Havana.

The arms had been smuggled as far as Santiago. Here half of the shipment was retained by the M-26 underground, for future use. The other half was to be delivered to Fidel at a rendezvous near the garrison city of Bayamo. These arrangements were completed at the end of April.

By the beginning of May, the Cuban army had begun to withdraw the last of its small outposts from the Sierra proper, retaining only a few garrisons at strategic points throughout the foothills. In consequence, there was considerable military movement in the Bayamo area. After some slight delay, the rebels hit on a new plan for receiving the arms.

They had been close to Bayamo. Now they turned back toward Manzanillo, forty miles away by air and perhaps two hundred miles over the devious, difficult trails of the Sierra. The following week, after a hard forced march, they moved down into the hills overlooking the port city. A few days later, a small schooner sailing from Santiago passed offshore under cover of darkness and put overboard a number of sealed oil drums, which were brought ashore by fishermen in small boats. Some local lumbermen whose work took them to the wooded slopes above Manzanillo completed the delivery.

In the drums were six heavy machine guns, a bazooka and rockets for it, ten light machine guns, a dozen U.S. Army M-1 semi-automatic rifles, and thousands of rounds of ammunition: sufficient equipment to turn the ragged M-26 irregulars into the potent striking force that Fidel had thought to have when he first landed in Oriente.

In the early hours of May 28th, the rebels made their first foray in strength outside of the mountains. Their objective was the small military post of Ubero,* with its garrison of seventy soldiers, on the Caribbean coast of Manzanillo.

"Suddenly," relates a contemporary account, "machine guns sounded and the night was filled with screams and panic. It was the terrible warfare of the guerrilla, combined with modern war in new commando tactics—an audacious *fidelista* stroke."

In a well planned and sharply executed action, the rebel vanguard penetrated past the eight sentry posts almost before the Ubero garrison was aware of what was happening. Rockets began to burst in the compound. The soldiers who responded to the attack were quickly pinned down by machine-gun and rifle fire, and the fight became a series of small, isolated duels between defenders and assailants. In a lull in the shooting, the guerrillas called on the troops to surrender, and promised that their lives would be spared.

The Ubero garrison was completely cut off from outside assistance, and outnumbered two to one. There was no question of anything but surrender.

The rebels entered the camp and helped to attend to the wounded. The leader of the guerrilla force was identified by soldiers who had previously seen his picture as Raúl Castro, boyish-looking beneath a big steel helmet, and businesslike as always.

Raúl promptly requisitioned a convoy of trucks belonging to a local timber merchant, had them loaded with foodstuffs, medicines, and radio-telegraphic equipment. When all was ready, the rebels departed, taking a truck full of pris-

* Also spelled Uvero.

oners with them. Shortly after their departure, a gunboat from the naval station at Chivirico approached the shore and began to shell the post, on the assumption that the raiders were still in possession.

A bulletin issued by the army high command in Havana reported that an encounter had occurred at Ubero and stated that there had been casualties on both sides. No figures were given. An undetermined number of military casualties were transported to Havana during the next several days. The bodies of eleven soldiers of the Maceo Regiment from Santiago were buried in that city's Santa Efigenia cemetery. A *fidelista* captain who participated in the fight, Victor Mora, later placed the army losses at thirty killed; rebel losses at eight dead.

As a battle, Ubero will not interest the military historian. As an indication of the new *fidelista* potential, marking the opening of a new phase in the Oriente campaign, it was both an embarrassment to the government and a source of considerable anxiety to the army high command.

An interview with Fidel Castro and some documentation of *fidelista* operations in the Sierra Maestra, filmed during April and shown on television in the United States in early May,* had created a mild sensation in Cuba, forcing the government to abandon its fiction that no rebel force existed in the mountains. But until Ubero, there had been no word of aggressive action on Fidel's part to sustain this propaganda coup.

To quote the popular Cuban weekly review, *Bohemia*:

The film documentary of the Columbia Broadcasting System* terminated a chapter in the record of developments in the Sierra Maestra. After that sensational report, lively testimony to the rebel presence in the mountains, it was known for certain that hostilities would break, putting an end to long weeks of doubt and rumors.

* P. 11.

No doubt hostilities would have broken eventually, that they should have broken at this time, and on the rebel initiative, was providential. Flags were lowered to half mast at Camp Columbia—in sign of pain, commented *Bohemia*.

There was reason for anguish in the *estado mayor* (general staff), quite aside from the disgrace of the defeat at Ubero. On the 25th of the month, the eighty-two-foot yacht *Corinthia,* sailing from Florida with twenty-seven members of Prío's *Organizacion Auténtica* and a heavy cargo of weapons and ammunition aboard, had landed at Cabonico Bay, on the northern coast of Oriente.

Four hundred soldiers under Colonel Fermin Cowley, commander of the Holguín district and author of the atrocities of "Batista's Christmas Gift" of the preceding December, had been dispatched in pursuit of the expeditionaries. The OA force, fleeing into the coastal mountains, broke up into several groups. The main body of the fugitives, sixteen men, was captured by a column of one hundred fifty soldiers two days after the landing, and the army officer in command of the column, a captain named Cárdenas, radioed to Colonel Cowley's field headquarters for instructions.

Cowley was off in the hills, leading another column. In his absence, an aide at the base camp, Captain Rosendo Abreu, radioed back the terse message: "Sacrifice them."

Cárdenas, aghast, refused to act, and a major in command of another unit, hurrying to join the captain after picking up the same radio message, agreed with him that it would be madness to kill the prisoners.

Certainly it appeared indiscreet, to say the least, since the prisoners had already been seen, in custody of the troops, by *campesinos* in the area, as well as by many soldiers from other units. Accordingly, their captors began to march the OA men out of the hills, toward Cabonico, disregarding Abreu's order.

They were on the way when a second radio message was received, this one from Colonel Cowley himself. Cowley confirmed the previous order. When Captain Cárdenas and the major continued to balk, another officer in the column subsequently identified as a Lieutenant Fernández Chirino, made his own decision to carry out the order.

It would appear that the two senior officers might have stopped him, had they dared. They did not.

The scene was a clearing in the woods near the mountain village of Levisa. It was dusk, and the prisoners were having their evening meal, apart from the troops, when the lieutenant casually picked up a submachine gun, approached the group, and without warning opened fire.

The slaughter was described in a terse bulletin issued by the *estado mayor* in Havana the next day as a "battle" between government troops and the insurgents. The bulletin was released on the same day as that reporting the fight at Ubero.

At a later news conference, Cowley had some difficulty in explaining to the Cuban press the circumstances of a "battle" which had resulted in sixteen rebel dead, no wounded, no prisoners and not a single casualty on the government side. The Colonel said that conditions were "different" in the mountainous area where the clash had occurred, and, in effect, had to be seen to be appreciated.

Only fifteen bodies were shown in the official army photographs which were made at the Cabonico cemetery, where the dead were taken for burial. The sixteenth victim, mortally wounded, had crawled away in the dark, and died the next day in a *guajiro's* hut. His body was not immediately recovered.

Among the slain was the leader of the *Corinthia* expedition, Calixto Sánchez White. The Glasgow-born son of a Cuban diplomat, Sánchez had been the secretary of the

Federation of Airway Workers in Havana, until his flight to Miami two months before his death.

His departure from Cuba had been dictated by the failure of the attack on the presidential palace, and no doubt by a declaration of the student *directorio,* in which he was specifically named as one of those responsible for the fiasco.

The denunciation had preyed on his mind. Four of the youths who had signed the accusation were no longer alive and, as an editorial post mortem, published in Havana after the massacre of the *Corinthia* expeditionaries, commented: "It had not been possible to argue with the dead." In Miami, Sánchez said that he would prove that he was not afraid to face physical peril. Forswearing polemics, he vindicated his honor by dying in Oriente. That, at any rate, seems to have been the judgment of his contemporaries. One must add that it is not at all certain that his honor required any such vindication.

The attack on Ubero was enough in itself to make May 28th a black-letter day on Batista's calendar. The developments on the north coast of Oriente did nothing to improve the situation.

Deepening the gloom in the capital in the most literal sense, *fidelista* saboteurs tunneled under the Calle Suárez and exploded a charge of dynamite during the pre-dawn hours of the same day, destroying seven main electrical conduits and plunging most of Havana into darkness.

Two thousand feet of cable had to be replaced. An emergency force of one hundred fifty men was put on the job, and it took them fifty-seven hours to complete repairs.

In the interim, offices and department stores deprived of air conditioning as well as all bars, cafes, and motion picture theatres and nightclubs in the downtown district remained closed; meat rotted and butter turned rancid in refrigerators; telephone service was cut off; newspapers were unable to go to press; and the economic life of the capital came to a virtual standstill.

The total financial loss was estimated at close to three million pesos, equivalent to that number of dollars.

The sabotage in Havana was the climax of a wave of bomb explosions and incendiary fires across the island, mocking the efforts of a government that still sought to convey the impression, outside of Cuba, that all was well.

Batista fought back in the only manner which he, or those who supported him, appeared to understand.

At dawn on May 29th, an electrical company maintenance crew driving through an isolated section of Havana encountered the macabre spectacle of two corpses, side by side on their knees, their heads fallen forward on their chests, in grotesque attitudes of supplication. Closer inspection disclosed that they had been hanged by their necks from the branches of two pines, in such a manner that their knees just touched the ground. The scene had been carefully arranged. Between the two corpses lay a package of dynamite, silently indicating the supposed offense of the hanged ones.

A third corpse was found in a gutter elsewhere in the city, riddled with bullets. On the curb was the same grim warning to saboteurs, a bundle of dynamite wrapped in brown paper.

In Santiago, four youths were seized at their homes by men in uniforms. The following morning they were found, shot to death, on the outskirts of the provincial capital.

The army high command confirmed its plans for a new campaign against the rebels in the Sierra Maestra. Warplanes were being sent to Camagüey, whence they would fly, laden with napalm and explosives, on dawn-to-dusk saturation bombing missions.

In consequence, it was announced, the civilian population would have to be evacuated from that part of the Sierra which was considered to be the rebel zone of operations.

Batista denied a report that he personally would assume command of the new campaign to extirpate the *fidelista* forces in the mountains. He likewise denied that so-called "zones of death" were to be established, remarking that such a phrase was, in any case, foreign to the military lexicon. He admitted, however, that it would be necessary to evacuate a large number of *guajiro* families.

The first evacuees, more than one hundred in number, were herded out of the foothills of the Sierra and brought by truck to Santiago on May 31st. They came clutching infants, chickens, blankets, small, squealing pigs, pots and pans, whatever they had been able to salvage of their few possessions, and were bedded down on the open docks near the Santiago customs station.

Las Instituciones Femeninas de Santiago de Cuba, representing twenty separate women's organizations and auxiliaries of civic and business groups such as the Lions Club and the League Against Cancer, sent an anguished appeal to Batista, expressing profound alarm at the sad and inhumane spectacle of families displaced from their homesteads of centuries, and imploring the president, "in the name of God, your own family, and our civilization," to countermand the order for the saturation bombing of the Sierra.

From the Cathedral in Santiago, the Archbishop Pérez Serantes issued a pastoral letter ordering prayers for peace in all of the churches of Oriente, and declaring that he was no longer able to remain silent before the terror that was unfolding in the province.

The *Instituciones Cívicas* of Santiago, comprised of some two score civic, social, business, professional, and religious associations, wired Batista, protesting the murder of the four youths and demanding an end to the "wave of terror" that had made it unsafe for peaceful citizens to venture out of their homes, the civic leaders declared, for fear of being seized and brutally beaten, or worse, by police and soldiers. The situation had become such, it was asserted, that no one was safe from attack, by day or night, whether in public or in the sanctity of his own home.

The attitude of the government was clearly expressed in a written reply from the Minister of Interior, Santiago Rey, suggesting that the signers of the civic protest might well consult their consciences, to see whether they themselves had not in some way contributed to the climate of violence of which they now complained.

The atmosphere of Oriente had been poisoned by false rumors, the minister declared, terrorists had been provided with dynamite, the forces of public security had been chivvied by insolent agitators, soldiers had been murdered in the peaceful pursuit of their duties, fugitives with bloody hands had found refuge in the homes of ostensibly respectable citizens, and none of all this, the government spokesman noted with some asperity, had been condemned by the persons who were now become supplicants.

In effect, he declared, the "boomerang" had returned to strike those who had cast it. It was the first duty of the security forces, he wrote, to maintain public order, and as for those who had thought to fight a war from the comfort of their homes and luxurious clubs (a pointed warning to the members of the Santiago Country Club and the Vista Alegre Tennis Club, who almost without exception belonged to the *Resistencia Cívica*) they would find themselves greatly in error.

It must be admitted that, whatever the desperate resolve of the palace guard that surrounded Batista or the dictator's own will to retain power, the regime in its ruthlessness lacked the thoroughness which one associates with a police state like that of, for example, Nazi Germany.

Secret police, paid assassins, torture chambers all existed in Cuba under Batista; many thousands of Cubans were tortured, many thousands were murdered; the overthrow of the regime brought to light ghastly examples of the insane viciousness and cruelty of the Venturas and Julio Laurents of the dictatorship. The sight of the barbaric instruments for crushing bones, piercing eyeballs, and extracting fingernails that were found in the secret interrogation chambers of the police after the revolution is enough to make the blood run cold.

Yet the theory of "torturable" and "non-torturable" classes expounded by Graham Greene in his novel "Our Man in Havana" is not entirely without validity.

Position, social station, familial relationships in the hierarchical Cuban society did make a difference, after all. Important persons and the sons of wealthy families, known beyond question to be involved in conspiracy against the government, were permitted, through the intervention of influential friends or relatives, to leave the country under safe conduct.

Armando Hart, the judge's son and chief coordinator of the *Movimiento 26* in Havana as well as a member of its "National Direction," survived three arrests in less than two years, once after having made a sensational escape from a courtroom, again on the way back from a trip to the Sierra, in circumstances where any ordinary *guajiro* would have been shot on the spot.

Nor was his good fortune unique.

The homes of three judges in Holguín were machine-gunned when the actions of the jurists displeased the district commander. On the other hand, Dr. Manuel Urrutia Lleó, later to become provisional president of the revolutionary government, defied Batista with seeming impunity in May of 1957, by voting to acquit one hundred twenty-three persons accused of insurrection, among them the surviving prisoners of the *Granma* expedition and participants of the Santiago uprising of November 30, 1956.

As a minority of one on a three-man court, Dr. Urrutia was overruled. Yet his minority decision, based on the constitutional right of the citizen to oppose tyranny, which had previously been cited by Fidel Castro at *his* trial, made a sensation. It is rather surprising to find that the judge was able to retain his post until November of 1957, when he finally resigned and flew into exile in New York.

Dr. Osvaldo Dorticós Torrado, who was to succeed Urrutia as provisional president in 1959, similarly survived three arrests as head of the M-26 underground in Cienfuegos, and was finally put aboard a military plane and forcibly sent into exile.

One may wonder why he was not simply assassinated, like Pelayo Cuervo. The answer probably is that he was too important to be shot, or too well connected. The murder of Dr. Cuervo no doubt had been considered "necessary" in view of the disclosures which he had threatened to make. Or perhaps the Cuervo assassination was merely an error of judgment.

In general, the regime tried to avoid creating such scandals, although it showed no compunction when it came to deal with obscure peasants and others whose death would cause no great outcry.

Such anomalies are explained to a degree by the fact that Batista was far more conscious of the scrutiny of the outside world than he had been two decades earlier. He felt that he had to maintain at least an appearance of "business as usual" for both economic and diplomatic reasons, whatever happened. Thus, it is strange but nevertheless a fact that, during a period of savage and unrelenting terror, censorship was not always in force, civil guarantees could be invoked with occasional success, an honest judge might sometimes do his duty, and the public press could praise him.

It was possible to spend weeks in Havana without becoming conscious of anything seriously amiss. Appearances were kept up, marred only by the explosion of an occasional petard or the appearance in the streets of a mutilated corpse. Visiting foreigners were usually unaware of such incidents. Residents became almost accustomed to them, as was indicated by the casual tone of the few foreign press reports which mentioned them.

Despite the foregoing, it was impossible for the observer who made it his business to look behind the facade *not* to discover the truth, daily becoming more evident as spring merged almost imperceptibly into the baking stillness of Cuban summer and the rhythm of revolution made itself felt in a quickening cycle of terror and counter-terror.

Tied to three palm trees were six individuals, two men and four women, all naked, their bodies soaked with gasoline and a fire built at their feet.
—*Congressional Record,* March 20, 1958

VIII

To THE American observer following the uncertain course
of Cuban affairs from abroad during the summer of 1957,
there were only a few visible highlights to illuminate a scene
of otherwise unrelieved gloom.

Ambassador Arthur Gardner resigned, to the undisguised joy of a large section of the Cuban press and public,
and the reception of his successor, Earl Smith, was the occasion of a diplomatic flare-up that raised hope that United
States policy vis-à-vis Cuba was about to take a promising
new turn.

There was a general strike in August.

In early September, a naval insurrection in the port city
of Cienfuegos laid bare the existence of a serious split in the
Cuban armed forces, posing a major threat to Batista.

These were the highlights.

Much else was happening both in the public arena and behind the scenes that failed to attract the notice of the foreign
press.

The arrest of one after another of the top leaders of the
26th of July organization, the innumerable clashes between
underground activities and government security forces that
were taking a heavy toll of Cuban youth, the quickened pace
of the rebel campaign on the perimeter of the Sierra Maestra
—none of this seemed to create a ripple outside of Cuba.

The saturation bombing of the Sierra announced by the
army in May was already an obvious failure. Bombers flying
from Camagüey daily unloaded their cargoes of explosives

and jellied gasoline on areas where the rebels were thought to be. Once they came close to the target, having been instructed by an agent who had infiltrated the rebel force and had then deserted, in order to report the location of Fidel's temporary headquarters to the army. The headquarters was bombed, but in vain. Fidel had moved on. The spy made the mistake of rejoining the rebels, and was court-martialed and shot.

The air attacks had little if any effect on the activities of the guerrillas. The only victims of the campaign were the innocent *guajiros* and their families remaining in the mountains. Batista's "scorched earth" strategy had proved to be far beyond the physical capability or financial resources of the government. The army high command seems not to have realized, when it spoke of evacuating the "zone of operations," that it was treating of any area of more than five thousand square miles, with a rural population of perhaps fifty thousand inhabitants.

The "zone of death plan" which had been disavowed by Batista was in force in the foothills. The margin between plain and mountains was a forbidden zone to all strangers, and anyone caught entering or leaving without an acceptable excuse was adjudged a rebel and executed on the spot. Couriers continued to come and go, passing through the army lines. The principal sufferers were the small *comerciantes* of the mountains, whose business it was to sell the sparse agricultural produce of the *guajiros* in the market towns and return with the few manufactured products— cloth, shoes, knives and implements, salt, sugar, tobacco, rum—that the mountain people were able to buy. The effort to cut off supplies to the rebels only created new enemies of the government, and made conspirators of those who were forced to outwit or bribe the troops.

By the end of June, the outlook was sufficiently promising to induce Fidel to approve plans made by the National Direction of the Movement for opening a "second front" in the mountains of northern Oriente.

In the interim, two of the key *Resistencia* leaders in Havana, Raúl Chibás and the economist Felipe Pazos, journeyed into the Sierra. Pazos emerged after a series of conferences with Fidel bearing a manifesto which was, to say the least, expedient in terms of the time and circumstances.

The civic institutions of the island, as distinguished from those of Santiago alone, had recently issued a statement in effect urging a truce between the rebels and the dictatorship, with the proviso that the government "demonstrate good faith by deeds," i.e., by calling free and honest elections.

The document drafted in the Sierra rejected the very notion that impartial elections could be conducted "with all the repressive apparatus of the state hanging like a sword over the heads of the oppositionists."

Proposed, instead, was the formation of a popular front, integrating all of the revolutionary, political, and civic groups aligned against Batista in a common aim and strategy to overthrow the dictatorship, install a provisional government, and call general elections—this last as a "formal promise"—within one year.

It was further proposed that a provisional president be designated at once, by a "non-political" civic committee.

The provisional government envisioned in the Sierra manifesto was to be pledged to a program that would guarantee civil rights under the Constitution, separate the military from politics, establish a sound fiscal policy, etc. The only major item of the *fidelista* social-revolutionary program retained in the manifesto was that relating to agrarian reform, the keystone of the program.

In other respects, the Sierra manifesto reflected a high degree of political realism. Fidel continued to have his reservations concerning the question of cooperation with the old-line politicos, or, for that matter, with any political faction.

At the same time, he saw the need to win the support of conservatives who still reposed confidence in the politicos, and to capture control of the respectable parties and institutions nominally representing the conservative elements—that is to say, the recognized, collective voice of what commonly passes for "public opinion."

The *Resistencia Cívica* did not entirely serve the purpose, being identified, correctly, as an instrument of the 26th of July movement, hence *fidelista* by definition.

Fidel's program was modified accordingly. The Sierra manifesto was his first formal political pronouncement since the *Granma* landing,* and it was cut to political expedience, stressing those objectives on which all might be expected to agree, without reference to matters on which agreement was unlikely.

Despite the compromise implicit here, the "civic revolutionary front" proposed by Fidel failed to materialize in any effective form until the Cuban struggle was close to its climax. A "Council of Liberation" was formed in Miami in November, nominally bringing the *fidelistas* and Prío's followers under one roof, along with the *ortodoxos* and other anti-Batista political elements. But the Miami pact was repudiated by Fidel in December, in an angry letter from the Sierra, after the Council had named Dr. Pazos as its candidate for provisional president of the projected coalition government that was to assume power following the overthrow of the Batista regime.

Fidel had his own plans, which included neither political coalitions nor Pazos as provisional president. He designated his own nominee, Dr. Manuel Urrutia, on a take-it-or-leave-it basis. Since his was the only force making any effective fight against the dictatorship, Fidel did not consider it unreasonable that he should dictate the terms of such post-

---

* Excepting, of course, the statements contained in *The New York Times* and CBS interviews.

revolutionary arrangements as the situation seemed to require.

It was not until July of 1958 that a new alliance was formed and a new pact signed in Caracas. And by that time the political conservatives had lost whatever influence they might have hoped to exert on the conduct of post-revolutionary affairs in Cuba.

The immediate advantage accruing to Fidel from the Sierra manifesto derived from the reassurance offered to the Cuban middle classes, whose interest was not in social revolution but in political reform, and whose sons were involved in the struggle.

The factionalists continued their interminable debate in Havana, Miami, New York, and elsewhere. The politically disinterested—and these were the majority—turned their energies into more productive channels. Members of the 26th of July clubs and the *Resistencia* picketed the United Nations Secretariat in New York in a "hunger march," until they grew weak from lack of nourishment and began to collapse in the street. Funds were collected at rallies; members of the movement subscribed to regular pay "check-offs," making regular contributions from their salaries. Avenues for the clandestine shipment of small quantities of arms were opened. For a time, a plan was under consideration to launch two fighter planes from the United States on a bombing run over Camp Columbia in Havana; but this idea was abandoned, in consideration of the risk of producing civilian casualties in the residential sections surrounding the military establishment and of the suicidal nature of what would have been essentially a bit of psychological warfare, yielding no certain results.

An accounting made by Dr. Charles Santos Buch* for the *Resistencia* in New York, with reference to this same period, notes also the stern rejection of a proposal to augment the

---

* Son of the *Resistencia* representative at Caracas.

meager funds of the movement by means of a series of assaults on Cuban banks—the method employed by the Irgun and other revolutionary groups in Israel. (It should be noted that the suggestion came from outside of the movement.)

The *fidelista* underground in Cuba had been hard hit during the spring of '57. For a period of some weeks, all of the top action leaders were behind bars, including three members of the National Direction, Faustino Perez and Armando Hart in Havana, and Frank País, the national action chief, in Santiago.

Nevertheless, the Santiago cells, at least, were vigorously engaged with the Batista repression forces on several sides. Sufficient arms and equipment had been accumulated to justify the opening of a second-front guerrilla campaign in northern Oriente, with manpower drawn mainly from the Santiago underground, and in June a force of about forty men under René Ramos Latour, known in the movement as "Daniel," was dispatched to the mountains in the neighborhood of a place called Miranda, near the large town of San Luis, to prepare for action on the 30th of the month, when the opening of the second front was to be announced.

The announcement was to be timed to coincide with a rally of government coalition parties in Santiago, extensively advertised by the notorious political *"cacique"* of the province, Senator Rolando Masferrer.

The underground had other surprises in store for the government, not the least of which was a fifty-pound time bomb, placed with great care and at no little risk in the park in front of the cathedral where the rally was to be held, precisely under the speaker's platform on which Masferrer was to stand, surrounded by his chief lieutenants.

The rally was boycotted, the townspeople being warned by members of the 26th and of the *Resistencia* to stay at home, for reasons which, although not made explicit, are obvious enough in view of the preparation which had been made. By afternoon, the streets of the city were deserted. "Even the dogs were kept indoors," says one account.

The audience in the park consisted of several hundred of Masferrer's own hired terrorists, identified by the peaked baseball caps which they wore in order to recognize one another, and a contingent of three thousand troops, policemen, and uniformed members of the *masferristas* vigilante organization. Many of the troops, including more than a thousand who had been imported from outside of the province, wore sports shirts and trousers to give the meeting a civilian character.

Efforts had been made to lure working-class residents of the city, principally the unemployed, to the rally, with promises of hard cash and free rum. There was even an attempt to form a congo line. But a dispute about the promised wage developed, and most of the working-class audience drifted away.

The boycott was successful. Virtually everything else went wrong, including the bomb, which failed to explode.

There was bad news from the projected second front. Most of the arms and weapons sent to the staging area by truck had been captured.

In Santiago, three young members of the M-26 militia were killed in a clash with security forces, several hours before the rally began. One of the slain was Josue País, the seventeen-year-old brother of the action chief.

Fidel had evidently sent several proposals of his own from the Sierra for breaking up the Santiago rally, an event of some importance on the national political scene. But as Frank País explained in a letter dated July 5th, referring to Josue's death and other set-backs, ideas that would have applied to an ordinary political rally had been scarcely applicable to a government meeting dominated by the presence of three thousand soldiers, backed by tanks. In fact, wrote the action leader, there would have been a massacre.

The letter, addressed to "Alejandro"—Fidel's code name —summed up:

I suppose you have already learned the latest news. Even the pen trembles in my hand when I have to record the events of this terrible week.*** All the things planned in such detail, so well disposed, all came out badly, all failed, the reports of bad news coming one after another until it seemed that they would never end. The time bomb so carefully prepared and placed, failed when it rained some hours earlier. The hand grenades failed.* The second front so secretly prepared was aborted and we lost arms worth more than $20,000 and the life of a comrade.

Here we lost three more comrades. They were surprised when they went to fulfill a delicate assignment and preferred to die fighting rather than to let themselves be arrested.

Among them, the smallest (a reference to Josue), whose death has left an emptiness in my chest and a very personal sorrow in my soul.

It is a measure of País, perhaps helping to explain the deep esteem in which he was held, that his letter makes no further mention of his personal loss. That is quickly put aside as he goes on to discuss news of a movement of government troops, tanks, and artillery near Palma Soriano, the trials of "Daniel" and his commandos in the countryside as they make their way back to Santiago on foot, the disposition of a truckload of arms and provisions salvaged from the quantity of material originally intended for the second front, and similar matters.

The same letter contains a passing reference to Armando Hart, who had produced a sensation in Havana on the previous day, July 4th, by escaping from the Urgency Court in the capital as he was being brought before the bar with a group of other political prisoners. The only clue to Hart's escape was his blue denim prisoner's jacket, dropped on the

* Reference obscure. Certainly there was no intention to use grenades at the political meeting in Santiago.

floor of an anteroom as he fled. He had been wearing a sweater under the jacket, and passed unnoticed down a rear stairway to an interior courtyard, through the court building, and out onto the busy street. It had been twenty minutes before he had been missed.

País' comment was, "Formidable, no?"

País had regained his own freedom in May, having been exonerated of insurrectionary acts against the government during the same trial, previously mentioned, at which Dr. Manuel Urrutia had distinguished himself. Urrutia's minority opinion, outweighed by the dissenting votes of his two colleagues of the vacation term of Santiago Urgency Court, had invoked the constitutional right to resist tyranny as adequate justification for the acts of twenty-two surviving prisoners of the *Granma* expedition and more than one hundred actual and alleged participants in the Santiago uprising of November 30, 1956.

Where Urrutia's effort failed of practical results, except as a magnificent and courageous reproach of the dictatorship, other considerations saved some of the defendants. In the case of Frank País, the judges voted for acquittal in view of the lack of evidence to connect him with the November insurrection, although it will be recalled that it was he who had directed the uprising.

The young action leader had gone immediately into hiding, on being released from prison, and had returned at once to the direction of underground activities throughout the island. In his letter of July 5th he wrote of plans to initiate a national campaign of intensive sabotage, beginning on July 10th. On July 26th, in another letter to "Alejandro," he writes:

The situation in Santiago is becoming more tense every day. The other day I escaped miraculously from a police cordon. There were some comrades near the house where we were. An imprudence, they were informed upon, the district was surrounded. Three were caught; one fled over the rooftops. He managed to escape, but they started to search the roofs and through the street. Just as my companion and I were beginning to think the search would reach us, they stopped, coming only as far as the house next door. Ours inspired confidence.

However, there is a wave of such searches, fantastic and absurd, but what is absurd is also dangerous . . .

And he goes on to tell of having had to move to three different hiding places within the space of four days.

The manhunt of which País himself was the object was rapidly drawing to a close. On July 30th, at about three o'clock in the afternoon, it ended.

The twenty-three-year-old fugitive's last hiding place was an apartment on the ground floor of a blue-washed concrete building on Calle German, also called Maximo Gomez, on a hill overlooking the dock district. The apartment was occupied by the wife and small children of a hardware merchant named Raúl Pujol whose store had been a source of supply for the movement, and in whom País had great personal confidence.

One of the "fantastic and absurd" but dangerous searches to which he had referred in his letter to "Alejandro" began in the district. Peering through a window, País saw several carloads of police and soldiers in the street. He quickly telephoned Pujol at his shop, thinking to have his friend come and take him out of the district by automobile. Then, seeing the searchers coming closer and apparently taking thought of the danger to Pujol's family and the other three families in the building if he were to be caught there, he suddenly decided to leave, alone and on foot.

He had started down the street, away from the search, when he recognized his friend approaching from the opposite direction. Before either of them could make a decision, whether to greet each other, to flee, to return to the house, the security forces were upon them.

It is not entirely clear what happened next, but a witness who had a view of the section from behind a shuttered window nearby says that both País and Pujol were knocked down.

Their assailants were identified as Lieutenant Colonel Jose María Salas Cañizares, the SIM commander in Santiago, one of Salas' aides, a notorious assassin known to the provincial capital as "Mano Negra," * and a young police informer named Arthur Randich, who had known País from his school days.

According to the account of the eye-witness, País regained his feet and, somehow evading his captors, turned into the narrow Callejon Muro, intersecting Calle San German at a distance of a few feet from the scene of the attack. The SIM chief, following, was seen to raise his pistol and fire twice, missing both times. "Mano Negra" then rushed after the youth and fired a bullet into his back at close range. País fell in the alley. The assassin turned back to where the hardware merchant Pujol lay dazed on the sidewalk, leaned over him, and fired again.

The corpses were removed to the mortuary of the Santa Efigenia cemetery, where they were later claimed by members of the respective families.

The body of Frank País was laid out in the home of his fiancée, América Terlebauca, whose brother Taras had been one of his closest friends and chief lieutenants in the revolutionary underground. Pictures taken at the wake show a slightly built youth, dark face hollow, eyes closed in death, the thin frame clothed in the olive-green uniform and red armband of the 26th, the insignia of a colonel on the shoulder-straps, a 26th of July banner draped across the casket. A guard of honor stands stiffly by the casket, shadowy in the candlelight.

* Black hand.

The house was crowded through the night with friends, relatives, former teachers, former schoolmates, former pupils coming to pay their respects to the young schoolmaster-turned-revolutionary. By afternoon of the following day, several thousand mourners were at hand, including virtually all of the *Resistencia Cívica* and most of the 26th militia and action squad members in Santiago.

The authorities might have seized the entire underground organization at a single swoop by raiding the Terlebauca residence; but the thought is not consistent with Spanish tradition, which pays solemn tribute to death, whatever it may make of life. If the idea occurred to anyone, it was left unspoken. Neither police nor soldiers were seen at the wake or at the funeral.

While the funeral was in preparation, Ambassador Earl E. T. Smith arrived in Santiago, on his first tour of the island since his appointment to the Havana embassy.

Plans had been made by the *Resistencia* to take advantage of the political opportunity presented by the ambassador's visit; and, despite the widespread consternation caused by the death of Frank País, the chance to embarrass the regime and to gain the attention of the outside world could not be lost.

The women of the *Resistencia* and the *Instituciones Femeninas* were determined to demonstrate. The repression forces, under Salas Cañizares, were equally determined to prevent the demonstration. They failed.

Hundreds of women poured into the shop district near the city hall during the morning, ostensibly on shopping tours. Efforts were made to discourage them; they were harried from store to store. The only effect was to keep them on the move, back and forth through the civic plaza, until 11 o'clock, when the official reception for the ambassador was to begin.

From a political point of view, the manifestation was all that could have been desired.

As the eight-car caravan bringing the ambassador and his wife to the civic reception passed Céspedes Park, a horde of women came pouring out of the side streets and across the park, screaming *"Libertad! Libertad!"* and when Smith raised his hand in an uncertain gesture of salute, an echoing chorus of applause broke out.

The officials inside of the city hall were scarcely able to make themselves heard above the clamor outside. The ambassador, distracted by what he was able to see of the demonstration, mechanically received the keys to the city and listened impatiently to the interminable speeches of the mayor's welcoming committee.

Troops outside were pressing the muzzles of their weapons into the front rank of the crowd of women in an effort to drive them back. Those who resisted were beaten with clubs and fists; more than forty were dragged away to waiting police vans and patrol cars and taken to the city jail.

The action only angered the women and spurred them to renewed resistance. In desperation, the officer in charge —as it happened, Salas Cañizares—summoned fire trucks, and the high pressure hoses were turned on the women, drenching them and driving them back.

It was at this point that Ambassador Smith emerged from the hall. Several of the women, dripping and pathetic, managed to get close enough to speak with him; and one thrust a pamphlet into his hands, while the troops stood back for the moment, hesitating to use force in his presence. The ambassador was too bewildered to know quite how to respond; he had little knowledge of the political situation, and no preconceptions, but his sensibilities were outraged.

After being questioned by reporters at an informal luncheon concerning the events of the morning, he conferred with the political officer and press attaché of the embassy, both on tour with him, and issued a formal statement.

Its substance was an expression of regret that his presence should have been the occasion of violence. He said that such police excesses were "repugnant" to him, and added the wish that the women who had been arrested might be put at liberty. With reference to a letter which had been given to him, an appeal from the mothers of Santiago for a review of the United States policy of support for the Batista dictatorship, Smith declared: "I can say that this document will receive my most careful consideration."

The statement was enthusiastically received by most of the Cuban press, and the entire incident was recounted in vivid detail by *Bohemia* when censorship was lifted, after a long blackout, in February of the following year. That section of the press which supported Batista, including Masferrer's two newspapers, launched an angry campaign against the United States envoy. In the Cuban Congress, several speeches were made, demanding his recall.

Santiago was seized in a great wave of emotion, produced by the slaying of Frank País and Raúl Pujol, the women's manifestation, the ambassador's statement; all of these things, coming after long months of repression, terror, lawlessness and abuse, seemed to open a floodgate.

The security forces wisely stood aside and let the torrent roll past. With the United States envoy in the city, and perhaps even without his presence, it would have been folly to act otherwise. No attempt was made to interfere with the huge procession that followed the flag-draped casket of Frank País to the grave.

Several thousand mourners had gathered about the residence where the body lay, waiting for the funeral march to begin. By the time the procession reached the center of the city, it had grown so great that nothing but the tops of heads was visible from street level, for as far as the eye could see.

The sun beat down on the burgeoning, slowly moving mass with a blazing heat, and bright umbrellas began to blossom like funeral flowers in the sea of people, these and the petals strewn on the passing hearse from the balconies above lending a color to the procession that belied its solemn, ritualistic character.

Several times men in the procession shouted some angry political slogan, but such outbursts were quickly silenced by the women, who began to chant, in mournful accents, the opening lines of the national anthem: *"Al combate, corred, bayameses, / que la Patria os contempla orgullosa; / no temais una muerte gloriosa, / que morir por la Patria es vivir . . ."* "To die for *La Patria* is to live"—the recurring article of faith.

A separate cortege following the mortal remains of Raúl Pujol to the place of burial joined the País funeral procession, and together the mourners continued on the two-and-a-half-mile route to Santa Efigenia cemetery, trudging silently along the dusty road. It was early evening when the graveside ceremonies began; dusk by the time the people began to disperse.

From its staff above the Tomb of the Armed Forces, members of the M-26 militia had pulled down the red-yellow-green-and-white banner of the Fourth of September, symbol of the Sergeants' Revolt of 1933 and emblem of the dictatorship. In its place fluttered the red-and-black banner of the 26th of July, symbol of revolt.

Youths returning to the city from the cemetery stoned buses along the road and ran through the street shouting "Strike!" A general strike, long discussed and decided upon on the day of País' death, was beginning. Shops in Santiago had been closed for the funeral. They remained closed.

The strike spread through the province, then through the

length of the island, taking effect in the capital on August 5th.

Santiago was paralyzed for five days, despite the efforts of the police to re-open the shops. The big United States government-owned nickel mines at Nicaro were shut down. Shops in Guantánamo were closed for a week. In Havana the bank tellers left their cages, and bus drivers refused to take their buses out of the central station. But imperfect coordination and in some cases the drastic action of the authorities doomed the strike. In Holguín, Colonel Cowley dealt with the situation in his own draconian fashion. The lights of the entire city were switched off at the power plant at 8 P.M. When they came on again at 2 A.M., nine civilians were dead, shot on the street by way of example to the rest of the population. One of the dead was a father who had gone out to get candles to light the sickroom of his young daughter.

Similar methods were applied elsewhere. Many members of the Havana underground were arrested in the streets, as they tried to persuade shopkeepers to close their doors. In most places, force quickly prevailed. The Oriente stood firm until it became clear that the strike had been crushed in Havana. Then the eastern province, too, lost hope and abandoned the effort.

The naval revolt at Cienfuegos began on the morning of September 5th, just a month after the collapse of the general strike.

The news of the insurrection must have come as a distant shock to Batista, threatening to shatter the illusion of the "monolithic unity" of the armed forces which he had been at such pains to maintain. The reference to "monolithic unity" was contained in a prideful speech made by the generalissimo at Camp Columbia only a few hours before the first report of the Cienfuegos uprising, the occasion being a celebration of the twenty-fourth anniversary of the coup of 1933, the so-called Sergeants' Revolt.

In truth, Batista had no personal illusions as to the loyalty of the officers and men on whom his career and indeed his life depended. In general, he was not a man to deceive himself about harsh realities. He was aware, as well he might have been, of the methods by which the all-important appearance of "monolithic unity" had been maintained: bribery, terrorism, blackmail, and periodic political purges of the armed forces, dating from the day of his 1952 power grab.

It should not be necessary to say that human decency was by no means the exclusive possession of civilians and revolutionaries in the Cuban struggle, nor that military monsters were the rule. Still, it may help to relieve the harsh blacks and glaring whites of the revolutionary scene to underline the fact that there were, after all, a great many decent and humane officers and enlisted men in the Cuban armed services; many who risked their lives to conspire against the dictator, and not a few who were cashiered, jailed, or murdered because they were unable to accept their position as unwilling instruments in the apparatus of tyranny.

Fidel Castro himself remarked, in early 1957, that the Navy, in particular, was a source of hope to him, as a force known still to harbor many men who were sympathetic to the revolution or, in any event, bitterly opposed to a regime that had disgraced the service by promoting such known assassins as Julio Laurent, the chief of the naval intelligence service (SIN).

That view was expressed at about the time that a United-States-born lieutenant in the Cuban Navy, a veteran of the second world war named Antonio Santa Cruz, resigned from the service "as a one-man protest," he said, "against the wholesale murders committed by fellow officers of the Navy in the farming communities of the Sierra Maestra."

Santa Cruz specifically accused Laurent, Lieutenant Alejandro Olayón, and an ensign named Pérez Mejides.

Santa Cruz's testimony is contained in a letter smuggled out of Cuba while he was in Havana's Príncipe prison, and was read into the Congressional Record of March 20, 1958, by Representative Adam Clayton Powell, Jr., of New York, who was then fighting to halt the shipment of American arms to the Batista government.

The letter was addressed to Santa Cruz's brother, Henry G. Santa Cruz, also a native-born citizen of the United States, and a resident of New York City. The testimony is of interest because it is illustrative both of the situation prevailing in eastern Cuba in 1957, and of the causes that finally led to the Cienfuegos mutiny in September.

Santa Cruz was serving aboard the Cuban frigate *José Martí,* patrolling the Caribbean coast from Cabo Cruz to Santiago de Cuba in the early part of the year, and putting in at the small fishing ports along the shore.

His letter relates:

On the morning of February 2, while in Pilón, I went ashore to relax a little along the outskirts of the village and I found a half-burned *bohío*. The inside was plainly visible. There were four bodies inside, three adults (two females and a male), mutilated beyond recognition, and in a crude crib a child about three or four years old . . .

Santa Cruz said that the SIN chief, Laurent, coming aboard the frigate later that day, boasted of having ordered and personally participated in the murders, having learned, according to Santa Cruz, that the head of the family had "expressed himself in favor of" Fidel Castro in one of the local bars.

The letter continues:

About two weeks later, we were again in Pilón. That night a group of officers from the ship (I was in the group) went ashore for a walk. Nearing the cane fields we saw a fire a short distance away. We ran toward the fire to try to help. What we saw still makes me sick, literally. Tied to three palm trees were six individuals, two men and four women, all naked, their bodies soaked with gasoline and a fire built at their feet. Twenty armed sailors with Lt. Olayón were conducting the affair.

The first thing they did was to point their guns at us (we were unarmed) and order us not to interfere and to go back to the ship. When we reached the pier, it was heavily patrolled by Laurent's men, who had orders to shoot anyone coming ashore. We were permitted to go aboard, but that was all. Next morning we saw the burnt bodies still tied with wires to the palm trees. Later we learned that the victims were a small merchant in the town, his nephew, his wife and three daughters, accused of having sold food to Castro (more than 100 miles away). The women had been brutally violated before death.

It is not entirely clear how Santa Cruz was able to learn all of these details, or to see the burned bodies from the ship. One can only remark that there has been ample documentation of similar atrocities, and worse. The point has been made by several American reporters, and can stand to be stressed, that the assassins of the regime, Laurent, Cowley, Ventura, José María Salas Cañizares, Olayón, Chaviano, to name a few, made no secret of their crimes, but boasted of them openly. Oriente is not Main Street; Cuba is not Indianapolis. One does not like to make too much of the fact, because it lends itself to prejudicial conclusions. Yet it is so.

Santa Cruz's letter concludes:

Upon arriving in Havana, I presented my resignation, stating plainly my motives, and in a personal interview with the Chief of the Navy (Admiral Rodríguez Calderón), I stated that I was unwilling to wear the same uniform as murderers like Olayón, Laurent, etc. Needless to say, my resignation was accepted immediately. Since then things have gone from bad to worse. All political suspects, whether innocent or not, are tortured beyond imagination, some killed afterward, and most kept in this so-called preventive prison against all law and order.

The "preventive prison" referred to was El Príncipe, where Santa Cruz was held for more than four months. He had become involved with several conspiratorial groups in Havana after leaving the naval service, and at the beginning of January, 1958, he was arrested by Captain Ventura, and taken to the latter's notorious 5th Precinct.

His survival marks one of the rare instances in which Ventura actually saved a life. Santa Cruz says that Laurent, the SIN chief, tried for a week to gain custody of him. Ventura stubbornly refused to surrender custody.

Ultimately he was sent to El Príncipe. In May the courts released him, there being no evidence against him; he went into hiding, and appealed to the U.S. Ambassador for protection. Santa Cruz had been born in Miami, and had served as an officer in the United States Navy for five years, being separated from service as a lieutenant commander. But he had forfeited his citizenship by entering the Cuban service in 1951, under the Prío administration, and his plea for sanctuary was denied. A similar plea to the Venezuelan Embassy produced better results. The Venezuelan Ambassador personally drove to the apartment where Santa Cruz was in hiding, concealed him in the trunk of the car, and conveyed him to the embassy. A few days later he left Cuba under a safe conduct, to return to the island in January, 1959, as naval chief of operations under the revolutionary government.

A sufficiently large number of navy men shared the sentiments of Santa Cruz in 1957 to create the potentiality of a far more serious insurrection than the one that actually occurred. Investigation discloses that there was, in fact, a widespread naval conspiracy, and that the plans of the conspirators were far more ambitious than the mutiny at Cienfuegos suggested.

Political reliability and a strong stomach being the prime qualifications for an officer's career under Batista, it is not surprising that by 1957 most of the conspirators against the regime should have been found outside of the service rather than still in uniform.

The heart of the naval conspiracy was in Havana, where some eighty men, most of them cashier junior officers, were privy to an ambitious plot to raise the navy against the dictatorship, and to launching daring blows in Cienfuegos, at the Mariel base and naval academy in Pinar del Río province, in Santiago de Cuba, and in the capital itself.

The conspirators were in communication with the *Movimiento 26,* with Prío's *Organizacion Auténtica,* and with revolutionary cells in the army, the army air force and the motorized police division in Havana.

The plan of action in Havana was to seize that part of the fleet to be found in the harbor there—the cruiser "El Cuba" and half a dozen smaller ships—train the naval guns on key military objectives, and then attempt to take the city itself, with such naval manpower as might be available, supported by the underground action groups and militia and an armed citizenry. Sabotage within the police force was expected to immobilize the patrol cars.

Similar plans were worked out in detail for Santiago, Cienfuegos and Mariel.

The planning and organization of the insurrection were the work of some months. At length, a date was set. The plans were confirmed at a final meeting in a private home in a suburb of Havana, with Faustino Pérez, released from prison a month before, representing the 26th of July movement. The naval conspirators were represented by their leader, a cashiered ensign named Juan Castiñeiras.

To plan a large-scale, coordinated uprising was one thing; to implement it another. As on previous occasions, excessive optimism, unrealistic appraisal, neglect of detail, and inadequate liaison combined to produce tragedy, in this instance, tragedy of a major order.

At virtually the eleventh hour, junior naval officers in the conspiracy leaving their duty stations aboard ships in the Havana harbor on the night of September 4th reported that it appeared doubtful that they would be able to carry out their commitments.

Leaders of the various conspiratorial factions met in a series of frantic conferences through the evening in Havana. It was midnight by the time they had reached a decision: to suspend all action until further notice. Castiñeiras argued that it was already too late to notify the many men throughout the island who were committed to strike within a matter of hours. He was overruled.

Messengers were hastily dispatched to the ships of the fleet in the harbor and to the various other places in the capital where action was impending. The conspirators at Mariel, thirty miles from Havana, were notified of the decision. By two o'clock in the morning, Santiago had been reached by telephone, and the uprising there had been cancelled. For reasons still not clear, the word failed to reach Cienfuegos.

One of the key figures in the plot was a cashiered naval lieutenant who had been stationed at the Cienfuegos base, and who is said to have had some connection with the Barquín conspiracy of 1956, Dionisio San Román Toledo.

San Román had made several clandestine visits to Cienfuegos during the spring and summer, had been in contact with both the M-26 underground and the OA in that city and, through them, with a group of twenty-nine conspirators at the naval base, headed by a petty officer known to him, one Santiago Ríos.

It had been agreed that Ríos' assignment would be to seize the sleeping naval station with its normal complement of one hundred twenty-four men and officers, and to open the gates and the vital arsenal to a Trojan horse of civilian revolutionaries from the town. The task was made less difficult by the fact that many of the married personnel customarily slept in the city. At a final conference in Cienfuegos it had been decided that San Román's next appearance in the city would be the signal for the insurrection.

He arrived on September 4th, hence was out of touch with Havana when the decision to postpone the uprising was reached. He contacted Emilio Aragonés, the 26th of July leader, Santiago Ríos was summoned from the naval station, and a meeting was held with the *Organizacion Auténtica* leaders, Miguel Merino and Raúl Coll.

By five o'clock of the following morning, September 5th, Ríos was back at the base on Cayo Loco, an egg-shaped, sandy key in Jagua Bay, linked to the city proper by a short causeway road.

At 5:20, Ríos and four other enlisted men approached the guard at the armory, told him that the navy was rising against the regime throughout the island, and that Batista and General Tabernilla were already under arrest in Havana. The sentry promptly joined the mutineers.

Ríos opened the armory with a duplicate key which he had made some while in advance. He was now ready to arm his co-conspirators, and any who might care to join them. A few minutes later, the officer and four enlisted men on duty at the main gatehouse were disarmed and locked in the brig. The eleven members of the guard who were off duty were awakened and given their choice: to take part in the insurrection or to be locked up. Most of them chose to participate.

Guards on duty at the inner sentry posts were seized, one by one, and replaced with mutineers. By 5:35, all the inner guard posts had been taken, and their guns turned inward on the base itself.

Ríos had the "general call" sounded to rout out the remainder of the sleeping garrison, some fifty men. Known Batista adherents were arrested. The others were enlisted in the mutiny. The base was secure.

Gray dawn was breaking and a light rain was falling as San Román drove across the causeway and through the main gate to take command. Shortly after six o'clock, the former lieutenant and two of the civilian revolutionary leaders roused the base commander in his quarters and apprised him of the situation. He was put under arrest.

Naval personnel living off the base now began straggling in to report for duty, and were given the same choice as the others. Most of the enlisted men elected to join the mutiny. Six officers also chose this course; eighteen other officers joined the prisoners in the brig.

Members of the 26th of July underground began to arrive at the naval station, some one hundred fifty in all. They were followed by about fifty members of the OA. All were issued weapons and ammunition from the naval armory.

By 8 o'clock insurgent forces from the base were moving purposefully into the city. A lieutenant of the harbor police who was a party to the conspiracy led a squad into the maritime police headquarters on Calle Dorticós and killed the superintendent in his office with a grenade, when the latter offered resistance. Nearby a navy jeep intercepted a police patrol car. The occupants were killed when they resisted arrest. There was a brief skirmish with troops of the *Guardia Rural* at the residence of the Cienfuegos military commander, Major Eugenio Fernández. He fled with his family to the *Guardia* headquarters, which was quickly surrounded by mutinous naval personnel and civilian revolutionaries.

The insurgents had been hastily arming civilians and giving them elementary instruction in the use of their weapons. Several hundred of the new recruits took part in laying siege to a force of about one hundred policemen in the headquarters of the National Police, located in the south wing of the two-story gray municipal building on the city park, the Parque Martí.

Men were posted behind the columns of the arcade on the

opposite side of the park, and at vantage points in surrounding buildings. A truce committee called on the police commander to surrender. He replied that he would have to telephone to Havana for instructions. In fact, he had already made a series of frantic telephone calls, to Santa Clara and elsewhere, describing the situation and making urgent appeals for aid.

The negotiations broke off. The insurgents opened a tremendous fusillade of rifle and machine-gun fire. A few of the besieged policemen returned the fire; and one of the attacking force, a navy man, was killed. At the first interval in the shooting, a white flag fluttered from a window of the building. The time was 9:55.

The policemen were disarmed and led into the park, their hands in the air, herded into trucks and jeeps, and driven to the naval station under guard. The insurgent leaders prevented the immediate lynching of the police commander, a Comandante Ruiz Beltrán. He, too, was driven to Cayo Loco, under arrest.

The shooting had long since awakened the entire city, and thousands of men, women, girls and small boys lined the sidewalks, and crowded the balconies, cheering wildly, as trucks carrying armed sailors and rebels and others filled with prisoners en route to Cayo Loco passed by.

Rebels wearing the red-and-black or red-and-white armbands of the *Movimiento 26* and the bright orange armbands of the OA patrolled the streets in trucks and jeeps with mounted machine guns ready for action. A delirium swept Cienfuegos as it became apparent that the insurgents had taken complete control.

Men and boys roamed the city with rifles in their hands, bandoliers across their chests, revolvers in their belts and pockets bulging with cartridges, bright-eyed, faces flushed, teeth glittering, in a scene reminiscent of the newsreels made in Budapest during the brief period of its liberation, before the return of the Russian tanks to that stricken capital.

There was this difference: discipline was maintained. No massacre occurred at the national police headquarters, or elsewhere. Crowds that clamored for the blood of known *"chivatos"* were restrained. In one instance, a member of the national Congress, Alonso Avila, was rescued from a mob by the M-26 militia and sent from the city by automobile, with his family.

A single point of danger remained within Cienfuegos—the *Guardia Rural* post on the Santa Clara road, at the northern edge of the city. The far greater threat lay without, and was rapidly approaching.

An ultimatum was sent to the *rurales:* surrender within half an hour, or face the consequences. In the interim, a telephone call was made to Cayo Loco, where mutineers monitoring the shortwave radio band confirmed the worst: government reinforcements were on the way, infantrymen of the Leoncio Vidal regiment from Santa Clara, an infantry unit from Matanzas, Army Air Force fighters and bombers from Camp Columbia and from Camagüey.

An amphibious navy Catalina PBY appeared over the city, sweeping low. It was thought to be with the mutineers, but, if so, could have put up little opposition to the government aircraft soon to appear.

At eleven o'clock, the first air force planes were seen over Cienfuegos. The Catalina had vanished. A plane was reported going down over the sea, trailing smoke. It was not known whether it was the Catalina, or an air force plane.

An account of the Cienfuegos uprising published by the *Movimiento 26* several months after the insurrection had been crushed, declares:

Cienfuegos remained a lone bastion, isolated from the rest of the island. The faint-hearted among the rebels retired from the struggle. Some officers fearfully tried to withdraw and parleyed with the enemy, and in this respect, San Román was very strict with the deserters.

Other sources say that San Román himself had already left the scene of battle.

Government ground forces attacked in strength at noon, with motorized infantry from Santa Clara under a Lieutenant Colonel Cándido Hernández spearheading the assault.

The first wave of the attacking force swept into the Parque Martí area and was ambushed there, coming under a hail of rifle and machine-gun fire from insurgent forces barricaded in buildings around the park. Most of the infantry force was destroyed. Dead and wounded littered the streets and the park. Colonel Hernández himself was gravely wounded.

Light twin-engine bombers and jet fighters had begun to bomb and strafe the city. The radio monitors at Cayo Loco overheard a conversation between a mobile military transmitter on the ground and one of the first B-26 bombers to appear over the city, demanding to know where the bombs had fallen, since no explosions had been heard. It developed that the bombs had been dropped in the bay and in an uncontested sparsely settled section of the city, between the naval station and the downtown section where fighting was in progress, the fliers evidently being unwilling to bomb civilian targets or, for that matter, their comrades-in-arms. During the course of the entire day, only one bomb hit Cayo Loco, exploding on the sandy beach, well away from the naval station.

Troops continued to arrive from Santa Clara, from Matanzas and Camagüey, and, by troop transport plane, from as far away as Camp Columbia. Heavy tanks were brought up on trailer trucks; light tanks and armored cars sped to Cienfuegos under their own power.

Infantry men backed by armor moved against the defenders with mortars and heavy machine guns. For a brief interval, a young boy named Enrique Crucet held back an entire infantry company, manning two machine guns on a rooftop, until he was killed by a strafing plane.

More reinforcements poured into the city, the roar of motor convoys and the rumble of tank treads sounding the death knell for the insurgents, the flames of battle making it truly "Cienfuegos," the city of a hundred fires. Slowly, the bright hope of the day turned to the black despair of a night of defeat and disaster, and the cheering crowds of the morning became a shattered army of fugitives, seeking shelter away from the smoking ruins of buildings where the whine and blast of mortar shells marked the last remaining pockets of resistance.

An insurgent leader telephoning to Cayo Loco to ask for more ammunition was answered by a strange voice, informing him that the mutineers there had surrendered. Control of the naval station had been restored to its commanding officer, Captain Roberto Comesañas, when it had become apparent that the situation was hopeless. Comesañas personally accepted the surrender of sixty-seven mutineers, saving them from massacre by refusing to permit army forces to enter the naval district. All were held for trial by courts martial.

The rebels in the city fought on through the night. The last resistance at the San Lorenzo school was stamped out at one o'clock in the morning, when some forty defenders surrendered. They were shot down outside of the school, and tanks rolled over their bodies.

Some thirty rebels in the national police headquarters surrendered at 3:00 A.M., and were machine-gunned as they left the building. Four members of the 26th militia remained inside, stubbornly holding the position for five more hours, until the last defender was killed at 8 A.M.

A few of the rebels escaped from the city, slipping through

the army lines. Their leader, San Román, was captured at sea aboard a navy submarine chaser, flown to Havana, and handed over to the tender mercies of the naval intelligence chief, Laurent. No more is seen of San Román.

In Cienfuegos, the maritime police were placed under the temporary command of the sinister Captain Alejandro García Olayón, and a house-to-house search began, under his direction. Suspected insurgents, all those found with arms in their possession, with wounds, with anything that could incriminate them, including the mere fact of youth, were led outside and shot in the street. Trucks following to pick up the corpses moved like grisly butcher carts through the city, leaving trails of bright blood in their wake.

No attempt was made to identify the dead. Bulldozers opened a trench twenty-five yards long in the Tomás Acea cemetery, and the bodies of some six hundred persons were flung into this mass grave. *Chicago Tribune* correspondent Jules Dubois, who was on the scene, said that he personally saw fifty-two corpses dumped into the mass grave, and was told by officials that these were the bodies of men who had been killed in battle, among them some sailors.

Atrocities at Cienfuegos and elsewhere were denounced before the World Medical Association at its Eleventh General Assembly in Istanbul in October by Dr. Augusto Fernández Conde, a Havana chest specialist and past president of the Cuban Medical Association. In January, *Medical News* published a report from Dr. Louis H. Bauer, secretary-general of the world organization, citing evidence in hand that government troops in Cienfuegos had buried two hundred wounded, *alive*.

The statement seems at first incredible. Yet in conjunction with other testimony put forward by the same sources— sworn eye-witness accounts of murder, torture, mutilation, supported by photostatic copies of coroners' reports and other official documents—it is not easily refuted.

Certainly Batista made no attempt to refute the charges. When the World Medical Association tried to send a commission to investigate conditions in Cuba, it was denied admittance.

The sixty-seven naval mutineers at Cienfuegos, saved by the intervention of the base commander, were court-martialed in October. Thirty-one were convicted and sent to the penitentiary on the Isle of Pines. The remaining thirty-six were discharged from the service. The ugly scars crisscrossing the backs of all of those who survived the revolution bear witness that none entirely escaped punishment.

The policy of non-intervention, which we strongly uphold, is one of the cornerstones of the Inter-American system. Our commitment to this policy, however, does not lessen our own dedication to democracy in its real, and I might add, American sense, and we are in a position to feel—and we do feel—satisfaction and pleasure when the people of any country determinedly choose the road of democracy and freedom.

—ROY R. RUBOTTOM, JR., Assistant Secretary of State for Inter-American Affairs

IX

NO VICTORY CELEBRATION in Havana marked the end of the Cienfuegos uprising, no grin of triumph illuminated the saturnine features of Batista in the newsreels. The naval mutiny had revealed a crack in the dictator's armor, and a chill wind was blowing through the chink.

The government vainly tried to disguise the nature of the insurrection, denying that naval personnel had mutinied at Cienfuegos. The only result was to lay the dictatorship open to the grave new charge of having used the weapons of total war, tanks, aircraft, high explosives, to crush a mere civil disorder. For the first time, U.S. Congressmen began to question the nature of diplomatic arrangements that put the United States in the position of providing a dictator with bombs to be hurled upon a defenseless civilian population.

The *Washington Post,* summing up with fair accuracy in an editorial published on September 9th, five days after the Cienfuegos insurrection, declared:

Although the uprising of rebel and naval forces at the Cuban port of Cienfuegos may now be under control, it is an ominous portent for the dictatorship and General Fulgencio Batista. The main source of Batista's power is the military forces, but despite government denials there is good evidence that naval troops defected at Cienfuegos and aided rebel forces.*** The Cienfuegos uprising affords a sign of internal weakness that cannot be shrugged off as easily as the ragtag guerrilla army of Fidel Castro in the Sierra Maestra.

In the past few months, Cuba has witnessed an assassination attempt on the presidential palace, an abortive general strike, police terror in Santiago, midnight bombings and shootings in Havana, and a blackout of the Cuban press.

General Batista deceives no one by blaming the unrest on the Communists. He has pledged a free election in June of 1958, but his repressive policies weaken faith in his promise. It seems clear that if Batista does not accede to an orderly transfer of power, trouble and revolt will continue to plague the freedom-hungry island of Cuba.

The "ominous portent" seen by the *Washington Post* failed to hearten the leaders of the 26th of July movement. If a general strike, a serious defection of the armed forces, and the pitched battle of an entire city against the army could not shake down the dictator, the question was—what could?

The revolutionary leaders had relied from the beginning on various forms of psychological warfare against the dictatorship, with but little apparent success. Fidel himself had "struck the spark," but the fire refused to spread to the desired quarter, nor had repeated "sparks"—the assault on the palace, the general strike, Cienfuegos—seemed to make any difference. The foundations of the government had no doubt been weakened. But the dramatic collapse anticipated had failed to come.

It was plain that a new and more powerful and concerted effort was required. On October 10th and 11th, *Resistencia Cívica* and M-26 underground leaders from every province but those of Pinar del Río and Matanzas met at "Chantilly," the summer cottage of the Santos Buch family outside of Santiago, to reorganize the entire top echelon of the movement.

Dr. Angel Santos Buch was appointed national secretary of the *Resistencia*. The National Direction of the 26th, heretofore a loose, informal, and shifting delegation of authority rather than an executive committee, now became a formal entity with at least nominal responsibility for making command decisions.

The word "nominal" must be stressed. Fidel subscribed

to the idea of group decision, in principle. In practice, he continued to issue the orders, both political and military, and to exercise his personal veto on plans of which he disapproved.

The principal effect of the reorganization was to accelerate the drive for funds with which to arm the revolutionary forces in Oriente. Chapters of the *Resistencia Cívica* were set up in a dozen cities in the United States, to supplement the fund-raising and arms-purchasing activities of the 26th of July "clubs," on a somewhat higher economic plane.

By spring, a committee of *Resistencia* leaders that included Dr. Santos Buch, Raúl Chibás, the former *Ortodoxo* presidential candidate Roberto Agramonte, and Fidel's nominee for provisional president, Dr. Urrutia, was touring the capitals of the hemisphere, seeking contributions and diplomatic support.

A Washington lobby was formed, to win Congressional support in a drive to shut off the flow of "Mutual Security" arms to Batista.

In Cuba fund collections were put on an organized basis, with Haydée Santamaría and later Manuel Suzarte in charge of national finance. Bonds were issued in a variety of denominations ranging upwards from one to a thousand dollars. A single issue of non-redeemable "salary day" bonds bearing the legend "For the Last 10th of March Under Tyranny" * yielded a quarter of a million dollars. Single private donations ranged as high as one hundred thousand dollars (a rare instance), and contributions from business, industry, and agriculture matched the popular donations and the proceeds of bond sales.

It may be noted without prejudice that, although the contributions in most instances reflected nothing more than simple patriotism, a natural tendency to seek to purchase "insurance" against strikes, sabotage, and the eventual day

* Anniversary of the Batista coup of 1952.

of reckoning can also be detected. By the time the rebel march on Havana began, sounding the death knell of the dictatorship, the *Movimiento 26* had three million dollars in hand, as yet unspent. And by that time, contributions in the vast *territorio libre* of Cuba which Batista no longer even pretended to control had become direct taxes, imposed by a revolutionary government the very existence of which, for reasons worth some later consideration, remained unaccountably unknown to the vast majority of Americans.

But this is to be beforehand. In the autumn of 1957, Batista still had a great many unpleasant surprises ahead of him.

One of the blows that hit him hardest was a personal thrust: the assassination at the end of November of the Holguín district commander, Colonel Fermin Cowley.

The author of "Batista's Christmas Gift" of the preceding winter had long been marked for death, the order for his execution having come directly from the Sierra. It was by no means an easy assignment. Other problems aside, Cowley was extremely erratic in his habits, as in his personal character.

As to his character, it is of some interest because the colonel was a close friend of Batista, a sometime revolutionary himself, who had had a part in the Sergeants' Revolt of 1933. At forty-seven he was slightly obese and soft from good living, but energetic and not unattractive in appearance and manner, capable of exercising a certain graciousness, a charm that was not lost on women, as witness the fact that he had acquired eight wives in twenty-five years (and had outworn seven).

His tastes were epicurean; he enjoyed classical music and had a large record library, flew his own airplane, dabbled in underwater photography, played with an elaborate model railway, and collected children's toys. His favorite toy is said to have been a soft black teddy bear.

It is hard to say whether murder was also one of his pleasures, or merely his business. The fact is that he was directly responsible for the slaying of more than one hundred persons. In the great majority of instances, he pulled the trigger or tightened the noose himself.

The responsibility for carrying out Cowley's execution—it cannot justly be called by any other name—was assumed by the M-26 action leader in the city of Holguín, a mechanic by trade, then thirty-three years old.*

The action chief put a watch on the colonel, and waited for opportunity to present itself. It came, finally, on the morning of November 23rd. A telephone call informed the underground leader that Cowley was at that moment in the Holguín business section, without his bodyguard, shopping on the premises of an air supply company.

The leader and three men who had been chosen for the execution drove immediately to the company store and warehouse, found the familiar blue sedan of the colonel's wife parked outside, empty, and looked into the office. Cowley was not there. The M-26 men drove around the corner, past the service entrance at the side of the store, and saw Cowley inside at a counter. They circled the block and returned to park behind a truck that was unloading cylinders of gas and compressed air at the loading ramp.

The squad leader got out of the car with an automatic shotgun in his hands. There was a moment's hesitation. The man glimpsed inside the air supply storeroom had been wearing glasses. Cowley was not known to wear or to need them. As the man with the shotgun mounted the loading ramp, one of the youths behind him shouted that he was making a mistake.

There was no mistake. The shout was heard by Cowley, examining an air meter at the counter. He turned to the open door as his executioner reached it. Perhaps the glare of light

* His name is withheld because of the continuing danger of reprisal.

kept the colonel from seeing what the man approaching held in his hands. Perhaps he was too shocked to react rationally. Whatever was in his mind, he turned back to the counter, hunching his shoulders as though to shut out an intrusion that he resented but felt helpless to prevent.

A young clerk with whom the underground leader was acquainted was standing on the other side of the counter. The action chief took a long step to one side, so as to put the boy out of the line of fire, raised the shotgun and, standing on the ramp at a level slightly below the motionless colonel, squeezed the trigger. There was no response. The colonel still stood with his back turned. The gunman lowered his weapon, released the safety catch, again took aim, and fired. The charge caught Cowley full in the back of the head.

On the street outside, the roar of the shotgun was echoed by another blast. One of the three youths waiting for the action leader had shot the colonel's chauffeur, who had been standing on the corner, and had turned around at the sound of the shot that killed his superior. The rebels fled.

The fatal shotgun blast reverberated in the presidential palace in Havana, where the news of Cowley's death brought personal anguish to Batista. "The dictator is no longer derisive," wrote *Time* magazine in its editions of December 9th. "Last week, in Colon Cemetery in Havana, he dropped his broad face in his hands and wept as a guard of honor buried Colonel Fermin Cowley, 47, one of his top commanders . . ."

Batista's tears do him more credit than most of his actions; no one can wish to strip him of all humanity. To do so would be to create a caricature. But comradely tears and soldiers' teddy bears weighed little in a war that mocked all misery and made jokes of the grim "ornaments" that Colonel Cowley swung from trees on Christmas Eve in Oriente.

A photograph published in *Bohemia* during the first weeks of 1959, after the liberation, shows a small boy in

Manzanillo playing with three human skulls given to him by his father, a lieutenant of the notorious Masferrer. This, like tears and teddy bears, is also incidental, signifying little except as a token of the bitterness and despair, the cynicism, the perversion of human values that are the by-products of war.

For, however it may have seemed from the outside, full-scale civil war was in progress in Oriente by the end of 1957. And the reprisals that followed the Cowley killing, quick, cold-blooded, and efficient, were only to be expected as part of the quickening conflict that had spread throughout the province and to all the cities of the island.

The "rag-tag guerrilla army" of Fidel Castro was giving Batista more trouble than was apparent to anyone outside of the province. Far-ranging guerrilla patrols, continuing the hit-and-run, fight-and-hide offensive that had begun in May, harried the government forces for a hundred miles along the Caribbean coast, and along the northern perimeter of the Sierra for another hundred miles, from Cape Cruz north to Niquero and Manzanillo and east to the garrison city of Bayamo.

One result of the reorganization of the rebel *Direccion Nacional* was to put pressure on Fidel to take fewer personal risks; to repress his impulse to supervise each action himself and persuade him to delegate more authority, confining himself to strategic planning in the relative safety of a rear echelon headquarters.

The effort was not entirely a success, but eventually a more or less permanent headquarters was established, in a *bohío* at La Plata,* on the southern slope of the Sierra, within two days' march of Pico Turquino.

The responsibilities of directing, simultaneously, an am-

* Not to be confused with the coastal village of La Plata indicated on most maps of Cuba.

bitious military campaign and a variety of political efforts were enough to keep Fidel in one place much of the time, of necessity if not by choice. A constant stream of messengers coming and going, visitors from the cities arriving for political consultations, unit commanders reporting for orders, underground leaders requiring instruction, all occupied him from early morning until far into the night.

The free-lance journalist Andrew St. George, coming out of the mountains in November after a long sojourn, explained: "You need to have an appointment to talk with Fidel now. It has become a big organization, and he's a very busy man."

Fidel no longer troubled to remove his heavy horn-rimmed glasses when his photograph was made: he was too preoccupied to be concerned about appearance, too sure of his position to bother striking poses, and by now too accustomed to being photographed to take notice.

His scraggly beard had grown untended. It is doubtful that he would have bothered to shave, even if *simbolismo* had not converted the earlier absence of razor blades and hot water into an asset, in terms of "public relations."

The term *"barbudos"* was becoming a familiar expression in Oriente as Fidel's bearded guerrillas began to strike into the villages and towns along the edge of the Sierra. The raids were becoming increasingly frequent. On rare occasions, the army still attempted some counter-measure.

In mid-September the *barbudos* ambushed a column of two hundred government troops at Palma Mocha, on the Caribbean side of the range, as they worked their way in the general direction of La Plata. The rebels had the advantage of surprise. Fifty-seven soldiers were killed in the clash. Fidel lost five men, and considered the rebel casualty rate excessive, the price too high for the weapons and ammunition that were captured.

The army did not mention the action in its bulletins. But no further attempt to penetrate the area was made throughout the remainder of the fall and winter.

The accelerated pace of the guerrilla campaign was matched by the efforts of the urban underground, and this activity in turn by the terrorism of government security forces and pro-Batista civilian elements, namely, the *"masferristas."*

Dynamite explosions temporarily cut off electric power and water supplies in Santiago and Havana. An army lieutenant who had been accused of selling rifles to the rebels was tortured to death. A loyalty check of the armed forces, begun in the wake of the Cienfuegos uprising, continued. Military rule, already a condition of life in Oriente, became more rigorous. Road blocks were increased in number; airports, rail terminals, and bus stations were closely guarded; and all travelers subjected to strict surveillance. Armed soldiers rode on all buses, both in the towns and in the countryside. Troops stood guard at radio stations, power plants, and public buildings; army jeeps and *micro-ondas* ceaselessly prowled the city streets; and armored cars patrolled the highways.

In Holguín, two days after Colonel Cowley's death, a special force of one hundred fifty SIM troops under Lieutenant Colonel Irenaldo García Baez,* the assistant chief of the military intelligence service, arrived to conduct an investigation.

The inquiry was carried out with Prussian thoroughness. All roads leading out of the city were blocked by the SIM men with their distinctive red-white-and-blue shoulder patches. Check points were established at intersections throughout the city. Residents wishing to move from one section to another were required to obtain special passes.

---

* Son of Pilar García, colonel at Matanzas, later made Brigadier and put in charge of National Police in Havana.

Every house and building in the city of eighty thousand population was searched, with the aid of regular troops and police; every citizen able to talk was questioned.

More than one thousand persons were taken to the 7th District military base for further interrogation. By the first week of December, all but eighteen suspects had been cleared.

Eleven whose association with the Holguín underground was uncertain were held for the courts, later released for lack of evidence against them. One, a youth who had had some connection with the underground but no knowledge of the circumstances of Cowley's death, was saved by his own good fortune and the intervention of his influential family.

Of the remaining six, five were members of the 26th of July movement, the sixth was a middle-aged automobile dealer, so unfortunate as to have been on the scene at the time of the shooting, and so unwise as to have denied it, in a moment of panic. Testimony that he had been in an ice-cream parlor across the street when Cowley was shot failed to convince García Baez of his innocence.

On the night of December 8th, an automobile left the military base with the six suspects. A carload of soldiers followed the automobile conveying the handcuffed prisoners to the city where, presumably, they were to be lodged in the civil prison.

En route, there was a brief halt. A short while later the soldiers arrived in Holguín and left six bullet-riddled bodies on the curb in front of the city hospital. The soldiers reported that rebels had fired on them on the drive into the city and had killed the prisoners—by mistake.

As it happened, none of the six had taken part in Cowley's execution. The four men actually responsible were far from Holguín. All four survived the revolution.

In November the call came from the Sierra for an intensive campaign of economic attrition, designed to exert pressure on the government in its most vulnerable quarter.

The guerrilla operation in Oriente was going well enough, the revolutionary movement was being strengthened throughout the country. More was required.

Batista, too, was reinforcing his position, both militarily and politically. The army was being built up; the government was emptying the reformatories and jails in order to fill military uniforms, seeming not to care what sort of human material was employed, so long as it could shoulder a rifle and be marched into the Sierra. Money was being poured into armaments, with the emphasis on the specialized weapons of mountain warfare, howitzers, mortars, rifle grenades, machine guns, napalm.

On the political level, Batista was seeking to provide fresh window dressing, with the cooperation of the legal opposition parties, including Grau San Martín's *auténticos,* and reactionary splinters of the no longer legal *Ortodoxo* party. General elections had been called for June 1st, 1958. Batista was willing to leave the presidential palace, as the Constitution required that he should, on condition that it be surrendered to a custodian of his choice. His interest was in real rather than apparent power. Having failed to win personal popularity, he was ready to revert to his long-held former role of president-maker.

The object was to provide a figurehead in the palace and yet retain control. If appearances required elections, as was beginning to appear to be the case, then, very well—he himself was prepared to finance the "election campaigns" of the nominal opposition candidates, which is to say, stalking-horses.

The political maneuvers in the capital worried Fidel far more than the efforts of the army in Oriente. The *fidelista* strategy from the start had been conceived in terms of psychological warfare. The sporadic and relatively harmless sabotage of the past had been intended largely for psychological effect. Fifty bombs exploded in the capital during one brief period, the rebels boasted, produced no more than four casualties. The trouble was that the squawking hen continued to lay eggs. The people responded to the alarms and excursions of the psychological campaign, and were savagely repressed by a regime that had contempt for weakness and respected only force and wealth. The interests that backed Batista, seeing no imminent military threat, feeling no tug at their purse strings, remained unmoved.

Baffled by the "business as usual" attitude that prevailed in the capital, impatient for quick, dramatic results at a minimal cost in lives, fearing a farcical election that would nevertheless consolidate the position of the regime in power under a new name, Fidel took a drastic step.

The order that came from the Sierra was: apply the torch to the ripening sugar cane crop—some six and a half million tons, a third of the world's entire sugar supply for the year, with an estimated value of more than half a billion dollars, the livelihood of seven hundred thousand Cubans employed in the annual cane harvest and grinding, the *zafra*.

It was a staggering, almost sacrilegious idea—like asking bankers to burn bank notes. Cane had been burned before, but mainly as a device to create disorder and to distract the attention of the government security forces; usually, also, with an eye to the political orientation and behavior of the mill owner. Now the cane was *all* to go. The call for the torch was firm: "There will be no *zafra* with Batista. After the tyrant is in the tomb . . . we will have a *zafra* of liberty."

Cane was the primary target, but the order applied to all income-producing crops and industry. The disorganized, "psychological" sabotage of the past now gave way to purposeful destruction on a broad scale.

Small guerrilla patrols from the Sierra moved into the

plains to spread fire through the canefields. Leaflets were circulated giving simple instructions for the preparation of gasoline bombs. Saboteurs crept out from the towns and villages at night to set the fields ablaze from one end of the island to the other.

In the western provinces of Havana and Pinar del Río, it was tobacco that burned. Fifty tobacco warehouses went up in smoke within a single week. A small airplane flying over the province of Havana destroyed one hundred fifty thousand tons of sugar in two days, by dropping small celluloid capsules filled with phosphorous that spread flames across five major sugar *centrales*.

The urban underground increased its effort. Huge oil refinery tanks on the outskirts of Santiago and Havana burned. The Havana Aqueduct was dynamited and began to lose five million gallons of water daily. Buses were burned in their terminal in Santiago. There were increasing interruptions of electrical power and water supplies from Guantánamo to Havana as power lines and water mains were wrecked.

"Embattled Cuba Gay for Yuletide," was the column heading of the Havana dispatch published in *The New York Times* of December 15th. The text went on to report that Cuban workers were earning higher wages than in many years, sugar producers were planning to distribute wage bonuses amounting to seventeen million dollars by government edict, "Santa Claus has become an important personality and the Christmas tree has been adopted wholeheartedly."

Glittering white Christmas trees adorned the presidential palace grounds where the insurgents of the March 13th attack had lain in their blood. Stores were crowded, cabarets and casinos were flourishing, and even motion picture houses were doing a "fair" trade, although the *Times* notes that there was scarcely a theater in Cuba that had not been bombed.

Fidel Castro did his Christmas "shopping" in the village of Veguitas, on the Manzanillo-Bayamo highway, disarming eight soldiers on duty at the small military barracks there and returning to the hills with four trucks laden with food and clothing from the village stores, paid for with cash.

In his letter of December 14th, in which he proposed Judge Urrutia as head of "a caretaker government" to succeed the Batista regime, Fidel reported no fewer than eight engagements with the army in the preceding week. The most important had been near Veguitas, where the rebels, two hundred strong, attacked a column of three hundred soldiers on December 11th, and—Fidel wrote—inflicted one hundred seventy casualties.

There was a series of raids in the Manzanillo area. On Christmas Eve, the rebels captured the Manzanillo airport, held it briefly while taking medical stores from a nearby hospital, and again withdrew into the hills.

In his New Year's message from the presidential palace, Batista expressed hope of "continued rising prosperity and happiness in all Cuban homes," and declared that the people had manifested "a deep desire to live in peace according to Christian principles."

The *Times* headed its dispatch of January 1st: "Bombs in Havana Greet New Year."

There was no abatement of the sabotage campaign, nor of the fighting in Oriente. The rebels again raided Veguitas, killed five soldiers of the reinforced garrison there, destroyed the telegraph office, and withdrew as a motorized column sped down the highway from Bayamo to relieve the besieged soldiers. An armored car at the head of the relief column ran over a mine in the road and was blown to bits.

Buses and trains were being stopped daily in the Manzanillo area, the passengers set afoot, and the buses burned. Private automobiles were halted for inspection by rebel patrols, trains were stopped and searched for arms and ammunition, their guards relieved of their weapons, the passengers instructed to stay home in the future. A diesel train was burned near Bayamo, a locomotive vanished from a sugar mill and later was discovered to have been blown up. Another train was sent running free along the tracks to crash into a string of empty cars in the Guantánamo station.

An exodus of civilians began from Manzanillo as a rebel attack on the city of forty thousand population daily appeared more imminent. The army poured reinforcements into the city and built concrete fortifications on its outskirts in anticipation of the assault.

More than five thousand troops had by now been committed to the Sierra Maestra zone of operations, and fresh troops continued to arrive, air-lifted from Havana, Matanzas, Santa Clara, and Camagüey.

The government forces were hopelessly inadequate for their task, their lines far over-extended, unable to maintain contact with the enemy, hard put to defend themselves from lightning attacks in unexpected quarters.

The rebel tactics were simple and seldom varied. A provocation would be created. Government troops would speed to the scene and run headlong into ambush or, avoiding the obvious trap, would find themselves in yet another, encircled and attacked on their flanks or from behind. Army commanders found it easy to enter the foothills, difficult to get out again with their units intact.

Rebel patrols moved along the perimeter of Fidel's proclaimed *territorio libre* over a distance of more than two hundred fifty miles on both sides of the mountain range, laying waste to the canefields and the rice crop, attacking the garrisons at the sugar mills, entering towns to make purchases of supplies and leaving at their leisure.

The army controlled the Manzanillo-Bayamo road during daylight, the rebels controlled it at night. The central highway itself was threatened as the *barbudos* extended their operations from Bayamo westward to the outskirts of Palma Soriano and southward to the port of Chivirico, across the broad bay from Santiago de Cuba.

Rebel casualties were low, one reason being that the rebels were able to depend on the civil population for warning of the approach of government troops, and did battle only when it seemed expedient.

It was the civilians who suffered, and the urban underground. Army commanders were under pressure from Havana to produce "victories"—and *evidence* of their achievement. In many instances, they took the easiest and safest course. On January 15th, a military bulletin issued by the *estado mayor* at Camp Columbia reported that twenty-three rebels had been killed in an encounter at Los Hombritos, near Bayamo. No army casualties were reported, for the very good reason that there had been no "encounter." The "rebels" had been taken from jail in Santiago, conveyed by truck to the Los Hombritos area, marched into the hills, and shot down by the soldiers.

The bodies of four unidentified young men were found hanging from trees outside of Guantánamo. Manuel Hevia, nephew of former President Carlos Hevia, was kidnapped on the street in Havana, beaten and burned on his arms and body with lighted cigarets, and told to "stay out of it," meaning, stay out of politics. Saboteurs caught in the canefields were shot on sight. The bodies of youths suspected of having any connection with the underground littered the roads. The residents of Manzanillo sent a petition to General Chaviano, asking for military intervention to protect their sons from a band of Senator Masferrer's vigilantes roaming the area, killing suspected rebel sympathizers.

Although the *barbudos* moved in relative security within

their own free territory, to pass into the fortified cities remained a hazardous undertaking for individuals. Those who were caught leaving the rebel zone and survived were the fortunate few.

On January 10th the fugitive underground leader Armando Hart was captured near Bayamo as he returned from consultations in the Sierra with Fidel. Seized with him were Felipe Pazos' son, Javier, and Antonio Buch, a cousin of Dr. Angel Santos Buch, the *Resistencia* leader. (The latter had already gone into exile, having fled the country after his Santiago laboratory was searched during his temporary absence by Salas Cañizares, the SIM chief.)

By good fortune, the arrest of the three prominent *fidelistas* was reported immediately to the *Resistencia*. The *Times* correspondent in Havana was notified at once, so as to publicize the capture and insure that the prisoners would not simply vanish. The United States vice consul in Santiago, Robert Wiecha, was prevailed upon to make inquiries on behalf of the families of the three men, with the result that General Chaviano was compelled to produce the prisoners, unharmed, to prove that they had not been tortured or killed.*

The foregoing is one of the several instances in which Wiecha rendered invaluable and humanitarian service to the Batista opposition. Similar services were performed by other individual members of the U.S. consular and diplomatic corps; in some cases as a matter of natural human sympathy, in others, apparently, as a simple consequence of the wish to maintain some semblance of contact with the leadership of a movement that daily seemed more certain of taking over the reins of government in Cuba.

Such contacts were not officially sanctioned. On the contrary, Ambassador Smith expressly ordered his staff to

---

* Buch and Pazos were later freed by the courts. Hart was sent to the Isle of Pines, where he remained until the liberation.

have *no* dealings with revolutionary elements, and subsequently the commandant at the United States naval base at Guantánamo Bay, Rear Admiral Robert B. Ellis, issued the same order to the officer in charge of naval intelligence on the base; i.e., learn what needs to be known about rebel strength and military intentions, but have no contact with the rebels.

The good offices of individual members of the consular and diplomatic services failed to offset the unfavorable impression made on the Cuban public at large by Ambassador Smith, a millionaire stockbroker and a political appointee, who had contributed generously to the Republican campaign fund during the 1952 presidential elections in the United States.

Smith lost what remained of his earlier popularity in Cuba when he flew to Washington for "routine" consultations during the first month of 1958, and after conferring with the State Department, issued a statement in which he expressed it as the "hope" of the United States that Batista would restore full constitutional guarantees, as promised, on January 27th, and would proceed in June with elections "acceptable to the people of Cuba."

The ambassador's remarks, coupled with an expression of strict neutrality in the Cuban struggle, were interpreted in Cuba as a declaration of support for Batista, the more so since it was obvious to all—and should have been clear to Smith—that elections conducted while the dictator remained in power could have but one result.

A report circulated in Washington concerning certain "off-the-record" statements said to have been made by the ambassador at his news conference did nothing to improve the impression.

Among other things, Smith was quoted as being of the opinion that the United States could not possibly "do business" with Fidel Castro's followers under any circumstances, that rebel raids on Manzanillo had been made because of criticism that the *fidelistas* had not been "active enough," that the cane burning had "boomeranged," and that although there was no evidence that Fidel Castro was a Communist, there was "no doubt that he has a questionable background."

Whatever the intention of the State Department, Smith's statement supporting the scheduled June electoral farce and U.S. protestations of "impartiality and non-intervention" infuriated the Batista oppositionists, who denounced it as "unwarranted intervention" and much else that was unfavorable besides.

As to the ambassador's reported off-the-cuff remarks vis-à-vis Fidel Castro, they were not easily dismissed. It was all too easy to recall other diplomatic *gaffes,* for example, Ambassador Arthur Gardner's characterization of Castro as a "rabble rouser" on the occasion of the formal delivery of seven Sherman tanks to the Cuban army,* and the decoration of Colonel Carlos Tabernilla, son of the army chief of staff, by a United States Air Force General, only a few weeks after the younger Tabernilla had directed the air attacks that had crushed the Cienfuegos uprising.†

Of even more concern to the Cuban revolutionaries than the pronouncements of the American ambassador were the policies actively being pursued by the United States government with respect to the Batista regime.

* February, 1957.

† USAF Major General Truman Landon flew to Havana to present Tabernilla the Legion of Merit. The accompanying citation, as recorded in the Library of Congress, reads: "Colonel Carlos M. Tabernilla y Palmero, Chief, Cuban Army Air Force, distinguished himself by exceptionally meritorious conduct in the furtherance of amicable relations between the Cuban Air Force and the United States Air Force from May, 1955, to February, 1957. During this period the leadership ability, diplomacy, and good will of Colonel Tabernilla have contributed immeasurably to the furtherance of Cuban-American friendship." The fact that the period cited antedates the Cienfuegos insurrection was lost on most Cubans. They were in no humor to make such fine distinctions.

The asserted neutrality of the United States could not be a reality, according to a statement issued by Ernesto Betancourt, a spokesman for the 26th of July movement in Washington, "as long as there is an American military mission in Cuba whose technical assistance is being used by the Batista regime to increase the proficiency of its repressive forces, and as long as planes, tanks, and ships over which the United States government still has control, weapons given by the American people to defend this hemisphere, are used by Batista to unleash total war on Cuban citizens."

An even more forceful statement came in February from the Sierra Maestra, where Fidel declared that a change in the attitude of the United States government had been noted since Ambassador Smith's Washington visit. A "secret agreement" had been made in January, Fidel charged, in which Batista had agreed to restore constitutional guarantees, in return for firmer U.S. support, namely, a pledge to take action against Cuban revolutionary groups soliciting funds and buying arms in the United States.

In evidence, Fidel cited the recent arrest in Miami of Dr. Prío, indicted February 13th for conspiracy to violate the U.S. Neutrality Act. Moreover, the rebel leader declared, it had been noted that the Batista air force had started using jet aircraft in Oriente for the first time following Smith's return from Washington, and that the Havana government had increased its arms budget.

As to the question of arms being purchased by Batista in the United States, the 26th of July movement was in certain possession of the facts, having, as it happened, an agent in the Cuban Embassy in Washington.

The agent was a Cuban army sergeant, Angel Saavedra, secretary to the military attaché, and so in a position to lay hands on virtually every document of interest to Fidel that passed through the Embassy—including arms purchase and delivery orders. Photographic copies of value to the *Movimiento 26* were passed on to Ernesto Betancourt, its registered agent in Washington, who took care in making use of the documents that suspicion should not fall on Saavedra. (The sergeant, for his part, posed as an ardent *batistiano,* so much so as to become a nuisance to less enthusiastic followers of Batista. He was still at work in the Embassy when Batista fled to Santo Domingo.)

The State Department was prompt to deny that any "secret agreement" had been made, or that the attitude of the United States government was other than scrupulously neutral.

Nevertheless, as the result of the interchange, and the lobbying of a number of eminently respectable and widely respected Cubans aligned against Batista, rising criticism of State Department policy began to be voiced in the American press, and several Congressmen—notably Oregon's Senator Wayne Morse and Representative Charles O. Porter, and New York Representative Adam Clayton Powell, Jr.—began to investigate the use to which armaments sent to Cuba under the Mutual Security program and the Mutual Assistance pact were being put.

The State Department regretfully refused to divulge the amounts and nature of the weapons shipped to Cuba. Within a short while, however, Powell contrived to provide Congress with a list of such arms, complete with the specific order numbers and delivery dates.

In so doing, the Congressman minced no words. "The United States," he declared, "is a partner with the dictator of Cuba, Fulgencio Batista, in the killing of close to four thousand Cubans so far, and it is time that we should get out and get out at once. We not only have been and are supplying arms to Batista, but we have a military mission established in Cuba, actively assisting the Cuban army. There should be an immediate stoppage of the flow of arms and ammunition from this country, and there should be an immediate withdrawal of the mission." *

The list of arms delivered during the preceding two years—"modest" in the opinion of the State Department —included:

3,000 M-1 caliber .30 semi-automatic rifles
15,000 hand grenades
5,000 mortar grenades
20 caliber .30 machine guns
20 caliber .50 machine guns
100,000 caliber .50 armor-piercing cartridges for machine guns
1,000 3.5-millimeter rockets
3,000 five-inch rockets
1 complete battery of light mountain howitzer artillery bombs for the Cuban Army Air Force valued at $328,931.48
7 M4A3 tanks with 76-millimeter guns

On order for June delivery were twenty armored cars, in the process of being rebuilt, and for August delivery communication equipment valued at $89,998.66.

Requests for which no contract number had been assigned included 1,000 rocket launchers, 24 mortars, 10,000 hand grenades, 6,000 M-1 rifles, and 2,000 M-1 carbines, among other items.

By the time the American public had begun to get a glimmering of what was happening in Cuba, a new crisis was approaching.

"Nations run fever charts like individuals," Herbert Matthews observed in one of his exceptionally perceptive reports from Havana in the early spring of 1958†—"A fever chart of Cuba started a year ago would show not only a steady rise but an increase in the last six weeks so steep and to such a height that one can only diagnose a crisis of the gravest nature."

* Congressional Record of March 20, 1958.
† March 22, 1958, *The New York Times.*

The developments of the late winter and early spring came at such a furious pace and in such profusion that it is difficult to separate the military from the political, the action from the reaction, the significant from the spectacular but merely incidental.

Both sides sustained losses, both suffered setbacks, both marked positive gains. What remained after debits and credits had been checked off, one against the other, was the undeniable circumstance that the Revolution had gained ground, both literally and in the political sense, and that Batista had retreated, both on the fighting front and in the political arena.

Only official Washington, absorbed in its own complex calculations, weighing and checking obscure factors on a global scale that were yet invisible to ordinary observers, or too complicated for ordinary understanding, seemed not to notice.

In rapid sequence, these were the salient developments:

Batista restored constitutional guarantees on January 25th to all of the six provinces but Oriente, and ten days later, under heavy pressure, to Oriente also.

Scarcely had censorship ended when fighting broke out on a new front in the center of the island, in Las Villas province, where Eloy Gutiérrez Menoyo, a survivor of the palace attack of 1957 and brother of the underground leader slain there, had quietly been building up a strong guerrilla force for two months past.

Fighters of *El Segundo Frente Nacional del Escambray*, trained in commando tactics by the American William Morgan, a war veteran from Toledo, Ohio, who was described as "particularly proficient with a knife," launched a series of lightning attacks on small army posts in the mountains around Sancti Spiritus and the Caribbean port of Trinidad. There was fighting at Fomento on the cross-island highway to the Atlantic coast and within fifteen miles of the all-important Central Highway. A rebel truck convoy was intercepted bringing arms to the mountains, and the *Directorio Revolucionario* leader from Sancti Spiritus was killed.

In February another veteran of the palace attack, Faure Chaumont, landed on the Caribbean coast with another small force and led his men into the *Sierra de Trinidad,* and the fighting spread, tying up more government troops.

A landing was reported at *Playa de las Coloradas* in Oriente, the scene of the original *Granma* landing. Fidel was there to receive, not men, but urgently needed arms. Other expeditions, too ambitious, met a harder fate. In March the U.S. Coast Guard seized the seventy-foot cruiser *Orion* off Brownsville, Texas, and with it thirty-five uniformed members of the *Movimiento 26* and armaments valued at thirty thousand dollars. Since the expedition had been the subject of discussion in every Spanish restaurant and bar in New York City since December, the capture should have come as no surprise.

"Some people may criticize," said Raúl Chibás, in exile in New York, "but the little trickle of arms that actually gets to Cuba, the few pistols in a sack of flour, the submachine gun in a tin of lard, counts for more than the big, noisy expedition that everyone boasts about, and that gets caught by the Customs the day before it sails."

Fidel was having better fortune finding his own weapons in Oriente. The government forces had continued to fall back. On February 16th, one of the last remaining toeholds in the foothills of the Sierra was eliminated at Pina del Agua, west of Bayamo. Rebel forces under the Argentine "Che" Guevara and Fidel himself attacked the Pina del Agua garrison at dawn. A column led by Raúl Castro ambushed the first small relief patrol to respond to the garrison's radioed alarm. Ten soldiers were killed, three wounded, and their officer captured. Motorized troops from Bayamo avoided road mines planted on their route, but failed to force an entrance to the area. The hundred-man garrison at Pina del Agua fled to the woods, leaving their fortified hill-top *cuartel* and four dead behind, along with five machine guns and three hundred thirteen rifles—sufficient to arm a new rebel column. The *barbudos* now rode openly through the foothills and along the edge of the plain in jeeps and trucks, no longer stealthy commando units but a growing guerrilla army.

Sabotage across the country began to paralyze transportation to the point where trains no longer ran on schedule east of Camagüey. A students' strike began in Santiago. The *"masferristas"* hanged three youths near the provincial capital. Police shot down Alfredo Gutiérrez, a member of the Santiago underground, and the women of Santiago followed his casket to the grave carrying the red-and-black flags of the *Movimiento 26* and singing *"Al combate, cubanos!"*

Arsonists invaded the courthouse in the city of Camagüey and burned the records of the Urgency Court. Armed men raided the central clearing office of the National Bank in Havana and applied the torch to thousands of cancelled checks and bank drafts, spreading chaos in the business and financial houses of the capital. Revolutionary exhortations were heard on thousands of radios, as radio stations were seized and regular programs interrupted by young men with pistols and prepared recordings.

Sugar cane no longer burned in the fields. Ambassador Smith had been right in one respect. The burning of the canefields "boomeranged" and the Movement was quick to respond to the outcries of *campesinos* whose entire livelihood depended on the *zafra*. But fire ravaged warehouses across the island, turning hundreds of tons of sugar to charred caramel, and David Salvador, the M-26 labor section leader in Havana, counted the cost of the overall campaign to sugar producers in five figures, estimating the sugar loss at two million tons, a sixth part of the entire crop.

Increasingly there was talk of a paralyzing general strike, to culminate the long struggle in one crushing blow. Batista impatiently shrugged his shoulders, and turned to more pressing business, confident of his control of the CTC and its bullnecked secretary-general, Eusebio Mujal.

A plague of stinging buzzing mosquitoes seemed to swarm about the dictator's head, none consequential in itself, but collectively infuriating, maddening, and—like mosquitoes —potentially capable of starting a fatal infection.

In the midst of all of the other threats and distractions of the heightening campaign of harassment, a daring under-ground "action" squad kidnapped Juan Manuel Fangio, the world auto-racing champion and a celebrity of a magni-tude sufficient to make headlines, where the rape of a city, the agony of a nation, could scarcely fill a column.

Fangio was seized in the lobby of the Hotel Lincoln in downtown Havana on the eve of the annual holiday* racing classic, the *Gran Premio,* forced at pistol point to enter a waiting automobile, and taken to an apartment where the Argentine driver had the reassurance of being introduced to the young wife of one of his abductors, at the moment busy telling a goodnight to her two-year-old daughter. He was shifted later to another apartment, and spent the night and the following day in a third.

The underground telephoned the newspapers in the interim, to make certain that the *Movimiento 26* received adequate credit for the action, and that its purpose—to underscore the revolutionary boycott of all amusement and frivolity—was understood. A later telephone call brought the Argentine ambassador to the outskirts of Havana, to pick up Fangio, who had been released.

* *"El Grito de Baire,"* February 24.

The *Gran Premio* had been run without the world champion. An accident at the track killed fourteen persons in his absence.

Fangio did nothing to lessen the government's embarrassment. He said he had been well treated, had seen part of the *Gran Premio* on television, and held no resentment against anyone, calling the incident "another adventure in my life."

More important developments were afoot. On the night of the *Gran Premio* disaster in Havana, while Fangio still was being guarded in a house in suburban Vedado, the first rebel radio broadcast from the Sierra Maestra was heard, crackling across the shortwave 40-meter band from Oriente to Pinar del Río: *"Aqui Radio Rebelde! Aqui Radio Rebelde, transmitiendo desde la Sierra Maestra en Territorio Libre de Cuba!"*

Rebel broadcasts purporting to be from the Sierra, actually from a small portable transmitter in Santiago, had been heard before. This one was authentic, coming from deep in the mountains and bringing news as well as revolutionary exhortations; in particular, the first on-the-scene report of the recent fighting at Pina del Agua and Oro de Guisa.

A new phase of the military campaign was opening. In early March, two small columns left the Sierra Maestra, one led by Raúl Castro, the other by Juan Almeida. Both emerged at San Lorenzo, on the eastern side of the Sierra. Almeida marched boldly toward Santiago, letting the word of his advance precede him by word of mouth, spread by the *campesinos*. Raúl's column, carrying the best of the small arms available, all that Fidel could spare, turned toward the north, moving cautiously in the direction of the Central Highway. The long-discussed second front, *"El Segundo Frente, Frank País,"* was about to be opened, finally, in the highlands of northern Oriente, in the Sierra Cristal.

A new and more serious and immediate threat to the regime was suddenly posed in an unexpected quarter. In a declaration that caught Batista completely by surprise, the hierarchy of the Roman Catholic Church called for the formation of "a government of national union" to prepare the way for "the restoration of normal political life" in Cuba.

The declaration—signed by Manuel Cardinal Arteaga and all of the members of the Cuban episcopate—caused consternation in the presidential palace, and elation elsewhere.

Batista's first reaction was to *ask* the press, in the absence of censorship, to withhold the news. The newspaper publishers refused. The editions of March 1st carried the episcopal message in full.

Batista, faced with what was tantamount to a demand for his abdication, chose to interpret the declaration as a call for a coalition government, i.e., a new *cabinet*. He said that he would remain in office until the June elections had chosen his successor. As for the cabinet, it was about to be reorganized in any event, since a new premier was to be named to replace Andrés Rivero Agüero, the presidential nominee of Batista's four-party government coalition.

The political opposition, the civic institutions, and the archbishop of Santiago, among other churchmen, rejected Batista's interpretation. Batista, blandly ignoring all protests, produced a "Commission of National Harmony," also described as a "Commission of Conciliation," headed by a priest who had been under-secretary of agriculture in the Batista regime before entering the priesthood. Other members were the former Cuban vice-president of Batista's first term, a former vice-president of the Grau regime, and the president of the Cuban Bank Association.

It was reported that the Commission would send agents to the Sierra Maestra to seek the basis of a compromise with Fidel Castro. In a further effort to allay the criticism now heard in even the most ultra-conservative quarters, Batista announced that he would be willing to approve elections conducted under the supervision of an international agency.

From the Sierra, Fidel sent a demand that Cuban journalists also be permitted to visit the zone of hostilities. He repeated the challenge, March 9th, in a letter broadcast the same night by Station CMKC in Santiago—an open letter in which he also called upon the episcopate to clarify its declaration, to state, categorically, whether it was possible "that any self-respecting Cuban is disposed to sit down in a Council of Ministers presided over by Fulgencio Batista."

The challenge to permit a commission of journalists to enter the liberated zone of Oriente was stated as an ultimatum, setting March 11th as a deadline on which, in the absence of a response from the government, the *Movimiento 26* would make "a definitive pronouncement to the nation, launching the final slogans of the struggle."

There was no response. On the 11th, the secretary of the archbishop of Santiago, the Reverend Angel Rivas, replied to the request for clarification of the episcopal declaration with an "Open Letter to Fidel," read on the air during the priest's evening editorial program "With the Cross and the Star," in which he asserted that the episcopate had called for "not a new cabinet," but a new, provisional government, to prepare the way for honest elections.

Batista's troubles were multiplying; the gamble that he had taken in restoring civil guarantees was lost. In Havana, thirteen eminent jurists addressed a petition to the Chamber of Administration of the Court of Appeals declaring that the courts were being flouted by the very officers sworn to serve them, that police refused to honor writs of *habeas corpus,* that political prisoners who *were* released were shot down on the streets, sometimes within sight of the courts that had freed them, that police officers fattened on the vices that they were employed to suppress, and that "violent death (by gunfire, torture, and hanging) are daily events" in Santiago, Guantánamo, Palma Soriano, Bayamo, El Cobre, Manzanillo, Niquero, and their environs.

A fearless Havana magistrate, Dr. Francisco Alabau Trelles, took a more dangerous step. Armed with the special authority of the Supreme Court, he signed orders for the immediate arrest and imprisonment of Esteban Ventura, head of the police bureau of subversive activities and by now a major, and the naval intelligence chief, Lieutenant Julio Laurent, on indictments of torture and murder stemming from the reprisals of the Cienfuegos uprising.

On the following day, March 12th, Batista suspended civil guarantees, reimposed censorship, and quashed the indictments by the simple process of transferring them to the jurisdiction of the military tribunals. Ventura, pistol in hand went seeking Judge Alabau. The jurist hastily obtained a leave of absence, and flew to Miami.

In the Sierra, Fidel issued a twenty-one-point manifesto, announcing the opening of a second front, and declaring "total, implacable war" on the dictatorship and a campaign of extermination against all bearing arms for it, to begin, full force, on the first day of April.

The red line on the Cuban fever chart was nearing its apex. The crisis was at hand.

Havana, April 3 (AP)—Dictator Batista's government today authorized workers to kill if necessary to stay on their jobs when rebel leader Fidel Castro issues his long-threatened call for a general strike.

X

A JUNCTURE has been reached at which political maneuvers cease to be meaningful and the voice of organized public opinion is as futile as all other voices. Masks are discarded. A test of strength is imminent. On one side is naked force. On the other, the people, truth, and the dragon seed of revolutionary doctrine, implanted most securely where the weight of military repression is most crushing, germinating best in blood-soaked soil, sprouting rebel soldiers overnight.

By the spring of 1958, Batista had but two choices: to get out, or to fight desperately with all of the weapons of his arsenal—the army, the treasury, the timidity or indifference of investors who preferred the devil they knew to the one unknown, the careful "neutrality" of the major foreign power whose single word of condemnation would have been sufficient to bring the dictatorship crashing down.

He chose to fight.

The army sent out a call for seven thousand more men, to bring its strength to twenty-nine thousand.

The forty national institutions—"whose names," said Congressman Porter, "read like a roster of *Who's Who Among Respectable Organizations*"—added their petition to that of the Church, abandoning all formulae of compromise and now demanding, in unmistakable terms "that the present regime shall cease to hold power . . ."

Batista's reply was to send police seeking the authors of the petition, who fled into hiding or into exile. (The president of the Havana Bar Association, Dr. José Miró Cardona, disguised himself as a priest and hid in a church.)

Ambassador Smith, insisting that he could obtain guarantees from Washington to safeguard the scheduled June elections under the existing government, asked to know why the members of the Joint Committee of Cuban Institutions had not signed their names to their petition. There is nothing to indicate that he was joking.

Batista would have found the question both grimly amusing and personally reassuring. He had his problems, multiplying on every hand, but he must have perceived that, if all of the pressures of Church and secular society could not crack the foundations of the dictatorship nor alienate his principal allies, then he had little to fear but force. And this he did not fear.

The capital seemed secure, despite the ravages of the revolutionary campaign in the countryside. The provincial cities remained under control. The big military garrisons were in safe hands, and Batista's military intelligence told him, quite accurately, that his enemies were as yet incapable of posing a serious military threat against him, however much they might harass him in the hinterland.

His concern, then, was with terrorism, sabotage, civil insurrection. Here, too, he felt confident, having leave, apparently, to fight fire with fire, so long as he did it discreetly, muffling the cries of the casualties under a blanket of censorship, hiding the true situation behind a smoke screen of "anti-Communist" propaganda, maintaining, above all, the myth of his military invulnerability. (Is any further explanation needed for the "victories" produced by slaughtering peasants?)

The *fidelistas,* and more particularly the strategists of the *Resistencia,* had hoped that a paper dragon would frighten away Batista's backers, that to create an atmosphere of insurrection, to threaten the economy without actually damaging it to any great degree, to militate all segments of society against the dictator and so discredit him, would be sufficient to destroy the regime. Now it was being discovered, bitterly, that force alone could win respect.

It is with this unhappy realization that the revolution moves into its final, military phase, opening in disaster and bitter anti-climax, ending in a triumph the more surprising and overwhelming because of what preceded it.

In March the resistance leaders in the cities were still looking for a short-cut to their objective. It was barely possible, at least in theory, that they might have found one. A general strike in the Thirties had given the Machado regime its *coup de grace*.* There was more recent encouragement to follow such a course, notably the overthrow of Perez Jiménez, the Venezuelan dictator, in January, 1958.

Batista's position had been appreciably weakened; rebel strength had increased throughout the island; revolutionary sentiment was running high among the people. The National Direction of the M-26, having better understanding of the actual situation in the Sierra Maestra than did Batista, and anxious to avoid the long campaign that seemed inevitable if based primarily on military strategy and growth, resolved to commit their entire resources to what they hoped would be a final, crushing blow against Batista, a revolutionary general strike.

Fidel was opposed. He may well have had political considerations in mind. He certainly had serious doubts as to the possibility of such a solution.

His own appraisal of the resources of the revolution and those of the dictator told him that only the steady growth of the process that had started in the Sierra Maestra, the gradual extension of *territorio libre*, the day by day ex-

---

* But not before Franklin Roosevelt, in one of the happier exercises of the Good Neighbor policy, had whisked the diplomatic rug out from under Machado's feet and the latter's army had deserted him. In Venezuela, too, military defection preceded a popular rising. It is, in fact, difficult to find a modern instance in which a mere rising of the people, unsupported by troops, has overthrown an entrenched regime.

pansion of the rebel fighting force and the elimination, one by one, of the government outposts, could cut the lifelines of the dictatorship.

He did not believe that the underground was adequately prepared for a general uprising, despite assurances to the contrary. He had little faith in Havana, with its large foreign population, its Spanish merchant class, which formed the backbone of Cuban conservatism, its traditional disaffection from the struggles of the nation, its historical position as the exploiter of the wealth-producing provinces.

He was well aware of the firm grip in which Batista held organized labor, under the domination of Eusebio Mujal and his C.T.C. and he recalled all too vividly the fiasco of the August strike. Having had some early experience of a similar disaster on a larger scale—as a youngster fighting briefly on the side of insurrectionary students and police against the Colombian armed forces in the *"bogotazo"* of 1947*—he had no illusions concerning such efforts.

He was nevertheless persuaded, against his better judgment.

The Sierra Maestra manifesto of March 12th, agreed upon by the National Direction of the *Movimiento 26,* called for a revolutionary general strike, backed by the armed action of the revolutionary fighting forces, as the basis of a final "decisive" blow against Batista.

Other articles in the 21-point declaration of war tended to support the impression that all would be gambled on a single cast of the dice—winner take all.

Directions were given for the organization and direction

* He says that his involvement was quite accidental. He was in Bogotá, Columbia, in the summer of 1947, as a delegate of the Havana FEU, to help make arrangements for an international student conference, and when fighting broke out, he went along with the Colombian students in whose company he happened to find himself at the moment, acting on pure impulse. The uprising was put down, a truce was declared, and Fidel, then nineteen years old, fled to the Cuban Embassy. The next day he was flown home, with some other Cuban students.

of the strike, and for instructing the public through the clandestine organs of the movement—*Revolución, Sierra Maestra, Resistencia, El Cubano Libre,* and *Vanguardia Obrera,* the last-named being produced by the M-26 labor section.

Cuban students, to constitute the vanguard of the strike, were forbidden to return to their classes until Batista had fallen.

All highway and rail traffic through Oriente Province was forbidden, as of April 1st, and travelers were warned that transport was liable to be fired on, indiscriminately, from that date.

From the same date, all payment of taxes was forbidden.

All members of the judiciary, all magistrates, all prosecutors, were called upon to resign before April 5th, on pain of later losing the right to hold such posts, under the post-revolutionary government.

The same warning was to apply to members of the armed services, who were called upon to mutiny or desert and join the revolutionary army, as a simple duty, and with the assurance that they would be well received, would be promoted in grade if they brought their rifles with them, and would not be required to fight against former comrades-at-arms.

Notice was served that any person enlisting in the armed forces would be subject to court martial, as a criminal.

To continue in any responsible post in the executive branch of government after April 5th was to be considered "an act of treason."

The preamble written by Fidel indicted the dictatorship on grounds of moral cowardice and military impotence for its refusal to permit the Cuban press to visit the area of operations. As to the reasons for that refusal:

The explanation . . . lies in the shameful defeats that the dictatorship has suffered, in the military offensives that we have destroyed one after the other, in the acts of unprecedented barbarism that have been committed on the defenseless civilian population, in the real and certain fact that the dictator's troops have been dislodged from the Sierra Maestra and that the Army of the 26th of July is in full offensive toward the north of the province. * * *

The dictatorship did not want the journalists to learn, on the scene and in a manner direct and irrefutable, that more than three hundred *campesinos* were murdered during the six months of the suspension of constitutional guarantees and censorship of the press, that in Oro de Guisa alone fifty-three *campesinos* were immolated in a single day, that they finished off a mother's nine children and her husband at a single stroke. It did not want the journalists to see the hundreds of humble homes, built by sacrifice, reduced to ashes in brutal reprisals, the children mutilated by the bombing and machine gunning of defenseless hamlets. Trying to deceive not only the people but the army itself, they did not want the falsity of the reports of the *Estado Mayor* on each single battle to be known. * * * For if all the truth of the Sierra Maestra were to be verified by Cuban journalists, the regime would fall, through the fearful discredit which it would suffer before the ranks of its own armed forces.

Such details of the opening military offensive as were to be made public were summed up in a single article of the March 12th manifesto, announcing:

. . . that rebel forces of Column 6 under Comandante* Raúl Castro Ruz have invaded the North of the Province of Oriente; that rebel forces of Column 3 under Comandante* Juan Almeida have invaded the East of said Province; that rebel patrols are moving in all directions through the length and breadth of the province, and that armed patrol action will be intensified in all of the National Territory.

The phrase "total war" carries somewhat different connotations in English than those intended; it had a grandilo-

---

* Although the rank of comandante in the Cuban army was equivalent to that of major in other forces, the derivation is from early Spanish military usage, where "comandante" meant simply commander, and it is in this sense that the title was first employed by Fidel.

quent ring in the ears of Americans who had seen two world wars and the destruction of several hundred thousand human lives with the explosion of a single bomb at Hiroshima. The American reaction, scepticism, ironic amusement, would have been even more pronounced had anyone known what Fidel's "columns" actually consisted of, or what slight force backed the threat of a "campaign of extermination" against all bearing arms for Batista.

Nevertheless, it was in the brief announcement of the military offensive rather than in the threat of revolutionary general strike that Batista might have read his future.

The proofs were yet to come. Much depended on faith, and more on illusion.

In Washington, diplomatic victory was won.

On March 26th, Charles O. Porter, the Democratic representative from Oregon, told Congress that his colleague, Representative Powell of New York, had performed a service in reporting "the grave matter" of the list of arms said to have been sent to the Cuban government during the past two years.

The weapons, said Porter, were being used by Batista to maintain power "in violation of our most solemn Mutual Assistance Pact," nor did the Congressman consider this to be anything less than the patent fact:

This is not a base rumor, spread by those opposed to Batista to compromise the position of his government with the United States. Nor is it a Communist-inspired rumor, intended to heap discredit upon the United States for its help to dictators. Indeed, although it may serve both purposes, it is not rumor at all.

As evidence, Porter cited the testimony of Roy R. Rubottom, Jr. "the able and conscientious Assistant Secretary for Inter-American Affairs," before the Senate Foreign Relations Committee on March 5th, in response to questioning by Oregon's Senator Wayne Morse:

Senator Morse: Would you say, in the case of Cuba, that our military aid strengthens the retention of that dictatorial form of government?

Rubottom: Sir, the Cuban government is certainly using the military equipment at its disposal to beat back armed insurrection, which as you know started, I believe, in November of 1956.

And from a letter directed to Porter on January 14th, 1958, by William B. Macomber, Jr., Assistant Secretary of State:

Cuba has received arms from the United States as grant aid, which arms, pursuant to Section 105 (b) (4) of the Mutual Security Act of 1954, as amended, may be used only in the implementation of defense plans agreed upon by the United States and Cuba, under which Cuba participates in missions important to the defense of the Hemisphere.

This condition is also included in the Mutual Defense Assistance Agreement with Cuba of March, 1952, which covers grant and military assistance. Article 2 of that agreement provides that this equipment will be used only for the purpose for which supplied, unless the prior consent of the United States has been obtained.

Accordingly Representative Porter argued:

Thus it follows that if Batista is using the military equipment to beat back armed insurrection, and if both Section 105 (b) (4) of the Mutual Assistance Pact of 1954 and the Mutual Assistance Agreement with Cuba specify that United States equipment cannot be used for such purposes, clearly the intent of Congress is being breached brazenly, and General Batista is violating the terms of his agreement.

Assistant Secretary Rubottom had testified, Porter said, that United States military aid made "little difference" as far as Batista's position was concerned.

The Congressman declared:

Be this as it may, the continued flow from the United States of lethal weapons to Batista only serves to identify us with his unpopular regime. If it is alleged that Batista can buy weapons elsewhere, anyway, I say, let him try. At least we will have the satisfaction of not being a party on any side to the deplorable fratricide in Cuba.

On March 31st, Porter was back to extend his remarks of March 26th, as follows:

Mr. Speaker. Last Wednesday in a special order I called, as others have called, on our government to stop shipping arms to Cuba. I pointed out that our arms were being used in violation of treaties between us and Cuba and were identifying us with the vicious police state ruled by Batista.

Today the State Department has made available to me a statement which declares that we have, finally, suspended shipments of arms to Cuba. It is a fine statement, another sign of a new and better Latin-American policy.

The statement:

In authorizing shipments of arms to other countries under the Mutual Security Program, it has been our consistent practice to weigh carefully those consigned to areas where political tensions have developed. We wish to be assured, for example, that the arms are destined for uses consistent with the objectives of our Mutual Security legislation. The shipment of 1,950 Garand rifles, purchased by the Cuban government, was temporarily suspended to allow us the opportunity of consulting further with the appropriate Cuban officials.

As for the situation in Cuba, it is a matter of sympathetic concern to all of us as friends and neighbors. It would be entirely contrary to our policy to intervene in its internal affairs, and we do not intend to become involved. We hope that the Cuban government and the people themselves will soon find a peaceful and democratic solution. They are the only ones who can, as well as being the only ones who should, resolve the issues.

Coming in the midst of other, more dramatic developments, the State Department announcement created scarcely a ripple in the United States. The *Times* gave it two paragraphs on March 31st, quoting Porter. On April 3rd, it was given more attention, in a Washington dispatch containing the additional information that the "arms embargo" —here identified as such for the first time—would not be lifted so long as the "current tensions" continued to exist in Cuba.

The latter report was attributed to unnamed "officials." Congressman Porter was quoted in the same dispatch as expressing—a trifle testily, one suspects—the wish that the Eisenhower administration would "stand up and announce its policies, instead of forcing us to infer their existence on the basis of reliable but anonymous sources."

The 1,950 Garand rifles to which the State Department referred had been on Representative Powell's list of March 20th, but had not yet been shipped to Cuba, as he had supposed.

The Cuban government now cancelled the purchase order, and turned to a new source of supply, namely, Batista's sometime and *pro tempore,* uneasy bedfellow, the Dominican dictator, Generalissimo Rafael Trujillo y Molina.*

The Garands that had been lost through the United States arms embargo were replaced by a shipment of excellent

* In the latter part of 1956, Trujillo began to plot with agents of Carlos Prío Socarrás to overthrow the Batista regime, perhaps foreseeing that the Cuban dictator would not be able to hold off a *fidelista* revolution, and preferring someone in the presidential palace in Havana with whom he might be able to do business, as he surely had no hope of doing with any radical revolutionary regime. Whatever his motives, the powerful radio *"Voz Dominicana"* launched a virulent propaganda campaign against Batista, and a group of Cuban expatriates actually began training on Dominican soil, in preparation for an invasion of Cuba. But Prío himself failed to reach agreement with Trujillo on mutual objectives, and the latter turned toward his erstwhile enemy. A rapproachment with Batista was reached in January, 1957, the Cuban trainees were expelled, and the radio attacks ceased. The Trujillo-Batista accord was a matter of scandal and indignation in Cuba. Prío himself suffered a loss of prestige by having been touched, however lightly, with the same tarbrush. An excellent account of Cuban-Dominican relations during this period is contained in Jules Dubois' well-documented book, "Fidel Castro: Rebel-Liberator or Dictator?" Bobbs-Merrill, 1959.

Cristobal automatic rifles of Dominican manufacture, copies of a weapon produced for Hitler at the end of World War II by the Skoda works in Hungary, and reproduced by refugee Hungarian craftsmen living in the Dominican Republic.

With the rifles came a more fearsome weapon—napalm, the clinging, searing, explosive jellied gasoline which is the substance of firebombs.

The State Department made inquiries through the U.S. Embassy in Ciudad Trujillo and declared that it had received assurances from the Dominican Government that none of the arms being sold to Cuba had come from the United States. The Cuban government, for its part, categorically denied that it was purchasing arms from Trujillo, a brazen lie, in view of the fact that eleven Cuban airline pilots had already flown to exile in the United States to avoid being forced to ferry the arms from Santo Domingo. The eleven civilian airline pilots—and four more who quickly joined them—all said that they had fled rather than be drafted into the Cuban Air Force and compelled to transport weapons to be used against their countrymen. Altogether, thirty-nine fliers, civilian and military, found political sanctuary in Miami, refusing to have a part in the transporting of arms and the bombing of civilian communities in Oriente.

A school strike had begun in Cuba, starting spontaneously in Santiago in protest against the murder of two sixteen-year-old boys there and spreading across the island with the announcement of a number of private schools and the National Confederation of Catholic Schools that school officials could not accept responsibility for the lives of pupils attending classes during the period of crisis ahead.

Wholesale arrests of teachers began; twenty-five teachers were seized at a single military school near Havana, accused of spreading subversion among their pupils.

The Universities of Oriente and Havana had been closed

for many months, but the University of Havana—with its constitutional extra-territorial status, won under Grau San Martín's first brief administration after the Machado revolution—continued to be a gathering place of students, and a focal point of revolutionary activity. Now, contravening the law, police raided the university to search for arms, and the teachers who had been retained were stricken from the payroll.

Two medical students suspected of revolutionary activity were killed, their bodies left, riddled with bullets, on the outskirts of Havana. The FEU, in retaliation, attacked a police patrol and critically wounded two policemen, one being Lieutenant Faustino Salas Cañizares, a brother of the former police chief killed in the Haitian Embassy in 1957.*

Despite earlier declarations of no further retreat on the political front, Batista found it necessary to postpone the scheduled June elections until November 3rd. Eleven days later, he obtained from the captive Congress virtually unlimited powers, under a state of "national emergency," to impose new taxes and to take whatever steps he might consider necessary to meet the threat of "total war."

The army had been organized, hundreds of soldiers transferred to police control to meet the anticipated general strike. Pilar García, who had crushed the assault on the Goicuría Barracks in Matanzas, was named head of the National Police in Havana, replacing Brigadier General Hernando Hernández, who was retired as "too soft."

* Another member of the same infamous family, the SIM chief José María Salas Cañizares, was paralyzed by the effects of a jeep "accident" in Oriente. The crash was actually a desperate expedient on the part of Salas' aide, a lieutenant named Chinea, who was suspected of having collaborated with the *fidelistas,* and was being taken to the Moncada Barracks, when, having no doubt as to his fate on arrival, he contrived to steer the jeep full speed into a tree. Chinea survived. Salas remained in a hospital until the following November, came out in time to participate, on crutches, in the final struggle, and fled the country when the end came.

Hundreds of new, khaki-colored military patrol cars were imported, and more than a thousand private vehicles were requisitioned for the use of the police and troops during the emergency.

The revolutionaries, too, were making preparations. The operational headquarters of the strike in Havana was to have a powerful long-wave radio transmitter, to instruct the general public on the day of the strike. Underground militia were to receive their orders through broadcasts from three powerful short-wave transmitters and twenty small portable units, "walkie-talkies," which had been smuggled in from the United States, with the aid of an official of the Havana public works department.

In an interview in his seaside home in Miramar, the "club on First Avenue," the broker Ignacio Mendoza, one of the architects of the Machado revolution and an advisor to the *fidelista* forces, said that the Havana underground was prepared to send eight thousand members into the streets, of which number, he said he had been told, perhaps two thousand would be fully armed and trained "first-line fighters." The remainder, according to his information, would be youngsters armed only with pistols, or unarmed, who would hurl gasoline bombs, build barricades, and canvass business districts to shut down the shops and offices.

Lest such a formidable build-up seem too much for belief, Mendoza expressed some personal doubt. "They keep telling me," he said, "that they have exactly two thousand one hundred twenty-one first line fighters, or some such precise figure, ready to move when they are called. Now, every day, some of these boys get arrested or killed by the police, some leave the city, others come in from the countryside. Then how is it that I keep getting the same exact figure?"

Plans were also being made in Santiago, Holguín, Santa Clara, Camagüey. Mimeographed instruction sheets were circulated by the underground, explaining how to make "Molotov cocktails" with four parts of gasoline and one of motor oil, how to cripple transport by strewing tacks and oil on the streets, how to sabotage industrial machinery, shop equipment, police vehicles and buses.

A letter from a Cuban visitor in Santiago to her husband in New York, written in mid-March and posted unsigned, suggests the atmosphere of the provincial capital as the crisis approached:

As of today, a most intense sabotage has begun, above all in Santiago. At about five o'clock this morning there was a fire in the Castillo rum distillery* and it's said to have burned down entirely. Since the suspension of guarantees began today, the facts are not entirely known, but the smoke could be seen in great quantity and at a tremendous height.

A wave of *micro-ondas* has come in. We'll see how long they last.

People coming from Mayarí, Palma, Contramaestre, etc., say that the *fidelistas* are already being seen in those places, and that they are fighting in the towns, so that we imagine they should be here very soon. We learned today that they are fighting and bombing near Miranda, where there is a sugar mill, and also near Guantánamo. One of the fronts is directed by Raúl Castro, the other we don't know.

Today the ministers resigned and Batista said for the first time that there were not going to be elections but that there will be fighting. Since censorship began again today, there isn't much news, but, nevertheless, Radio Bemba† keeps functioning.

This afternoon the body of a boy was found behind Ferreiro (?). The details aren't known. Every day bodies appear, but I don't have the names.

It seems that the general strike is approaching, above all in Havana, so that on that side it appears there's no problem. The

* Owned, as it happened, by Raúl Chibás' wife.

† Bemba: "big lips," i.e., a way of saying word-of-mouth intelligence, rumor.

situation in general is very tense, and everyone expects something at any moment. Everyone is buying quantities of food and provisions in general, since they don't know when the thing begins.

The M-26-7 makes telephone calls and says "M-26-7 calling. Don't go out on the streets. The chains are about to break." They called here. Laureano's garage has sandbags and perhaps three or four men visible. As to those who may be hidden, we don't know.

They say that Masferrer's men, who rented a house near the Colegio de Hijas de Maria (a girls' school), went up to the roof of the school today and have taken it as an observatory, for when the strike begins.

There was an attack at Mayarí* and it was phenomenal, the more so since I was told about it by a *chivato* and not one of our own. A group of some seventy rebels came in a truck, well armed, and the soldiers didn't fire a single shot. They jumped out of the back of the barracks into a stream and one of them broke a leg!

As to the politicos who came to meet here, three days ago, to form the parties (for the subsequently-postponed June elections) a bomb was set off, no shrapnel, just a petard, and they say that A. was so frightened that he—well, I won't tell you what he did.

There isn't a class in a single school, and the buses are empty. After dark, no one. The buses stop running at 11 o'clock at night.

We are well here. Send us your news.

The rumors of intensified fighting were correct. Fidel's guerrillas moved in force to the very edge of Manzanillo, attacked the jail, withdrew, and returned to attack a police station, in a vain effort to draw out troops from the Manzanillo garrison. The troops refused to rise to the bait.

Renewed attacks were reported at Veguitas and at Yara on the Manzanillo highway. At the *America* sugar mill

---

* Probably Mayarí Arriba, south of the Sierra Cristal, taken by Raúl early in his northern campaign.

near Contramaestre, two hundred men left their work and fled to the *Territorio Libre*.

Raúl Castro had crossed the Central Highway near Contramaestre on March 10th, and the "Second Front, Frank País," in the vast mountainous area north and east of Santiago was now a reality. Rebel forces were destroying communications on the northern edge of the new front. There was fighting near the mines at Moa on the north coast, fighting in the south near the Soledad sugar mill, within an hour by jeep from Guantánamo. Raúl himself was reported to be leading a column of a thousand men (a great exaggeration) on Santiago, and Juan Almeida, who had returned to the Sierra and set out again, was said to be leading a column of equal strength toward the provincial capital from the west.

Reports of the two columns supposedly converging on Santiago reached Havana on April 3rd. On the same day, Batista issued a series of unprecedented decrees:

1. Government ministers were empowered to issue arms licenses to 160,000 public employes and to any other "reliable" workers, such workers being absolved, in advance, of legal responsibility for whatever use they might make of their weapons in resisting any effort to keep them from their employment.
2. Judges were forbidden to issue judicial rulings against any government official, government agency, or leader of a legal political party, (e.g., Masferrer) under pain of instant dismissal.
3. Employers were forbidden to close their premises during normal working hours, on pain of imprisonment.
4. Workers were forbidden to strike, on pain of permanent loss of employment.

Fidel's orders to halt all movement of transport in Oriente had already gone into effect. Trains leaving Havana for Oriente ended their journey in the city of Camagüey, reportedly because the train crews refused to go farther, but actually, a railway official said, because most of the railway bridges east of Camagüey had been blown up or destroyed by fire.

Only military convoys and fuel and provision trucks guarded by military vehicles moved on the Central Highway in Oriente. Shortages of fresh vegetables, meat, and milk were developing in Santiago.

Manzanillo and all of the other cities on the perimeter of Fidel's zone of operations were cut off completely from sources of outside supply, except by air. Fighting was in progress at Baracoa, the capital of the revolutionaries during the War of Independence, and commercial flights to that city were halted after rebels fired on a transport plane trying to land there and the pilot returned to Santiago, to report that he had seen rebels and government troops fighting on the outskirts. A subsequent order cancelled *all* commercial flights in Oriente.

Government planes strafed the small village of Aguacate, northwest of Santiago, killing three civilians, after a rebel patrol ambushed an army convoy there. Rebel positions were being bombed daily near Manzanillo. Ground troops at Río Cauto, north of Bayamo, killed five guerrillas in a clash, after the rebels had burned a bridge over the Río Cauto, which Fidel had once called the natural line of defense against any invasion from the western provinces.

Nearby a rebel platoon, fighting in formation for the first time in the *llano,* the open, shelterless plain, drove a Rural Guard force from the village of Cauto Embarcadero. Government aircraft, called in by the Bayamo command, bombed and strafed the village, driving the civilian population into the river. The *Guardia* returned in force, seized seventeen *campesinos,* men and boys, and distributed their corpses along the road leading to Bayamo, as "proofs" of a battle fought and won.

A bulletin issued by the *Estado Mayor* at Camp Columbia described the slaughter thus:

Forces of Squadron 13 of the *Guardia Rural* of Bayamo sustained an encounter with a party of outlaws . . . in the zone of Cauto Embarcadero, killing seventeen. On our part, no casualties.

As reparation for the damage caused by the air attack, Batista personally ordered the appropriate government agency to build twenty-two houses in the village, to replace those destroyed.

An Easter Sunday radio broadcast from Santiago, shouted over a telephone in an echoing room in the Casa Granda hotel and recorded in New York, described the situation of April 6th as follows:

Rumors of fighting within five miles of Santiago were heard last night as the fifth day of the "total war" declared by Fidel Castro drew to a close. Reports, still lacking official confirmation, said that government troops had engaged a column of rebels believed to be led by Castro's younger brother, Raúl— one of two columns said earlier in the week to be converging on this provincial capital.

Here in the city, the streets are empty of motor traffic by eight o'clock in the evening, except for the security patrols, constantly on the prowl. The turrets of Moncada Barracks, against which Castro launched his first attack in 1953, bristle with helmeted soldiers. The few civilian vehicles leaving for nearby suburbs are stopped at checkpoints on the outskirts of the city, and in town, reluctant cab drivers travel the dark streets with the interiors of their taxis lighted—just to be sure there are no mistakes. Many of the estimated five thousand soldiers in the city are new recruits, and with tension running high here, there is fear that the jittery young soldiers may shoot first, and ask questions afterwards.

There is also the very real fear that Castro's guerrillas will carry the fight to the edge of the city, even before the anticipated general strike call.

Oil and gasoline trucks from the big Texas Company refinery across the bay continue to travel the main highway but they now travel in convoy, for fear the gasoline, a dangerous weapon in the hands of saboteurs, will be captured by the rebels.

As to measures for preventing the impending general strike, people here are bitter about President Batista's emergency decree, absolving of guilt any Cuban who kills in *defense* of his right not to strike. They point out that this measure, which Batista calls "mainly psychological," is in effect a hunting license for anyone who wants to get rid of a personal or political enemy. As one Santiagan remarked last evening—"Suppose someone owes me some money and would rather not have me around to collect?" *

The general strike came, finally, on April 9th, preceded in Santiago on the night of the 8th by a shattering explosion that wrecked three adjacent brick storage buildings, arousing the entire city, and, in the early morning hours, by a rebel attack on an army post at Puerto Boniato, just north of the provincial capital.

The explosion was the result of an ingenious plot that went somewhat amiss. Santiago underground members had filled an empty compressed-air cylinder with explosives, attached a time mechanism, and left it with several others like it, in a stolen pick-up truck, parked on a side street near the Cuartel Moncada. The underground leaders had hoped that soldiers, finding the truck, would simply drive it into the fortress.

The patrol that found the truck was either more or less suspicious than had been hoped. Instead of taking the cylinders into the military compound, the soldiers removed them to the place from which they assumed, correctly, that

* Taber, CBS.

the tanks had been stolen: one of the three storage buildings where several hundred other such cylinders were stored. The ensuing explosion sent 120-pound metal cylinders hurtling through the roof and walls of the buildings. One tank wrecked the roof of a dwelling across the street. But there were no casualties, military or civilian.

At Puerto Boniato, M-26 militia from the Santiago underground attacked in sufficient force to take the small *cuartel,* defended by ten soldiers, and shortly afterward engaged troops dispatched from Moncada, summoned by a telephone call from the wife of an army captain residing near the Boniato post.

The engagement lasted for an hour and a half. Three soldiers were killed. The army claimed to have killed fifteen rebels; the M-26 leaders put their losses at three. The clash was inconclusive, except in lending substance to current rumors that *fidelista* forces were actually fighting on the outskirts of the provincial capital.

Tellers and clerks in the banks of Santiago began to go out on strike at 11 o'clock in the morning, leaving their account books untallied. The word that the strike was starting was spread by telephone. Father Rivas, the archbishop's secretary, was in the Cathedral talking with a foreign correspondent, when his telephone rang. In a moment he returned to announce: "It is beginning."

M-26 militia hurled "Molotov cocktails" that started fires in five gasoline stations. A soldier near the city hall was killed by a rebel sniper on a rooftop. Four youths in a car were machine-gunned by security forces in a *micro-onda,* and two blocks from the Cathedral, a boy going from shop to shop, telling storekeepers to close their doors, was shot to death on the sidewalk before he had reached the fourth door.

Buses filled with soldiers hurtled through the narrow

streets, rifles protruding from the windows. By noon the city was silent, the streets empty, except for the prowling, ominous khaki-colored patrol cars.

Fifteen hundred workers failed to return to their jobs in the Bacardi rum distillery after the mid-day rest period, and the distillery closed down. Three foreign banks remained open, their managers having been summoned to Moncada and told that the army would send soldiers to replace any absent employes. No soldiers appeared in the banks.

Sporadic shooting was heard in scattered districts of the city as police and security troops hunted down strike agitators and rebel saboteurs. In the early afternoon there was rifle fire in the Céspedes Park area. No casualties were visible. A short while later, a khaki patrol car filled with civilians —Masferrer's men—came careening through the street on which the Casa Granda hotel faced, and loosed a volley of rifle shots in the general direction of the Cathedral.

By nightfall, the death toll in Santiago had reached thirty. Most of the dead were youths, members of the M-26 militia. The underground, making a brave fight of it, continued to snipe from rooftops at security patrols. There was blood on the sidewalk outside of the Casa Granda. Hysterical young *masferristas,* accompanied by troops, invaded the hotel lobby, and for an hour fired through the potted palms at real or imagined enemies in the darkness of the park outside and the unfinished buildings beyond, where it was believed that rebels were lurking.

As in the strike of the previous August, Santiago became a silent city, without industry, commerce, or movement in the streets and public places. Soldiers going from door to door in the morning to force open the shops found no employes to serve customers, no patrons, and often no proprietors. The gasoline refinery across the bay, producing twenty-five per cent of Cuba's motor fuel, was closed.

The strike continued. It was a useless sacrifice.

The national capital was the pivot on which all else turned. The M-26 leaders had been optimistic, predicting that it would be "all over with Batista" by the 15th of the month. In Havana, the strike itself was "all over" within a few hours.

It appeared to have begun well enough. Small action units seized Radio CMQ and another commercial station at 10 o'clock in the morning and broadcast recorded announcements, exhorting workers to leave their jobs, employers to close their shops, revolutionary fighters to fulfill their missions.

On the Prado, in the heart of the city, a bomb exploded under a gas main, setting a fire that flared high above the street through the day, a banner of defiance streaming in the breeze.

The banks and a few shops closed. Workers in factories and the public utilities left their jobs, and some of them gathered to receive arms at appointed places. But the arms failed to come. No one arrived to direct the volunteers. Few of the supposed "two thousand front-line fighters" came into the streets, and those who did were quickly destroyed by the massive, swift efficiency of the murderous machine of repression into which Pilar García had welded seven thousand soldiers and police.

More than two thousand patrol cars and civilian vehicles carrying security agents armed with submachine guns patrolled the city, instantly present at any sign of disorder, any potential threat.

Six youths who tried to obtain arms and ammunition from a weapons store were shot down before they reached the door. Machine gunners in a *micro-onda* pursuing an automobile that had fled from the scene of the gas fire killed four of the occupants on the outskirts of the city.

Bomb blasts wrecked electrical conduits, and power was cut off in downtown Havana. For a few brief hours, shooting could be heard at scattered points throughout the capital and its suburbs, indicating clashes between the security forces and small groups of resistance fighters. By evening, only occasional, isolated shots echoed in the streets, signaling, not combat, but execution.

Pilar García took personal command of the repression, and his orders were carried out with brutal dispatch. Reporters at several places, monitoring the short-wave radio band used by the National Police recorded some of the chilling messages* that went back and forth between patrol cars and the police dispatcher's office:

"We have a doctor here in his automobile. He has a pistol."

"Kill him." A dull detonation is heard on the air, instantaneously.

"We have ten prisoners."

"No prisoners. Kill them."

"We have a suspect, unarmed. Prisoner? Wounded?"

"No prisoners. No wounded. Kill him."

First reports put the death toll for the day at forty. Pilar García told a news conference, five days later, that thirteen insurgents and two policemen had been killed. The probable toll—still undetermined because in most instances the bodies were buried in unmarked graves—approached one hundred.

The strike was crushed in Havana, Matanzas, Santa Clara, Camagüey, Holguín, and finally, after five days, in Santiago de Cuba. Disorders continued on the eastern end of the island, but made little difference, since the revolutionary general strike, the supreme gamble, had failed.

No real purpose is served in seeking to analyze the causes of the failure. Faustino Pérez, who directed the M-26 operation in the capital, said in an interview at "the club on First

---

* Among the several foreign correspondents to bear witness to such incredible conversations are the Chilean journalist, Rafael Otero Echeverría, and Jules Dubois, the Chicago Tribune Syndicate reporter.

Avenue," that the failure had been the result of confusion, attendant on an eleventh-hour change of strategy, designed to avert bloodshed.

Whatever Fidel Castro's initial reluctance, he seems to have expected much of the strike. The Argentine journalist Jorge Masetti, who was with him in the Sierra Maestra when he received the news, says that Fidel embraced him and danced about shouting: "The general strike has exploded! The hour of liberation has arrived! You are going to Havana with us!" or words to that effect.

When the strike failed, he blamed the secrecy with which the underground had carried out its preparations, saying that security had been maintained to such a degree that the various revolutionary sections had been unable to coordinate their actions, and that insufficient confidence had been placed in "the people," who would have risen in full strength against the dictatorship, had they been properly prepared.

Some merit may be found in this argument, but it does not take account of the situation which existed in Havana, where it was dangerous in the extreme even to use the word "strike." Nor did anyone mention an equally grim fact: the two thousand adequately armed and trained "front line fighters" did not exist. It is doubtful that there were *two hundred*.

Is there a revolution here? I hadn't noticed any trouble.
—SENATOR ALLEN J. ELLENDER (D-Louisiana),
Havana, December 12, 1958

XI

THE ESTIMATE of the effective fighting strength of the Havana underground of April, 1958, closing the last chapter, should come, at this point, as no great surprise.

Lacking arms, the *fidelistas* continued to lack an army, as the term is understood in military academies, and however great their popular support they had no means to raise one, except by the slow and painful process seen in Oriente, each small military victory adding to the rebel arsenal, arming a new patrol, each small extension of *territorio libre* increasing the potential of manpower and supplies.

No such expansion was possible for the urban underground. Batista's *conservative* opposition had ample financial resources, to be sure; but this does not imply a willingness to arm or finance those who were ready to do the fighting, who were, in fact, already doing it.

There is no paradox here, but rather a dilemma that confronted the conservatives: to leave Batista in power and risk eventual chaos and collapse, or, an equally dangerous and distasteful alternative, to arm a host of radical revolutionaries and be presented, on the day of bitter triumph, with an orderly—and unwanted—new social order.

Most of those who understood the alternatives postponed the choice, and hoped that all would turn out for the best. A few* hoped for revolution and took their chances, also hoping for the best. Still others looked to the tradi-

* e.g., Pepín Bosch, head of the family which controls the great Bacardi distilleries.

tional solution, a mercenary force, or one that could be controlled, in any event.

The *fidelistas* clearly could not be controlled, and those among their number who urged "cooperation" with Prío —i.e., to give him a voice in the councils of the revolution in exchange for his material assistance—were repudiated by Fidel.

Prío, who had been arming the *Organization Auténtica** and aiding other groups which he thought to be well disposed toward himself, announced that his followers would have nothing to do with a revolutionary general strike called by the *Movimiento 26* unless they were given representation on the strike council. His opinion, expressed in an interview in March, was that the April strike would end in tragic failure without his assistance. And in this instance, as has been seen, he was perfectly correct.

The *fidelistas* continued the struggle alone, or with such support as they could win without compromising their objectives. All but the bare skeleton of the M-26 underground was withdrawn from the cities at the end of April. The failure of the general strike had made it bitterly clear, as perhaps nothing else could have done, that the battle could not be won in the capital until it had been won in the field, a point which Fidel had been trying to make from the beginning.†

* Why? The question had been asked, and the explanation suggested, by Fidel in his letter of December 14, denouncing the Miami pact: "How can an agreement be reached without first having defined the strategy of battle? Are the *'auténticos'* thinking about a 'putsch' in the capital? Will they continue storing arms and more arms which sooner or later will fall into the hands of the police before they can be delivered to those who are fighting? *** While the peasantry here (in the Sierra) see their homes burned and their families murdered and beg desperately for rifles, there are arms hidden in Cuba which are not being used and are waiting for the police to pick them up, or for the tyranny to fall, or for the rebels to be exterminated . . ."

† "The last battle will be fought in the capital, of that you may be sure." April, 1957.

The revolution moves now into the classic course of the war of independence, gathering in Oriente, the cradle of Cuban liberty, challenging the mercenary armies of the capital, and marching against them in full defiance, with a mad confidence that makes Fidel at times seem to have been suffering from delusions of grandeur.

He was not. At the risk of being included among those whom *Life* magazine considers the "militarily naive," one must make the assertion that, in the end, the revolution is won by force of arms, all other efforts having failed. That other factors contributed is self-evident.

Some extraordinary sleight of hand was, indeed, required at times, to equip and train a potent military striking force while simultaneously sustaining the illusion that one already existed, and the process to inflict almost as much injury on the enemy as might have been done by a superior force.

All in all, it was a brilliant performance. But mere sleight of hand and "psychological" warfare in themselves could not have accomplished all of this.

Fidel's own simple explanation is the better one: the entire population of Oriente was in rebellion, and in such a circumstance no army could prevail against him, except by first depopulating the province. (A few lunatic army officers seem to have operated on precisely this premise. Fortunately their authority was limited and their resources small.)

The final campaign is beginning at this point, where all seems lost. Before turning to it, let us examine the resources of the *fidelistas* and their achievement up to April, 1958.

In little more than a year, beginning with a force that had been reduced to twelve men and that did not rise, for many months, to more than a hundred, the guerrillas of the M-26 won complete military control of a mountain range the size of the Adirondacks, which extends nearly half the length of New York State, and threw an army of more than five thousand men, supported by aircraft, armor, and artillery, completely on the defensive, around the entire perimeter of an area of some five thousand square miles.

The task was completed by the end of March, 1958. At that time, the rebel forces in the Sierra Maestra numbered *not more than four hundred* adequately armed men. In reserve, being trained in an encampment deep in the southern Sierra, were perhaps five hundred volunteers, unarmed.

On the basis of their accomplishment, prior to the April strike, Batista actually offered a political amnesty to all forces fighting against him, and several of the members of the government opposition, one of whom visited Fidel at his La Plata headquarters, recommended in all seriousness, that the government accept Fidel's terms of the time: the removal of all government troops from Oriente, to be followed by free elections.

The article of the manifesto of March 12th, announcing that Raúl Castro was marching into the north country, that Juan Almeida was in the east, that rebel patrols were moving in all directions "throughout the length and breadth of the province . . ." this stern and warlike bulletin—what did it mean?

Raúl had set out, crossing the Central Highway on March 10th near Contramaestre, to conquer a populated mining and agricultural region larger than the entire state of Massachusetts, with just *sixty-five* men, of whom fifty-four were armed with military weapons. Their heaviest armament was a Browning automatic rifle.

Juan Almeida was setting out toward Santiago, and subsequently received orders to capture that key garrison city, with *seventy men,* of whom just twenty-eight had military weapons—rifles or submachine guns.

The patrols? A small commando force under Camilo Cienfuegos, operating on the plain near Holguín. A few smaller units, some of only four or five men, engaged in harassing transport on the highway, blowing up railway bridges, and sniping at small military posts and convoys.

These and the *fidelista* column fighting on the margin of the Sierra Maestra, scarcely a battalion altogether, comprised the entire rebel army of Oriente: a few hundred ragged riflemen, without artillery, air support, or any armament of modern war heavier than a few mortars and machine guns.

In such numbers it is admittedly difficult to see the potential of an armed conflict of major proportions for the control of a country nearly as great in land area as England, more populous than Scotland, with greater per capita wealth than any nation of the Americas outside of the United States and Canada, and with a modern army of nearly thirty thousand men. Yet this is what existed. It shall be seen how the potential was employed.

The *Times* of April 18th describes the period immediately following the end of the general strike as "a period of ebb tide" for the revolutionaries, and more particularly the *fidelistas*. "The dust of recent flurries has settled," said the *Times*, "and revealed only too clearly the strength of General Batista's position and the weakness of his opponents."

True enough insofar as it went. And a brief look at what was happening near Santiago, a few days earlier, discloses what was meant:

On April 9th, the day of the general strike, Juan Almeida and his "column" were encamped on the hills westward of Santiago, in the vicinity of the national Catholic retreat of the Virgin of Cobre, and the town of that name, El Cobre, when the column commander received his incredible orders: to march forthwith on Santiago, seizing en route El Cobre, the Texas Company refinery with its garrison of several hundred soldiers, and all strategic objectives in and around the capital city of Oriente—water works, power plants, major industrial establishments.

It bears repeating that he had but seventy men. Almeida understandably felt that his military capabilities had been over-estimated, to say the least. He moved eastward to survey the situation, he says, came close enough on the evening of the 9th to perceive that all was quiet in the city, lights burning, no sign of battle or disorder, and discreetly retired, deciding to interpret his orders liberally; that is, as orders simply to do his best.

The result of his decision was a battle in the town of El Cobre, and the explosion of a government powder deposit there—April 11th—that set off thirty *tons* of dynamite, stored for the use of mining companies in the area. The magazine was set afire by some of Almeida's men as they withdrew from El Cobre, under heavy attack by army forces. Quite apparently the rebels had not realized the tremendous power of the explosion that would be produced. The blast was heard in Santiago, fifteen miles away, and shattered windows in Puerto Boniato on the outskirts of that city. The only image that remained intact in the sanctuary of the Virgin of Cobre was the wooden figure of the Virgin, herself, intact in a glass case.

A government bulletin of March 12th, from the office of the chief of staff at Camp Columbia in Havana:

In Oriente Province widespread indignation against the Fidel Castro group was expressed today as the result of yesterday's profane attack against the sanctuary of the Virgin of Cobre, Cuba's patron saint.

Details of the attack were received in Havana today. It was reported that approximately 200 members of the Castro gang stormed the sanctuary with the hope that they could seize the sacred relic and carry it off to the Sierra Maestra.

Soldiers on duty at the sanctuary, although greatly outnumbered, succeeded in frustrating the attempt. Later the Castro group set off a nearby powder magazine and burned the little city hall at the town of Cobre. There are indications that the casualties among the Castro group were substantial.

Other bulletins of the date are of the same character:

The Armed Forces headquarters in Havana was advised today that on a road leading to the Charco Mono mines in Oriente Province a group of outlaws tried without success to force simple countrymen to take up arms against the army detachments in the area. When an automobile with members of the armed forces passed along the road the insurgents ambushed the vehicle and wounded three military men. In the exchange of gunfire, the countrymen abandoned the group which had threatened their lives. Two of the bandits were killed and a quantity of arms and documents were found in the nearby woods. The farmers later reported to army officers that they had been threatened and intimidated by the bandits.

Troops in the Estrada Palma zone in the Manzanillo area reported today that the bodies of three outlaws had been found at a place known as the Cerro, Barrio de Jibacoa. The bodies were not yet identified.

A group of saboteurs surrendered to the Rural Guard Station at Ciego de Avila today, after having engaged in terrorist activities in the Palma Dumenico neighborhood. Only one of those surrendering turned in a rifle. The others said that although they were offered arms by the insurgent elements, they had refused to accept them.

It did, indeed, seem to be a period of ebb tide for the *fidelistas*. But this is not to say that it was a time of rising fortunes for Batista. On the 17th of the month he demonstrated that he knew better by decreeing drastic penalties for all opposition to or criticism of the regime, in any form, and drafted all employes and officials of the public service companies into the military reserves, subject to call for active duty. A new military offensive against the *Movimiento 26* in Oriente was beginning, not withstanding Batista's recently stated opinion that it was "not worth the trouble" to try to flush the rebels out of the Sierra Maestra.

The quote again from the *Times* editorial of April 18th:

The fundamental conflict in Cuba continues. It is a struggle for liberty against a harsh and corrupt military dictatorship. There is no reason whatever to doubt that an overwhelming number of Cubans are against the Batista regime. The hatreds, the bitterness, the frustrations, the despair of today are merely proof that the tensions and struggle must go on. The extraordinary measures that the government took yesterday show that President Batista has no illusions about having crushed the revolutionary resistance.

The opposition has lost a major battle and may well take months to recover, but Cuba is in the midst of a long civil war. There is one fight that the Cuban people will not and cannot lose, and that is the fight for freedom.

Fierce fighting was reported at Baire, on the Central Highway between Bayamo and Palma Soriano, and elsewhere along the perimeter of the *Territorio Libre*. Fidel had recalled his roving patrols—Almeida's group, the commando force under Cienfuegos near Holguín—and there was a series of clashes with army forces as these units made their way back into the Sierra Maestra. No attempt was being made at concealment, except from aircraft. The army was exerting pressure, and the *fidelista* strategy was to give ground, but gradually, and in such a manner as to lead the government troops into the mountains, to conduct the impending battle on Fidel's chosen ground.

Given the terrain of his choosing, densely forested mountains in which manpower was no match for mobility, his assets were greater than appeared. Although he had insufficient arms, there was ammunition, and to spare. A shipment had arrived during the period of "total war," transported aboard a twin-engine plane from Mexico by way of Costa Rica. Aboard the plane was Pedro Miret—the veteran of Moncada and chief arms procurement officer abroad—and nearly one hundred thousand rounds of rifle, submachine-gun, and mortar ammunition, along with sixty rifles, some submachine guns, and two .50-caliber machine guns.

The rebels had established their own machine shop, their

own arms repair facilities, and were even producing, in small quantities, their own grenades, molded from light metal and filled with shrapnel and explosives from unexploded aerial bombs, courtesy of Batista. There was even a crude telephone system, a "party line," linking the several M-26 command posts in Fidel's headquarters area at La Plata, near Turquino and atop the third highest mountain of the range.

Herds of cattle, driven deep into the mountains, grazed on sheltered pastures as a source of provisions for the future, against the day when rebel supply lines might be cut. New rebel hospitals were built, and stocked with medicines and bandages.

Fidel was perfectly aware that he was facing the most desperate, unrelenting, and prolonged offensive of the civil war to date; all his strategy was based on turning it to his advantage.

His general orders to all unit commanders indicated what was in his mind:

This offensive will be the longest of all. *After its failure,* Batista will be irredeemably lost, as he knows, and therefore he will make his maximum effort. This is a decisive battle being fought precisely on the terrain known best by us. * * * The task is to make our resistance stronger at each stage, and that will be in the measure that their lines are extended and ours are shortened, as we withdraw to the most strategic positions . . .

Batista appointed General Eulogio Cantillo, whose name becomes important later, in another context, as supreme commander of operations in Oriente. Fresh troops were poured into the Caribbean coastal area on the south of the Sierra Maestra, and into the towns and villages along the northern edge of the range, from Bayamo west and south to Manzanillo and Niquero.

The army, spending millions on new equipment, sent armored trucks and half-tracks to protect the government

column slowly pushing into the Sierra foothills. New fortified posts were built, with concrete gun emplacements. Light
artillery was moved up. Armored helicopters, bought from
Britain, began to carry soldiers deeper into the mountains.

The *fidelista* forces were withdrawn, gradually, into a tight
defensive perimeter centering on the headquarters area of
La Plata—not to be confused with the coastal village of that
name indicated on most maps, but high above it on the
southern slope of the mountain range, with access to the
natural fortress of Pico Turquino, from which no defender
could be dislodged.

In all, thirteen army combat teams of three hundred fifty
men each—more than forty-five hundred government troops
—were thrown into the final decisive contest, odds of more
than twelve to one.

No decision is seen until the summer.

In the interim, Raúl's forces in the northern highlands
were in the midst of a crucial battle of their own. The
original expedition from the Sierra, that crossed the Central
Highway on March 10th, had been reinforced by rebel
militia from the Santiago underground, the same forces that
fought at Puerto Boniato, now campaigning in the countryside. The territory was much more heavily populated than
the Sierra, and easier of access. There were scores of villages,
ranging in size from tiny *caseríos* to settlements of several
thousand population, and hundreds of farms and coffee
fincas; in each of the larger villages, a rural guard post;
visible from the air, a hundred rutted roads, several small
landing fields for private planes, the great nickel and
manganese mines, of the north coast, and in the south,
the canefields of the plains above Guantánamo and Santiago;
between, not one mountain range, but half a dozen, providing a refuge and base of operations.

All of these things were assets. The army could not keep
transport from entering and leaving the district without cut-

ting off a vital commerce, the movement of virtually the entire Cuban coffee crop and much cane, timber, and other produce to the towns, the return flow of supplies on which the welfare of the inhabitants of the region and the outside tradesmen and banks with whom they did business depended.

The rural military posts were hopeless to defend; too numerous, vulnerable, and difficult of access for an army already spread far too thin. Raúl, with nearly a hundred men in the beginning, and perhaps six times that many in the end, was able to move undetected through the hills and forest, and to concentrate virtually his entire force on any single contested point. The posts fell one by one, under swift and devastating night attacks. Most of them within the Second Front area had been captured by the end of April.

The army, making a determined effort to regain control, dispatched large motorized columns from its big garrisons at Mayarí in the north, Baracoa in the east, Guantánamo in the south, and Alto Songo in the west.

The column commanders found that they could enter the new *territorio libre* and control the roads—but only the portion of road they happened to be on, and only for so long as they remained there.

A strong army column driving eastward from Alto Songo was unopposed at the railway town of San Benito a few miles away, but came under heavy attack from snipers in the hills beyond, fought its way through to La Maya, burning the coffee terminal there (and so in the end making it all the more imperative not to interfere with the mule trains carrying coffee that now had to travel on all the way to Alto Songo itself), and was driven back again, not by numbers, but by a host of hazards, road mines, sniping, ambuscades at every turn.

Troops coming from Baracoa into the Sierra de Purial had a similar experience, and those from Guantánamo at

Jamaica and the great sugar *central* and village of Soledad nearby. Troops from Mayarí were able to proceed as far as the big manganese mines at Ocujal, but attempts to maintain a garrison there were futile and costly, since a night march of an hour could bring the entire rebel force to the attack, and army reinforcements from Mayarí would be ambushed on the road.

Conditions on the edge of the north coast mining district were typical of the military situation that confronted army commanders all around the second front perimeter. The nature of the fighting and of the tactics employed by Raúl's *barbudos* may be best understood in the details of one of several clashes at the manganese mines.*

The rebels, about one hundred fifty strong, began moving up over the rutted, tortuous roads of the Sierra Cristal by jeep and truck on the afternoon preceding the attack, reaching the northern edge of the range by dusk. Several times, aircraft were seen in the distance, but the planes did not come near enough to be a threat. The rebel vehicles traveled slowly in open formation, each at an interval of half a mile or more from the other. The vehicles were hidden along the sides of the road and in small clearings, and camouflaged with leaves and branches.

A few of the officers went forward to make a reconnaissance. From the top of the farthest hill the big open-face mines could be seen, the service roads cutting from one excavation to another, the main road leading to the small mining community itself, beyond, the lights of Mayarí, to the right, the nickel mines and processing plant at Nicaro, to the left, the great bay of Nipe.

With darkness the rebels moved up to the edge of the hill, and an hour before midnight they began the descent, walking silently in a long, single file, their rifles glistening in the moonlight. The file made a long detour around one of

---

* One at which the author happened to be present, July 30-31.

the mines, where big excavators were still operating, under arc lights. When an ore truck passed, the *barbudos* flattened themselves against the ground, and when it was gone, they continued swiftly on.

The column entered the mining community at midnight, the first rebels to arrive accosting a middle-aged, worried watchman and relieving him of his revolver. Lights were blazing in the big sheds where earth-moving equipment and ore trucks were garaged, and there were dim lights in the several frame buildings that housed the administrative of-fices of the mines, but, aside from the watchman, no life stirred.

About a hundred of the rebel force continued on, to prepare a series of ambuscades along the Mayarí road, in anticipation of the arrival of troop reinforcements from Mayarí, when the fighting should begin. About a third of the original force was left behind to deal with the small detachment of soldiers who had recently been installed to guard the mines.

The original *cuartel* had been burned long since. The new detachment, seventeen soldiers, was quartered in one of three frame buildings at the farther end of the com-munity.

A .30-caliber machine gun was placed in a command-ing position, riflemen were disposed on several sides, and shortly after midnight, the rebels opened a heavy barrage. The first fusillade was directed at the wrong building. It proved to be empty. The soldiers promptly began to return the fire from the one which they actually occupied, and it presently developed that they had the benefit of a deep trench and sand-bagged parapet around the outside of the building.

A long siege began. The soldiers, firing at the muzzle flashes of the rebel rifles, wounded one of the attackers in the leg. Another was grazed by a ricocheting bullet.

The rebels had prepared a fifty-gallon drum of gasoline with a bomb and fuse attached, in effect, a giant "Molotov cocktail," the plan being to drive it, attached to the front of a bulldozer, directly against the *cuartel*. The bulldozer was overlong in coming. It had broken down on the road.

At four o'clock in the morning, abandoning thought of other expedients, the rebels made an open assault on the building, hurling flaming bottles of gasoline as they advanced under the protective fire of their machine gun. One of the attackers was hit in the abdomen, a grave but not, as it turned out, fatal wound.

The first *barbudo* to enter the blazing barracks found five frightened soldiers inside, weaponless and holding their arms in the air in sign of surrender. Seven others lay dead in the *cuartel* and in the trench outside.

The wounded were put in an ambulance that immediately started back up the mountain, lights on and siren screaming. (By way of celebration, and nothing of necessity.) The jeeps in which the rebels had reached their jumping-off point had been brought down to the mines, and the *barbudos* now drove back up the mountain, in triumphal procession, with their prisoners.

Army forces from Mayarí did not approach until daylight, and then at a cautious pace. They were permitted to pass the first ambuscade, and then the second, a force of about one hundred soldiers, in trucks and jeeps. A small scouting patrol was sent ahead on foot. The soldiers, rounding a bend in the road, came on the rebels in the third ambuscade, stood indecisive a moment, unable, apparently, to move, and were shot down in the road before they had recovered.

The remainder of the army force, taking alarm, began to retreat and were caught in ambush at two points as they withdrew. A jeep carrying eight soldiers was blown up by a land-mine. Thirty-seven soldiers were killed. The rest of the government force withdrew in disorder.

Two hours later, a flight of three fighter-bombers came swooping low over the mountains, passing within a thousand yards of the lumber mill where most of the rebel force now lay hidden, sleeping. Nothing was visible from the air but green pine forest, the saw mill shed, and a clearing in which a few men worked among the tree stumps, piling new-hewn planks.

Five of the rebels who had taken part in the battle on the Mayarí road were missing. A week later, they limped into Raúl's headquarters at Las Calabazas, on the other side of the range, footsore, ragged, and still stained red with the dust of the mines, apologizing for their absence, which had been unavoidable.

By May 10th, the last of the government forces had been driven from Raúl's second front, and the consolidation of the considerable economic assets of the great new *territorio libre* was beginning.

As to those assets, they included a ripening coffee crop valued at some sixty million dollars, a wealth of subsidiary food crops, and cattle country in which a ranch of seventy thousand acres was not considered remarkable. A tax of ten per cent was imposed on all produce leaving the territory, payable in advance in cash or kind. Batista's soldiers, for their part, imposed their own tax—fifty cents for each two-hundred-fifty-pound bag of coffee leaving the region, ten per cent of the value of all commodities brought in by the merchants of the villages within the *territorio libre*.

Of more importance than the income gathered by the revolutionary tax collectors were two other factors: airfields, where small cargos of arms and ammunition aboard chartered planes from Florida could be landed, and time and space in which to organize and grow stronger.

The most rigid censorship in Cuban history, reinforced under Batista's emergency decrees by severe penalties for spreading "false propaganda," explains in part, at least, why little of the fighting of the spring and early summer was reported outside of Oriente. Word of "furious fighting" did leak out, but the details were lacking.

The crucial part of the campaign on Raúl Castro's front came during the period of Vice President Nixon's tour of South America, a good-will tour that elicited some disconcerting displays of ill will, and took up most of the headlines in the American press from April 28th through May 14th, when he arrived safely back on U.S. territory, in Puerto Rico.

The Vice President faced hostile demonstrations on his tour (in Lima, where he was barraged with fruit and stones; in Caracas, where a mob tried to drag him from his limousine) with great personal courage and good sense. Less fortunate was the presidential emergency order that sent airborne troops to Puerto Rico and two companies of Marines to Guantánamo Bay as "a precautionary measure," when the Vice President seemed to be in peril.

The display of force, recalling the worst days of "gunboat diplomacy," tended to reinforce the increasing anti-American sentiment among the *fidelistas,* who had followed the developments of the Nixon tour with great interest. They were already persuaded—by the American-made warplanes overhead, the bombs stamped "U.S.A." that burst about them, if by nothing else—that they had an enemy in Washington, despite the arms embargo of March.

In June, two unfortunate incidents occurred to support that opinion. Two Cuban air force planes, presumably employed on bombing runs over the Sierra Maestra, made emergency landings at the Guantánamo naval base, and were refueled there. From Washington, about the same time, came copies of documents, obtained by the M-26 agent in the Cuban Embassy, Angel Saavedra, relating to a matter of three hundred rocket warheads, delivered to the Cuban air force on May 19th, at the U.S. naval base.

As the State Department subsequently explained, the rockets had been purchased and delivered before the arms embargo became effective. It seemed that the warheads delivered with the rockets had been, by some error, non-explosive dummies for practice use. The Batista government complained of the mistake, and it was rectified, explosive warheads being shipped to replace the harmless ones, so Washington declared.

It is doubtful that the rebels would have made any fine distinction, had they been given the explanation in advance. Having discovered the affair by their own efforts, they assumed the worst, and, partly in protest, partly for other, expedient reasons, took retaliatory action.

On June 26th, Raúl's rebels invaded the properties of the Moa Bay Mining Company, where a nickel-processing plant was being built, and kidnapped twelve mining engineers, two of them Canadians and ten United States citizens, from the plant and from their homes in the village of Moa, where a military post was attacked.

Three soldiers were killed in the fighting and, before it was over, eight rebels were dead. The *barbudos* emptied the local hospital of supplies, and drove back into *territorio libre* with nineteen jeeps and trucks. On the 28th, thirty United States sailors and marines were seized on the road between the Guantánamo base and the city itself. Raids on the Nicaro nickel mines, the United Fruit Sugar Company agricultural station at Guaro on the north coast, and elsewhere brought the total of hostages to fifty.

The *barbudos* made a considerable show of courteous regret and gallantry, actually running some risk to safeguard the hostages from harm, to make them comfortable, and to assure their families that they would be safe. The hostages were informed that they were "international witnesses" to evidence of the matters under protest, mainly fragments of bomb and napalm casing stamped with U.S. identification marks.

Raúl later entered in his account book an item of fourteen hundred dollars, explained as *"gastos por los Americanos,"* covering expenditures for beer, soft drinks, and similar small luxuries.

Although they politely refrained from comment, the *fidelistas* took some ironical satisfaction from the experience of Grant Wollam, the U.S. consul from Santiago, who was strafed and rocketed by a government fighter-bomber plane as he made his way by jeep into the highlands to negotiate for the release of the "international witnesses." Wollam, scrambling out of a ditch, unhurt except in his dignity, was much embarrassed, and his hosts not unamused, to think that the rockets which had been fired at him had been, in all probability, armed with explosive warheads delivered to the Cuban air command by the United States Navy at Guantánamo Bay.

One of the objects of the kidnapping seemed to have been to obtain some degree of formal United States recognition of the revolutionary force. Raúl demanded that the ambassador or some other responsible diplomatic representative be sent. The State Department made no such concession, and the distinction between diplomatic and consular representation was maintained.

Nevertheless, the United States government *was* forced to negotiate with the rebels, on their terms, whether on a consular or a diplomatic level, and this in itself was a major propaganda victory, of considerable importance in the relations of the *fidelistas* with other forces outside of Cuba, adding much to their prestige.

The rebels took advantage of the interlude in the hostilities to extend their advance positions on all sides, and to continue the work of administrative organization within the *territorio libre*. As a subsidiary gain, the publicity attendant on the kidnapping and subsequent negotiations served to open a window on the Second Front, giving the world a glimpse of the new territory that had been won.

The hostages took their experience in good part, with few exceptions. The last of them, the sailors and marines, were air-lifted by helicopter from a field near Puriales, one of the largest villages held by the rebels, back to Guantánamo Bay on July 18th.

There had been much talk about an impending government offensive against the Second Front rebel forces, to begin as soon as the hostages might be released. The rebels had been busy preparing new ambuscades and building roads with equipment taken from the mines (Raúl argued that if the Americans could help Batista, the rebels had the right to help themselves, and would, in any event, make reparations after the war).

No offensive materialized. A page from a reporter's notebook,* written July 24th at Las Calabazas, may be of interest:

Back to Calabazas at 2 A.M. Much to-do, and Raúl is off again, but (Captain Felix) Pena says only to a meeting; no action expected immediately. Needless to say, I'm very impatient and a bad guest. Raúl and Lucas (Dr. Lucas Moran) planning big farmers' meeting here, 1,000 coming, and I said would be of interest for economic story. But hope something happens meantime, because time's wasting. My impression growing that rebels hold here by government default, because government, knowing it lacks popular support, is willing to write off large rural areas in order to maintain "business as usual" in the cities, or appearance thereof. But of course such a policy is foolish. In two weeks, rebels have taken control of perhaps another 600 square miles, without firing a shot. So it goes. Each week the army pulls out of

* The author flew into rebel territory aboard a private plane piloted by a member of the revolutionary forces, on July 1st, landing on an M-26 air strip at Mayarí Arriba, and remained at the Second Front through the summer except for one brief weekend visit to the naval base.

one or two small *cuartels* which uneconomic to hold, and so goes
Oriente! I suppose the army must pray that the rebels will come
to the cities. But they will not; need not, at least for a long time.
If the army attempts an offensive, it will lose arms and men; the
rebels will grow stronger. New rebel tax program will, of course,
add to rebel arms, but government hasn't guts to shut off contra-
band trade which bringing individual officers big revenues while
aiding rebels. Much talk about airplanes, but this is purely
psychological and intended to make rebels unpopular with
civilian population. (Succeeding to a degree; some merchants
very uneasy.) It can't work. Army has few big bombs mainly
anti-personnel and incendiary. People will realize that big noise
does not mean big casualties, necessarily.

There was some bombing, but little effect from it, possibly because many of the pilots were on the point of
defecting. A single large bomb exploded outside of Las
Calabazas, creating a crater twelve feet deep and twenty
feet wide in a pasture half a mile from the village. Nearby,
a *campesino* was seriously burned by white phosphorous
and his home was destroyed. But for the time, no serious
action developed.

Raúl was well satisfied with his progress, as well he might
have been. The rebels were already in control of most of
the province east of Guantánamo, outside of the cities and
the airports, and were, in fact, posting guards outside of
the main gate of the U.S. naval base, inspecting all traffic
coming and going. The Cuban customs officer on duty
there, an aged, tired man, shrugged his thin shoulders and
went about his business.

For a reporter, looking for signs of war inside the rebel
territory, it was an exasperating interlude:

July 26—Spent the night at Anibal's post near Andre. Morning
at Andre itself, at memorial service for six killed, June 28, at
Moa Bay. Afternoon tour of northern perimeter by miserable
jeep, outpost overlooking Sagua de Tánamo where 700 soldiers.
Could see soldiers on roof of *cuartel.*

Actually, all of this is too tiresome for words, because of the heat, difficulty of preserving equipment, the preoccupation with meals and coffee and socializing in general. My friends accept words and symbols more readily than facts. A happy dinner is a victory, a speech is as good as a war won. Right now, there's much ado about roast pig, this being the joyous 26th of July. A speech of course, later the pigs, although we had lunch only an hour or so ago. As usual, we'll get where we're going at 2 o'clock in the morning. Meanwhile I'll drag around a ton of gear and sweat like a horse, because the only alternative is to leave it in the jeep, which could be borrowed at any minute and might never return.

Met Raúl en route. Stopped to listen to radio, also visited rebel radio station, where I heard Radio Venezuela hook-up with Sierra Maestra, relayed through several other Latin-American countries. Very good.

The situation was apparently static. But this was merely a surface impression. The *barbudos* had good reason to celebrate. On the *Segundo Frente,* a diplomatic victory had been won, the military gains of months of struggle had been consolidated, and the news from the Sierra Maestra was not merely good, but wonderful, although this was scarcely appreciated in the following journal entry, of July 27th, date-lined El Naranjo:

Last night I finally managed to get a good and honest appraisal of the situation here. The substance of Anibal's analysis is as follows: the *barbudos* here were hard-pressed, from the opening of the second front, by the April strike and their efforts to aid it. Scarcely had they begun to organize the front, when the affair of the Americans again captured their energies. For the moment, they welcome the lull which has set in, as an opportunity for intensive internal organization—of the people, revenue sources, supplies, health facilities, propaganda, communications, etc. This being so, they will not initiate any military action for a while. Nor do they expect the army, having been repulsed in two major attempts, and *having recently lost a battalion in the Sierra Maestra,* to try to enter again. The army, too, is expected to play a waiting game.

News last night by radio that five Cuban army pilots had fled to Venezuela, and this item added much to the joy of a 26th of July celebration that kept all hands up until 2 A.M., singing songs and socializing, after the big dinner of roast pig. It was all very jolly, after all.

The important item was, of course, not the news of the flight of Batista airmen to Venezuela, although this was certainly encouraging, but the reference to the battle in the Sierra.

The captured army battalion referred to was that of Major José Quevedo, a young army officer who had studied law with Fidel at the University of Havana. The surrender of Quevedo's battalion, July 21st, after a ten-day battle, heralded the complete and final failure of the army offensive that had begun in the spring.

The fighting was of a different character than that seen in Raúl's second front territory, for two reasons: the difference in terrain, and the fact that for several months Fidel was on the defensive, whereas most of the fighting in the north had been on the rebel initiative. As to the terrain, there was nothing of the roads, the broad valleys, rolling hills, tall shade trees, rich coffee groves and settled farms and villages of the north, but, in the Sierra, a tangle of jungle growth, thicket, scrub forest, rocky river beds, and precipitous mountain paths which even mules sometimes could not ascend.

Again, the rebels in the Sierra were fighting within a much more tightly drawn perimeter, under attack on several sides. The army, nevertheless, had an all but impossible task before it. The rocky southern shoreline did not invite amphibious landings. Several such were attempted, and easily frustrated. To drive across the mountain range from bases in the north was an even more difficult and hazardous enterprise.

Two full battalions taking this route, led by Lieutenant

Colonel Angel Sánchez Mosquera, were harried all the way by Juan Almeida's small guerrilla force, which closed the avenue of retreat behind them. The government troops were gradually led, in a series of skirmishes with Fidel's and "Che" Guevara's columns, into a trap at Santo Domingo, due north of Fidel's La Plata headquarters, and there, surrounded on all sides by riflemen occupying higher ground, the two battalions were cut to pieces in a three-day battle. Sánchez Mosquera himself was gravely wounded, but escaped, leaving a third of his shattered force behind.

The destruction of Company M of Sánchez Mosquera's 22nd Infantry Battalion had more disastrous consequences for the government forces than the *Estado Mayor* realized at the time. As Fidel explained in a broadcast on *Radio Rebelde, M* Company's shortwave radio equipment was captured, and with it the army code. The army, seeming not to realize what had happened, or its significance, continued to use the code, and thus the *fidelistas* were anticipating every subsequent move of the offensive, from June 5th on. The code was not changed until July 25th, and on the same day, another company was captured, and the new code fell into rebel hands, along with more shortwave equipment. On several occasions when enemy units were out of communication because their transmitters had broken down, the rebels, said Fidel, were themselves able to direct air attacks on army positions.

For the most part, the aircraft did little damage on either side, because of the steepness and height of the mountains, which kept the army planes from flying too low, and the thickness of the jungle growth which provided protection and absorbed the force and shrapnel of the bomb explosions.

The rebels had been long prepared for the offensive, and held all points of vantage. As Fidel had predicted, the strength of the rebels increased as their lines shortened, and those of the enemy extended.

The efforts of the offensive forces and the tactics employed to frustrate them may be judged from Fidel's own report on the battle of El Jiguí, against the army's 18th Infantry Battalion, and the recollections of its commander, José Quevedo.

Quevedo had been assigned in early March to command a company of cadets and quartermaster troops at Maffo, just below the Central Highway between Bayamo and Palma Soriano. The army was building up its forces for the Sierra offensive with all speed, and within two months Quevedo found himself commanding a full battalion on the Caribbean shore at the foot of the Sierra Maestra.

His mission seems to have been to try to establish a *cordon sanitaire* around the rebel zone of operations. He says that his orders at the end of May were to rescue military and civilian prisoners held by the *fidelistas,* the civilian "prisoners" referred to presumably being the inhabitants of the tiny hamlets and *caseríos* of the region. He touched briefly at Palma Mocha, where Fidel had formerly had his headquarters, and pushed on toward the La Plata area.

His first contact with the rebels was on the 9th of June. There were thirteen subsequent contacts in the next thirty days, each consisting of a brief exchange of fire with unseen rebel snipers on higher ground, each leading him on in the direction chosen by the rebels.

On July 11th, the major found himself encamped in a depression at El Jiguí, the name of the place at which the river of that name enters the Rio de la Plata, flowing south to the sea, some four miles below.

Quevedo had left his supply company (G-4) at the mouth of the Rio de la Plata, and had been out of contact with it for eight days. His provisions were exhausted; the men were growing hungry. In these circumstances, at about six o'clock in the morning, the encampment came under rebel fire. The attack was a light one, lasting only a few minutes. It was enough to worry the major, but not a sufficiently serious threat to put him into motion, as had been intended. He was, however, concerned about the lack of provisions, and sent out a patrol, in the direction of the coast.

He had not long to wait. The patrol came under fire almost immediately. One man was killed; the others returned.

Quevedo was aware that he was operating dangerously close to the rebel stronghold. Pico Turquino itself rose majestically above him, six or seven miles to the west. He did not yet realize the full extent of his peril, but, growing fearful, decided to send out a stronger force, two platoons, with orders to reach the mouth of the river. Six men were lost; five killed, one captured.

Quevedo now saw that he was in a trap from which it was possible that he might not escape. The rebels surrounding him, still unseen, held their fire and awaited developments.

Three days passed, with no move on either side. On the afternoon of July 14th, Quevedo resolved to make a strong and determined effort to break the encirclement. He divided his best company, the 103rd, into three platoons, and dispatched them by separate routes, in the direction of the coast. The effort failed.

"Two of the platoons returned intact," says Quevedo in his account of the battle, "the third remained in the hands of the rebel army, with heavy casualties. Only ten or twelve men could escape."

The fighting lasted until nine o'clock at night. Five soldiers were killed; twenty-one remained in rebel hands, along with most of the company's arms, and all of its transport, thirty-nine mules.

Fidel, whose view of the battle was more intimate, because he had mobility, and controlled the situation, said in his report:

Simultaneously our forces advanced from all directions and took firing positions within rifleshot of the enemy encampment. From then on the fire on both sides was unceasing. The battalion had been immobilized and without food for four days. The success of the operation was going to depend on the fight against the enemy reinforcements (that might be expected to come). On the morning of the 15th, aircraft appeared. The air attack against our positions, with machine guns, explosive bombs of five hundred pounds, and napalm, lasted uninterrupted from six in the morning until one in the afternoon. * * * On the 16th, the attack was repeated, while enemy transports carried reinforcements to the mouth of the river La Plata.

Fidel called a cease-fire for three hours on the same day and asked for Quevedo's surrender. The troops took advantage of the truce to get out of the trenches where they had been crouched for days without relief, but returned to their positions when the cease-fire ended.

The army aircraft had been brought to the attack by Quevedo, who had successfully sent a courier undetected through the rebel lines, to reach the beach and relay a message to the navy frigate *Maximo Gomez,* cruising off shore. The entrapped battalion was now in communication with the frigate, through shortwave radio relay via the aircraft overhead. The major issued an urgent call for reinforcements, and was told that his own G-4 company would be sent to his relief, while other reinforcements were brought up to the beach. Quevedo says he begged the military command to rescind the order, arguing that the supply company was lightly armed and inexperienced, and would only fall into the rebel trap. His arguments were ignored.

To return to Fidel's account:

On the 17th, the G-4 company left the beach, marching slowly, watching the road (actually the rocky margin of the river bed). At 2:30 in the afternoon, fifty automatic rifles and two .50-caliber machine guns opened fire against the company.

Within fifteen minutes, the first two platoons were shot to pieces, and the rest were retreating.

Reinforcements were being landed.

On the 19th, an entire battalion supported by artillery fire from land and sea, and by aircraft, advanced from the beach. The hardest combat of the struggle then began, lasting without interruption for almost twenty-four hours. The rebel forces counter-attacked, and forced the retreat of the enemy to the beach again.

A rebel captain, Andrés Cuevas, and three of his men were killed, four others gravely wounded. On the enemy side: seventeen killed, twenty-one wounded.

Quevedo's last hope of rescue had been decisively destroyed; no further attempt was made to save him. The rebels now moved down to within fifty yards of the encampment, cutting the encircled soldiers off from their only source of water, the river. The situation was hopeless. Efforts to airdrop supplies to Quevedo had failed; the packages had fallen into rebel hands.

A prisoner was sent to Quevedo, with a formal, written demand for the surrender of the battalion. In the morning, Fidel called a cease-fire for four hours. Cautiously, the troops left their positions and, finding that they were not being fired upon, approached the nearest rebel foxholes, to ask for food and water. The *barbudos* shared with them the very food packages that had been dropped by the airplanes, and overcome by such kindness, the soldiers, relates Fidel, "embraced our soldiers and wept with emotion."

Although the matter was not mentioned in the report on *Radio Rebelde,* for reasons of discretion, Quevedo had joined Fidel the night before, and, after many hours of serious discussion, had decided to defect to the rebel side. He returned to his command and explained his decision and the reasons for it, and told his men that they were at liberty to make their own choice, individually. The men, says Quevedo, received the idea of joining the victorious rebels "with enthusiasm."

In fact, they were not permitted to do so. The formal surrender of the one hundred sixty-three men remaining under Quevedo's command was made on the following day, July 21st; the many wounded were given medical attention, and arrangements were made to deliver both wounded and unwounded prisoners to representatives of the Cuban and the International Red Cross.

Quevedo remained with Fidel, and accompanied him to La Plata where, he says, he received a letter which had been directed to him on June 9th, and had failed to reach him until now. It was a brief note from Fidel, remarking on the coincidence that brought them to the same area, so remote from the University of Havana and the other places where they might have expected to meet in normal circumstances, and expressing regret for the course of events which had disposed them on opposite sides. It closed with a simple expression of continued good will and "good luck."

The weapons which had been captured during the battle at El Jiguí were distributed among rebel volunteers who had long been awaiting arms. In effect, the government battalion became a *fidelista* battalion, and with this strong new force in the field, no possibility remained that the long drawn army offensive could succeed.

Fighting continued briefly in the north, where two new battalions returned to the attack. But again a defeat was inflicted on the Batista forces at Santo Domingo; another company was destroyed, more arms captured. By mid-August, the fighting was over in the Sierra.

In all, Fidel delivered four hundred forty-three prisoners to the Red Cross, and released one hundred twenty-one elsewhere.

The government forces moved gradually back into their fortified *cuartels,* abandoning the villages and the secondary roads. By the end of the summer, the *Movimiento 26* effectively controlled two-thirds of the province, a *territorio libre* of some fifteen thousand miles, and Fidel turned his attention westward, toward Havana, where he had said the last battle would be fought.

Havana, Dec. 31 (AP)—Government troops, backed by armor and planes, hammered retreating rebel forces around Santa Clara tonight and drove them eastward out of Las Villas Province. * * * A source close to President Batista said: "There will be no New Year's holiday and no truces or respites for the rebels."

XII

SUMMER'S END brought hurricanes to eastern Cuba, and torrential rains that filled the rivers to overflowing, delaying the difficult passage of two small *fidelista* columns moving slowly out of Oriente, toward the broad and empty plains of the province of Camagüey.

In an entry in his war journal on September 5th, the Argentine physician Ernesto "Che" Guevara says his men are so exhausted after a nine-day march that he has to find horses to carry them to the Río Jobabo, known in the north as Río Cabreras, the boundary line between Oriente and Camagüey. On the following day he notes that almost all of the men—some one hundred eighty in his column and perhaps half that number in the smaller group led by Camilo Cienfuegos—are now barefoot, their feet being so raw and swollen that they are unable to put on their broken and water-soaked boots.

"Che's" advance guard was ambushed the following day, the main body of his column attacked by army reinforcements arriving in trucks to support the few soldiers of the post where the shooting started. The troops were repelled, but the rebels were bombed by army aircraft, giving Guevara some serious problems and the slight satisfaction of noting in his journal: "A small airplane that relieved the army in its attacks on us was reached by our fire and knocked down in the vicinity of the Francisco *central.*"

There was another, more serious clash on September 13th, near the small village of Cuatro Compañeros, with the rebels again under attack on the ground and from the

272

air, a day-long battle in which Guevara's column lost contact with Camilo's group.

By the 30th of the month, Guevara's "Column 8, Ciro Redondo" had tramped to within thirty miles of the border of Las Villas, more than one hundred miles across the plains and through the salt marshes of Camagüey's Caribbean coast. The column was lost, ground artillery and ships offshore had been bombarding the swampland where the rebels were thought, correctly, to be, and for several days there had been nothing to eat but the heart of a small and edible variety of palm, which Guevara pronounced "very sweet."

They were approaching a railroad line terminating in a long lagoon, in the Baraguá zone south and east of Ciego de Avila. A small army scout plane was searching for them, soldiers were moving along the railroad embankment ahead, and there seemed no recourse but to go *around* the railway at its terminus, through the lagoon.

From Guevara's journal:

September 30—We advance into the swamp about two kilometers, parallel with the railroad, and camp with the water up to our knees. We endure two days without food and shivering with cold, drinking this pestilential water that is our only nourishment. The tortures that we are suffering are terrible. Scouts are sent out, who bring us news that the entire railway embankment is a firing line. Lieutenant Rogelio Acevedo, who is an excellent swimmer, goes out to inspect the line, swimming through the lagoon. On his return he informs me that a handcar passed, leaving provisions for the soldiers posted at intervals of fifty meters, but on reaching the edge of the lagoon the car departed without making any more stops (i.e., along its farther shore). It is unguarded below that point.

Guevara's diary entry of October 1st:

At 5 P.M. I called the captains together, explaining to them the extreme precautions that we had to take to cross the railway line.

Captain Manuel Hernández, with an advance guard, crosses the lagoon and occupies the embankment, placing the machine guns to protect our passage. We advance slowly, trying to make no noise, but the splashing seems that of a troop of elephants. We are only fifty meters from the enemy lines: from the last post a voice breaks the night: "Who goes there?" The column stops, sunk in mud to the ankles and in water to the neck, arms overhead protecting the weapons and ammunition. We cannot endure the position more than three minutes, and continue the march. We cross the lagoon, and camp on a key where we sleep in the mud.

By the 4th of October, Column 8 is out of the swamps, on dry land again, and although the rebels are scarcely able to walk, because of their weakness and the ravages of fungus infection in their feet, they go on, finding horses to carry the ten men in worst condition. On the 6th they are met in a thicket south of Ciego de Avila by three officers coming from the mountains of Las Villas province to meet them, and now, procuring fresh horses, they make better progress, crossing the storm-swollen Río Jatibonico into Las Villas at dawn on October 12th. Three days later, struggling through the mud in a teeming downpour, and under air attack again, they evaded a pursuit force of some one thousand soldiers and reached their destination—the sheltering hills of the Sierra de Sancti Spiritus on the edge of the complex of mountain ranges collectively known as the Escambray. Camilo Cienfuegos' "Column 2, Antonio Maceo," reaching the railway line by-passed by Guevara's column, had taken another direction. Led by a captured corporal, the guerrillas moved far to the north, crossing the Central Highway near Ciego de Avila and continuing on in trucks requisitioned from a sugar mill in the area.

"Unquestionably," relates Cienfuegos, "the corporal turned out to be the best of guides, for he passed us without any problem at all close to an infinity of ambuscades and the *cuartel* of Baraguá, where there were more than two hundred soldiers."

They burned the pumping plant at the Ciego de Avila waterworks after clashing with the guard there and killing a soldier. Thirty miles to the northwest, near Marroquí, army aircraft discovered their trucks and they were afoot again, under attack as they moved into a small range of mountains lying on either side of the Río Jatibonico del Norte, more than sixty miles north of the point where Guevara had crossed the river.

On October 9th, in a written report to Fidel, Camilo said that the province of Camagüey had bid them farewell as it had welcomed them "with a cyclone." He had received no word from Guevara in twenty-two days, he wrote. For the rest:

I will tell you that since we left the zone of Cauto, westward bound, we have traveled without resting a single night, for forty days, many of them without guides, with the coastline for our orientation and a compass for direction. For fifteen days we marched with the mud and water up to our knees, each night evading ambushes and troops situated on the crossings that we had to make. In the thirty-one days that the trip through Camagüey dragged on, we ate only eleven times, this being the foremost cattle zone of Cuba. After four days without tasting any food at all, we had to eat a mare, she being the best of our poor cavalry.

And to emphasize the point, Camilo adds that they had eaten the mare raw; moreover, without salt.

His report closes with a cryptic reference to his ultimate goal; he says he is sure that his column, "A-1" troops, will reach Pinar del Río, the westernmost province of the island.

In this he was mistaken. The revolutionaries were on the offensive, and although the offensive was slow in getting under way, the hour was already too advanced to permit any more long marches, nor was any such effort required.

What was behind the maneuvers that brought veterans of the Sierra Maestra into Las Villas? Quite evidently, an understanding that the end was near. Fidel had announced on *Radio Rebelde,* August 21st, that *fidelista* forces were moving out of Oriente, as indeed they were, to carry the war to the rest of the national territory. Within a few weeks or a few months, he warned, any town or zone of the island could become a battlefield. And with some slight exaggeration but nevertheless with a keen appreciation of the ignorance in which the government troops were kept, he asked:

What will the *Estado Mayor* tell the soldiers when they see a flood of rebel troops over the length and breadth of the island? Does not the general staff believe that in that moment their soldiers are going to have the most terrible surprise and the bitterest disillusionment. . . ?

There was no "flood of rebel troops" at any time, but a trickle was made to resemble a flood, by furious effort, and served as well. The censorship imposed by Batista worked against him, leading the Cubans to believe any report or rumor, so long as its source was not official. The army general staff, fabricating fairy tales of battles fought and won, was deceived by the soldiers as it deceived them, and they by each other, so that no one knew for sure whether the rebels were a few platoons or a few divisions.

As to the actual situation, it was clear to anyone who understood it that, if a few hundred mountain-based guerrillas could hold off any army and paralyze the busy trading towns and cities of Oriente by isolating them from the countryside on which their whole existence was predicated, then the same could be done wherever there were mountains, forests, farmlands, and trading centers to be isolated.

What could the army do to combat the practice, against an enemy that could be neither contained nor destroyed? In Fidel's informed opinion: very little. How long could the regime endure, supported only by a confused, discredited, and impotent military force? In his considered judgment: not very long.

Batista had by this time lost all vestige of political power, his name anathema with the Church, his trade relations breaking, his diplomatic standing extremely shaky despite the good offices of his public relations advisor, Edmund Chester, and the continuing cordiality of Ambassador Smith.

In short, there was not much left but a police force commanded by criminals, a military force commanded by knaves and incompetent fools, an unhappy and reluctant army of occupation, as it were, garrisoned on a hostile population, surrounded by unfriendly faces, uneasy outside of the big fortified *cuartels,* the soldiers distrustful of their officers, and the officers distrustful of a high command which had no strategy but opportunism, no certain tenure, no visible future.

Fidel's strategy was based on all of the foregoing considerations, and just possibly on one other. The regime was plainly crumbling, the victory was at hand. It was important to make it a *fidelista* victory: to prevent a *coup d'état* or any other sort of power grab in Havana. And it was a long way from Oriente to the national capital.

The only M-26 force close to the capital was a group of about thirty guerrillas, survivors of an April landing from Florida, who were fighting in the mountains of Pinar del Río, in the Sierra de los Organos. In Las Villas, the only *fidelista* military force prior to the arrival of "Che" and Camilo Cienfuegos was a small guerrilla column under Victor Bordon, far outnumbered by the combined forces of the *Directorio Revolucionario,* the *Organizacion Auténtica,* and Eloy Gutiérrez Menoyo's *Segundo Frente Nacional del Escambray.*

All things considered, there was every reason, both military and political, to strengthen the *fidelista* forces in these strategic areas.

The men that Fidel sent to do the job were not merely the best that he could spare, but from any point of view, his best and most experienced and reliable. With Guevara in the south of Las Villas and Cienfuegos in the north, the *fidelista* offensive began full force, both in that province and in Oriente.

Fighters from the Sierra Maestra had again moved up to threaten the towns along the Central Highway. In late September, raiders under Comandante Huber Matos marched through Maffo, entered Contramaestre, burned the police post and the railway station and drove on to the key highway town of Palma Soriano, where they held the military garrison immobilized for six hours while they burned the post office and telegraph station and replenished their provisions.

Raúl Castro's *"Mau Mau,"* so-called by the *campesinos* and one another (with no derogation intended), were ranging as far west as Victoria de las Tunas, and there was fighting again at Sagua de Tánamo in the north, for the first time since April. Rebel patrols were roaming the outskirts of Guantánamo, and harassing transport above Santiago, burning buses and gasoline tanker trucks.

Batista was determined to have elections and, having subsidized the "election campaigns" of the nominal opposition candidates, proceeded to go through the motions. The November ballot could not be prevented, but could be, and was, ignored. Despite the law which made voting mandatory, it was estimated that seventy-five per cent of the eligible electorate of Havana stayed away from the polls on November 3rd, and in Santiago, at the opposite end of the embattled island, scarcely two per cent of population—i.e., soldiers and government officials—made a pretense of voting.

It had been thought that Batista would be intelligent enough to surrender something, by letting the victory go to one of the stalking horses, Carlos Márquez Sterling. Amazingly, even this possibly saving concession was withheld, and the announcement that came, after a solemn farce of counting slips of paper from stuffed ballot boxes, was that the regime's chosen candidate, Andres Rivero Agüero, had won.

His margin of victory was astounding: he had won by a far greater number of votes than there had been voters. In this connection, some interesting evidence remains available to any investigator requiring proofs: hundreds of sets of certified voting registration cards, each card bearing a different name, occupation, and addresses, and dozens bearing identical photographs, i.e., the photograph of the same purported "voter." The question is, why go to such lengths to manufacture false evidence of an election "victory" which could have no credence in Cuba in any event? To convince whom?

The revolutionaries had made considerable effort to prevent the election. When it came, the electoral tragi-comedy made scarcely a ripple against the rising tide of revolution. It was far too late for any such ridiculous shadow play. The battle against Batista was in its final weeks.

A series of forays into the rural villages and towns of Oriente made plain, within a space of a month, that the army had no intention of leaving the big *cuartels* unless forced to do so. The cities themselves were threatened now, and the army's entire effort was to keep the Central Highway open, so that no big garrison could be isolated. The smaller garrisons were left to their own resources.

With the war now in the open country, Fidel marched

out of the mountains with two hundred riflemen and a hundred *escopeteros*, occupied the mines of Bueycito in the foothills and moved north to capture the town itself. Guisa, ten miles east of Bueycito and about the same distance south of the big garrison of Bayamo was next to be attacked.

The army, correctly interpreting the assault as the first step toward cutting the highway between Bayamo and Santiago, opposed it with all available force.

Bueycito had fallen on November 17th, without a shot, the small garrison retiring after vainly appealing to Bayamo for support, which was refused. The encirclement of Guisa began. On the morning of the 20th, a government patrol driving south from Bayamo was fired upon. Two hours later, more troops from Bayamo arrived, and ran into ambush. A truckload of soldiers was blown up and a six-hour fight ensued.

The Bayamo commander, beginning to realize the gravity of the threat, sent a stronger force, preceded by a thirty-ton tank. The tank ran over a land mine and was lifted into the air by so powerful an explosion that it landed upside down, burying its steel turret in the pavement of the road.

On the 21st, army reinforcements supported by tanks succeeded in breaking through to strengthen the encircled Guisa garrison, only to find that the rebels had closed the road behind them, cutting off their only avenue of retreat.

More troops were sent by way of El Corojo, five miles to the west, and were thrown back. On the 25th, the Bayamo commander launched another frontal assault, committing a full battalion to the effort, a thousand men in seventeen trucks, led by two medium tanks. The lead tank was put out of action by a mine explosion. The rebels, shooting from good cover on either side of the road, raked the column with a devastating hail of rifle and machine-gun fire, forcing the troops to leave their trucks.

A rebel mortar battery began to drop mortar shells in the midst of the column, driving the soldiers back.

A small task force armed with picks and shovels, finding cover behind the tank that had been overturned on the first day, dug into the roadway and opened a deep ditch across the road, isolating the two tanks that had led the battalion in its attack. The Bayamo commander threw another battalion into the battle, committing virtually all of his entire force. The troops, under fire from rebel entrenchments on higher ground, were unable to advance. A Sherman tank was able to pull out one of the two trapped medium tanks, but the other remained behind and the crew, cut off and without water for two days, surrendered.

The *fidelistas,* now in possession of their first tank, with a 37-millimeter gun, opened a strong counter-attack and the army, retreating, abandoned fourteen trucks on the road and sufficient small arms to increase the effective rebel force by nearly fifty per cent, as the *escopeteros* exchanged their shotguns for military weapons.

Having driven the army back to within rifle shot of the Central Highway, Fidel now turned his new tank on Guisa. The garrison held out for two days, immobilizing the tank by scoring two direct hits on it with light artillery, and army reinforcements from Palma Soriano and as far away as Manzanillo joined the shattered Bayamo force in launching a new series of assaults. None was successful. The road had been effectively cut; there was no other avenue of approach. The rebels continued to hold the high ground, and on November 30th, under the weight of a determined attack, the Guisa garrison fled into the surrounding countryside, leaving the town in rebel hands. Army casualties came to more than two hundred; the rebels lost eight men killed and seven wounded, a far smaller but not necessarily disproportionate number, considering the numerical disparity of the opposing forces.

The text of the bulletin announcing the victory, signed by Fidel, concluded: "Guisa, twelve kilometers from the command post of Bayamo, is now in *territorio libre*."

A significant development: the third largest military garrison in the province had ceased to be a serious threat. This clearly established, Fidel struck north toward Santa Rita and Jiguaní, cutting the Central Highway east of Bayamo, and turned his attention to the task of bottling up the Maceo Regiment in its stronghold, Santiago.

He had closed one exit, or was about to close it. *Barbudos* led by Huber Matos had already closed another, severing the Santiago-Guantánamo road at Cristo, just above the provincial capital, on November 26th, capturing the *cuartel* there and taking eighty prisoners.

Rebels on the southern edge of Raúl Castro's *Segundo Frente* had moved down to Alto Songo, on the same road, a few miles above Cristo.

Fidel's column rolled down the Central Highway through Baire and Contramaestre toward Palma Soriano, breaking the highway link between that city and the army training camp at Maffo, where Fidel engaged a powerful government force supported by aircraft and artillery.

From Songo, Raúl's "Mau Mau" now drove westward across country to join forces with Juan Almeida's command, and toward the captured San Luis, closing the last remaining road to Santiago from the north.

The Maceo Regiment made five successive attempts during early December to break the encirclement, and failed each time. The roads were ambuscaded and the villages and their fortified barracks and guard posts were in rebel hands.

Rebel advance units moved up to the Country Club on the edge of Santiago and remained there, too small and well dispersed to be dislodged by aircraft or artillery from their foxholes among the trees, too mobile and well informed to be surprised by infantry, for which they were able to lay a dozen traps.

For the army, it was like trying to combat an invasion of intelligent and dangerous squirrels. Any small force sent out was in danger of being encircled and destroyed. Any large force leaving its base could be evaded, flanked, harassed from several sides, and perhaps maneuvered into an exposed position from which there might be no retreat.

The tactics that had been applied to the small village garrisons and rural posts of northern Oriente were now being applied with equal success to the larger villages, the towns, the cities themselves.

Almeida's fighters had cut off Bayamo on the north, completing its isolation. Holguín was cut off on the south. Cauto Cristo, in between, was captured, and an army pilot landing on the Central Highway en route from Holguín to Bayamo in the midst of storm, found himself in *territorio rebelde*.

Baracoa, far to the east, had been encircled and neutralized. The Southern port of Caimanera fell, and the encirclement of Guantánamo was complete.

The big garrisons, separated like the links of a broken chain, continued to hold the cities, but that was all, and even that much was uncertain.

The air force, with new Sea Furies, purchased from Britain, bombed and strafed rebel positions where it could find them, but it was the civilian population that suffered.

Armored cars could leave the cities, but, being confined to the roads, offered no serious threat to the rebels, who had only to pull back a short distance and then close in behind them, as soon as they were gone.

A few commanders of small mobile columns roamed the countryside, but their forays had little effect on the rebel fighting forces; their war was against the *campesinos,* whom they believed, correctly, to be rebel sympathizers and potential *barbudos,* waiting to be armed. It was said of Jesús Sosa Blanco, a captain promoted to major for his many "victories" on such excursions, that his progress across the country could be followed by watching the columns of smoke rising from the burning hamlets that he left behind. In the Gibara zone alone he burned one hundred thirty homes, not forgetting to loot them first of all saleable property.

In at least one incontestably authenticated instance, December 15th, near Bocas de Gibara, he burned a man alive inside of a house, first binding him with wire. Atrocities of this kind were by no means rare, nor was Sosa alone in committing them. But such mad dog measures of desperation, perpetrated by lunatics whose lives were already forfeit, could accomplish nothing, except to make the final struggle more bitter and costly.

The rebels now controlled all of Oriente up to the very outskirts of the cities; the ripening canefields, three quarters of the entire Cuban sugar crop, were in *territorio libre,* the industries of the province were closing down, the huge nickel, cobalt, and manganese mines were idle; Holguín was without electric power and its eighty-five thousand people went to bed by candlelight; horse-drawn carts replaced automobiles and trucks in Bayamo and Guantánamo because there was no gasoline, and eggs sold for ten cents apiece in Santiago, when they were to be obtained at any price.

It was in these circumstances that United States Senator Ellender of Louisiana asked, in a news conference in Havana, December 12th: "Is there a revolution here?" and went on to give it as his opinion that Fidel Castro and his followers were "a bunch of bandits" burning sugar plantations. His conclusion: "It would be a great pity if civil war should occur here . . . Only the poor would suffer."

Why did not Batista send reinforcements to Oriente and open a determined, full-scale counter-offensive? He could not. There were no troops to be spared. He had found new sources of arms in Europe, where his agents were spending money like water, but the planes and armored cars coming from Britain, the rifles, machine guns, mortars and grenades purchased in Italy, Belgium, and France arrived too late. There were more aircraft than willing pilots, more armored cars than drivers, more rifles than soldiers to fire them.

Nor were Batista's troubles confined to Oriente. The island was now in open insurrection from end to end. Guerrilla forces were fighting on the outskirts of the city of Camagüey. An active underground was wrecking communications in Matanzas and Cardenas. The *fidelista* force in Pinar del Río was growing, and its powerful shortwave transmitter, one of more than a score in operation on the island, was speaking nightly to the people of Havana, reporting the developments which Batista thought to conceal, instructing the M-26 militia, preparing them for action in the city where Senator Ellender said he had not noticed any "unrest."

In Las Villas, Camilo Cienfuegos and "Che" Guevara had made radio contact for the first time on December 2nd, and now revolutionary columns as strong as those in Oriente were beginning to drive from north and south, to cut the vital rail and highway arteries at their juncture in Santa Clara.

Fidel had been building an air force in Oriente. He already had two planes large enough to use as bombers—Cubana DC-3 airliners, captured in transit by *fidelista* action squads that had boarded the planes as passengers, one group at Camagüey, and the other at Moa in northern Oriente. His plan: to bomb the Moncada Barracks, and capture Santiago. The necessity did not arise. The struggle was almost over.

On December 12th, the day after *Radio Rebelde* had announced the return from exile of Dr. Manuel Urrutia Lleó, the rubber-stamp Cuban Congress accorded Batista sweeping new emergency powers, authority to do what he wished with the economy in order to fill a new war chest, authority to draft into the armed services an unlimited number of conscripts, and to commit the nation to total war.

For nearly two months Batista had allowed his emergency powers to lapse, in order to give a semblance of normality to the elections. The pretense had gone on too long. The new decrees, like Fidel's plan to bomb Moncada, came too late.

The offensive in Las Villas was in full stride, and there was no way to halt it. The tactics applied were those seen in Oriente, to cut the smaller roads, strike through to the main artery, the Central Highway, and then spread out, taking first the small *cuartels* and then the larger ones, a process of encirclement repeated again and again, the object in all cases being to isolate, divide, and conquer.

Driving north from the Sierra de Sancti Spiritus, "Che" Guevara's first objective was Santa Lucia, a village with a small fortified post on a narrow connecting road between the city of Sancti Spiritus in the south and the north-south artery that intersects the Central Highway at Placetas, fifteen miles or so east of Santa Clara.

Santa Lucia seized, and with it several machine guns, the rebels moved across the triangle to take the Escambray sugar *central* and then the town of Fomento, capturing one hundred thirty-six soldiers there, and arming an equal number of eager volunteers with their rifles.

These points secured, Guevara turned east again, and cut the Central Highway at Guayos and Cabaiguán, a column under Victor Bordón capturing the *cuartel* at the latter place after a hard, two-day battle. Small ambuscades had been set up outside of Sancti Spiritus in the south and Placetas in the north.

With his rear secure, "Che" now opened a drive, full force, into Placetas, along two roads, the one from Fomento and the Central Highway. Placetas fell, and a rebel headquarters was established there, where recruits pouring in from other towns and from the countryside were armed and given rudimentary instruction.

In Sancti Spiritus, a strong M-26 underground militia opened the battle within the city, and the townspeople came out on the streets to fight with such weapons as they could find, opening the way for a small rebel column under Captain Erasmo Rodríguez.

On Christmas Eve, the rebels took full possession of the city, and the radio station there broadcast the stirring news, heard in thousands of homes throughout the island, that Sancti Spiritus was now a part of the great and growing *territorio libre* of Cuba.

Fidel's advance had been held up at Maffo. That strongpoint finally reduced, the rebels pushed into Palma Soriano on Christmas Day, after two days of hard fighting, and began a battle from house to house and street to street, gradually forcing the soldiers back into their fortress.

Some garrison commanders surrendered when it became apparent that nothing was to be gained by continued resistance. Their hearts were not in the fight, and those who felt that they had nothing to fear accepted the fortunes of war with stoical good grace.

Others—those who had long since been warned that revolutionary tribunals awaited them—fought on with the ferocity of desperation. Holguín, under siege for sixty-seven days, was not secured until the night of January 2nd, and army fliers leaving it the day before the garrison surrendered took their revenge by attacking the rebel-held village of Tacamara nearby with napalm and rockets, as they fled.

Sagua de Tánamo, north and east of the Sierra Cristal, had been encircled since early October. The troops and police there fortified the city hall and built up a series of smaller posts around it, created a formidable defense in depth against an incursion. The townspeople became captives; all commerce with the countryside was halted; and, by December, starvation faced the town, despite the efforts of the air force to air-drop provisions. The supplies, in great crates, crashed through rooftops with the effect of bombs. The people, terrorized, dug trenches, and lived in them, abandoning their homes, as the planes began to bomb and strafe rebel positions on the outskirts.

A rebel column commanded by Enrique Lusson, one of the heroes of the April battle of Puerto Boniato, forced an entrance to Sagua on December 17th, and began to evacuate the civilian population.

Thousands of people, empty-handed and starving, fled into the countryside, as the government planes opened a dawn-to-dusk bombardment and the soldiers, falling back, burned the houses and shops about them to clear lanes of fire for their machine guns and to halt the rebel advance.

In nine tragic days of battle, the city became a blackened shell, once prosperous businesses destroyed, homes burned and bombed to rubble, corpses littering the street, and no life moving in the streets, except the *fidelista* commandos, slowly closing their circle.

The surrender came on Christmas, after a parley arranged by the wife of a soldier, who entered the ruined city hall with an infant in her arms to plead with her husband, and found him so starved and thirsty that he drank the milk from the baby's bottle before he was able to talk.

Guantánamo fell, and, in Las Villas, Remedios and Caibarién on the north coast and Trinidad on the south. The rebels of the *Directorio* and the *Segundo Frente Nacional del Escambray* moved up to help take Cruces, and continued north and west, along with *fidelistas* under Victor Bordón, in an effort to encircle Santa Clara. Bordón was held up at Manacas on the Central Highway west of Santa Clara, and other rebel elements taking Santo Domingo, a few miles east, were pushed out again on December 28th, by army reinforcements coming from Havana and Matanzas.

The commander of the Leoncio Vidal 3rd Tactical Regiment in Santa Clara (the same used to put down the Cienfuegos uprising of 1957) was Colonel Joaquin Casillas Lumpuy, who had recently relieved General Chaviano, the latter having been given the command in September, presumably on the basis of his proven incompetence in more active areas.

Casillas was responsible for the defense of the city, but most of the orders came directly from Camp Columbia, where the general staff was trying, typically, to mastermind the battle from afar. A new chief of staff was in control, General José Euletorio Pedraza, a sometime chief of police and dreaded "enforcer" of an earlier Batista era, who had been recalled from affluent retirement in the emergency.

Pedraza, for lack of a better idea, had sent an armored train to Santa Clara. The train was outfitted with electric kitchens, and carried several of the new British armored cars, four hundred soldiers, a million rounds of ammunition, and provisions sufficient for a two-month campaign.

The general seemed to have the notion that he was directing a pacification campaign among the rebellious savages of some remote frontier. There was, however, some logic to his plan. In theory, at least, the armored train could have served as a mobile fortress, shuttling up and down on the railroad tracks to meet any threat that might be presented.

In practice, it proved to be nothing more than a steel trap for the soldiers inside of it, firing through slits in the armor, and demonstrated as well as anything could the basic flaw of an essentially defensive psychology.

Guevara blocked the tracks near the Public Works building, immediately north of the Capiro district, with several gasoline tank trucks, which would have made a funeral pyre of the armored train had its commander tried to push his way through.

Perceiving the danger, the engineer began to back up, only to find that the track had been destroyed behind him. Armor-piercing machine-gun bullets and bazooka rockets began to burst against the train; it was derailed by a dynamite blast, and Guevara's guerrillas, approaching closer, began to hurl Molotov cocktails against its sides and under it, turning the seventeen armored cars into so many ovens.

The troops, who had refused to leave the train to carry the fight to the numerically inferior rebel force, waved white flags from their firing slits in sign of surrender, were disarmed, and put under guard in the nearby Public Works building.

Their surrender had put a million dollars worth of arms and ammunition in Guevara's hands, and he found willing fighters to use them. Hundreds of members of the Santa Clara militia and other volunteers were armed, and the fight in the streets began, with civilians using their automobiles to make barricades, and women cheerfully manufacturing gasoline bombs, to be thrown from the windows of buildings at the armored vehicles of the police and soldiers.

The railway station was taken, the fortified Gran Hotel, and finally, on the night of December 31st, the police headquarters, defended by one hundred policemen, who surrendered on condition of being permitted to go to the Leoncia Videl Cuartel, pledged not to take up arms again.

The fortress was encircled, and there was no necessity to take it. Santa Clara was *territorio rebelde,* and the island had been cut in half. For all practical purposes, the war was over.

Where was Batista's well equipped and well trained "modern army," so often mentioned by the press? Where was Batista?

On a large electric map of Cuba, an expensive plaything of the generals at Camp Columbia, the lights that marked a thousand military posts and fortresses were being extinguished, one by one.

The officers of the general staff watched them go, first the tiny lights indicating village garrisons and rural guard posts, then the brighter lights, failing one after another, as the big fortresses fell and the hand of revolution spread darkness over the map from east to west.

The lights at Santa Clara flickered and went out, and the generals sighed and turned to their personal affairs, each seeking to salvage what he might.

Some of them, Batista included, had already been so occupied for many days.

On December 24th, the day before the rebels entered Palma Soriano, the regimental commander at Moncada in Santiago, Major General Eulogio Cantillo, made contact with the movement through a priest, and arranged a parley with Fidel. The meeting took place at Fidel's headquarters on a nearby sugar plantation on the 28th, the general arriving in an armored helicopter.

Cantillo indicated that Batista could be persuaded to leave the country, provided he were assured that the army command would be left substantially intact. The offer was flatly rejected. Further discussion, with Raúl Castro, Raúl Chibás, Vilma Espin, and Fidel's assistant and chief advisor, Celia Sánchez, in attendance, produced an agreement under which Cantillo was to deliver the Moncada and Bayamo garrisons, on December 31st.

It is clear, in retrospect, that he had no such intention. Cantillo flew on to Havana, skirting embattled Las Villas, where government planes were strafing and bombing Santa Clara, and joined the generals at Camp Columbia, watching their electric map.

On December 30th, two of Batista's young sons arrived in New York, "for the New Year's celebration," according to their escort.

The Cuban ambassador to the United States, arrived in New York on the following day, returning from consultations in Havana, with the report that, although his government was confident of victory, he gathered from talks with Batista that the president was, to quote the Associated Press, "worried at the growing signs of Communism."

It would have been pleasant for Batista if that had been his only anxiety. On the same day, in response to inquiries made by Senator Wayne Morse of Oregon, the assistant secretary of state for inter-American affairs, Roy Rubottom, Jr., assured a Senate foreign relations sub-committee in Washington that the United States government did *not* contemplate any intervention in the Cuban struggle.

The news bulletins from Havana, following one another in rapid succession on New Year's Eve and on into the morning of the first day of 1959 quoted army dispatches telling of government armored columns smashing through to Santa Clara, the rebels being routed, fierce fighting in progress, thousands on both sides killed, and, finally—"President Fulgencio Batista and his government fled the country today . . ."

All of the lights on the map had been extinguished. What follows is only denouement.

Batista had left his Kuquine estate with his wife and three children shortly before midnight on New Year's Eve. An hour later he was meeting with his military chiefs and political henchmen at Camp Columbia, putting in order the minutes of a final, futile strategy through which to preserve the essential structure of the state. Shortly after two o'clock in the morning he was gone, flying to exile in Ciudad Trujillo.

Behind him he left a worthless document, signed by himself, delivering his executive powers to the senior justice of the Supreme Court, Carlos Manuel Piedra, as "constitutional substitute," and his armed forces to General Cantillo. With him went General Tabernilla, the president-elect, Rivero Agüero, General Pedraza, and, altogether, five planeloads of bodyguards, retainers, and erstwhile military and political accomplices and their families. There is a story, perhaps apocryphal, that Esteban Ventura, the police assassin and torturer, was told that there would be no space for him on the planes. Ventura is said to have drawn his pistol and declared that Batista would have to *make* space, or he, Ventura, would make it with a bullet. True or not, he was among those who flew to Santo Domingo with the deposed dictator.

Some fifty other officers, left behind, commandeered a transport plane and flew to Florida. Senator Masferrer escaped on his yacht to the same haven, abandoning his private army, whose members now went into hiding, and prepared to sell their lives dearly, as many of them subsequently did.

Cuban flags and the red-and-black banners of the 26th of July blossomed across the country as the news of Batista's flight spread. Crowds ran riot in Havana, smashing parking meters, wrecking the gambling casinos, setting fire to Masferrer's *Tiempo* newspaper plants, and briefly battling the police, before M-26 militia appeared on the streets to restore order and prevent looting.

In Las Villas, a rebel column under William Morgan entered Cienfuegos and occupied the Cayo Loco naval base. The Santa Clara garrison surrendered, finally, and Colonel Casillas was caught trying to flee the city in civilian clothes.

Fidel, receiving the news in Oriente, ordered all available

units to march on Santiago, forthwith, and, denouncing the attempted *coup d'état* in Havana on *Radio Rebelde,* called a revolutionary general strike and warned that the *fidelista* military offensive would continue until all elements of the Cuban armed forces had agreed to unconditional surrender, nothing less.

The surrender came almost immediately in Santiago, and the *barbudos* marched in to celebrate a bloodless final victory.

In Havana the Supreme Court refused to administer the oath of office to Justice Piedra as provisional president. Within a matter of hours, army officers flying to the Isle of Pines had released Armando Hart, and with him Colonel Ramón Barquín and Lieutenant Colonel Enrique Borbonet, the heroes of the *Montecristi* plot of 1956. General Cantillo was put under arrest. Barquín, still wearing his prisoner's coveralls, replaced Cantillo at Camp Columbia, but not for long.

In the northeastern part of the province, Camilo Cienfuegos had been held up since December 19th at Yaguajay. The town's approaches to the beach were cut, preventing naval units offshore from landing reinforcements, which they showed little eagerness to do, in any event. The railway and the road above and below the town were severed. A house-to-house battle inside the town began on the 23rd, the two hundred soldiers defending it being driven slowly back. The last diehards of the garrison were not starved out until the 31st.

The army, meanwhile, was sending planes from Camagüey and Camp Columbia in Havana, armed with five-hundred-pound bombs, part of the war materiel purchased from Britain. All of the rebel-held towns around Santa Clara were subjected to heavy bombardment.

Up to this point, the rebels had met no large military force in Las Villas, the largest having been the garrison at

Yaquajay and an equal number of troops, two hundred at Placetas. The objective immediately ahead of them, the vital point at which all roads crossed, was Santa Clara, defended by fifteen times that number.

The Central Highway was secure on both sides of the city. *Directorio* troops under Rolando Cubela and elements of the *Movimiento 26* now moved up from the south to exert pressure on the garrison of the 31st battalion on that side of the city, and "Che" Guevara, who had occupied the University of Santa Clara, came in with the bulk of his force, three hundred men, to the north of the highway, along the Camajuaní-Santa Clara road, circling Capiro hill in the eastern suburbs, where a line of trenches and machine-gun positions had been established, and striking toward the public works building and the railroad.

Fidel, having proclaimed Dr. Urrutia provisional president and Santiago the provisional capital (a brief-lived, precautionary measure), put his captured tanks on huge trailer trucks, and began a triumphal procession overland, across the island to Havana. Dr. Urrutia flew on ahead to form a cabinet.

The rebels from Las Villas were also moving rapidly westward. "Che" Guevara occupied the military fortress of La Cabana. Camilo Cienfuegos, arriving at Camp Columbia, assumed command of the armed forces, including the air force, disarmed the troops, and stationed his bearded riflemen at the gates and in the sentry posts. Barquín was relieved.

Faure Chaumont's DR troops, preceding the *fidelistas,* caused a *contretemps* by seizing arms from an airport and seizing the presidential palace, but with the armed forces in hand, there was no longer any danger of a *coup,* and the problem was quickly settled by negotiation.

Air traffic to and from the States, briefly interrupted, resumed, and the great airlines again moved majestically on the runways at the Rancho Boyeros airport on the edge of the capital; newspapers appeared on the stands again, with banner headlines hailing the liberation, as the business of the nation began to return to normal; several thousand Americans who had fled aboard the Key West ferry began to arrive with the thousands of Cuban refugees flying back from long exile in Miami, Tampa, Chicago, Bridgeport, and New York.

To the reporter flying over the Central Highway to meet Fidel's caravan it seemed that the entire population of the island lined the roads; droves of laughing schoolgirls, reckless of whirling propellers, besieged the plane as it landed on the road, ready to make a fiesta of any incident, and their bubbling pleasure and high spirits was a token of the joy and vast relief of an entire people after seven years of gloom and social blight.

In Matanzas, searchlights played over a cheering crowd that filled the plaza and jammed all streets around the provincial palace until two o'clock in the morning, to hear Fidel shout through a microphone, in a voice made hoarse by a hundred such speeches, the promises and program of the victorious revolution.

In Cárdenas, thousands of people ran through the streets, to follow the rebels on a ceremonial visit to the grave of the student martyr, José Antonio Echevarría; and on the outskirts of Havana, the multitude was so closely packed that it took hours to enter the city, more hours to reach the presidential palace, and it was almost nightfall when the caravan reached Camp Columbia, now called *"Libertad."*

In the general euphoria, every passing vehicle was hailed as though it carried a conqueror. A journalist (whose name was not Hoffman) was startled to hear, among the cries of "Viva Fidel!" a burst of applause and happy shouts of "Hello, Meester Hoffman! *Viva* Wendell Hoffman!" in tribute to the cameraman of the Sierra Maestra, who happened to be elsewhere at the time.

In an unprecedented demonstration of confidence, the gates of the military city, no longer to be known as Camp Columbia, were opened to the people, and that fact in itself, far better than the speeches delivered there, made clear whose fortress and army it was.

The dozen men of the Sierra Maestra had become a multitude. How heart-lifting to hear the deep-throated roar of the crowd, to see the silent barracks, the tanks in array, girls with their arms around the waists of *barbudos,* the searchlights sweeping the field, and Fidel in a flutter of peace doves, released by some inspired publicity man, speaking to "the only troops that I care to command . . . the people."

How easy to understand Camilo Cienfuegos, gaunt, ready to drop with the fatigue of a hundred sleepless nights, but with happiness shining in his eyes, putting his hands on the shoulders of a friend and saying, in almost forgotten English: "We did it! We did it!"

The full extent of their achievement is better understood in facts than in rhetoric. At the hour of Batista's flight, Fidel had, of armed and disciplined fighters in all of Cuba, not more than fifteen hundred.

We did it.
                    —CAMILO CIENFUEGOS

XIII

THE CURTAIN falls, then rises again on a new scene. For a moment, the old Cuba is seen disintegrating, decaying stage properties collapse, the improbably painted actors flee in disorder, and one perceives the artificiality of the old order, which had been thought to be so solid, permanent, inevitable.

It proves to have been none of these things. Military tribunals and revolutionary firing squads sweep away the debris of the dictatorship; some six hundred assassins of the Batista regime, those unable to escape, die in a matter of weeks. Bulldozers raze the walls of Cuartel Moncada and a sunlit school city rises over the dungeons where Abel Santamaría and so many others were tortured to death.

A new Cuba is born, vigorously creative and proudly independent. Fidel Castro's promise of so long ago, "a transformation in the entire order of things," comes to pass so swiftly that the Cubans themselves can scarcely grasp what is happening.

In a word: revolution.

When I first set out to write a history of the Cuban Revolution in early 1959, what I had in mind was no more than the account of a successful insurrection. The foregoing chapters cover the main events and some of the significant details of that struggle. But revolution turns out to be something more important and more complex than any mere struggle for political power. The Cuban Revolution begins, in fact, where the insurrection leaves off.

One cannot pretend to analyze in a chapter the proper subject matter of volumes; but, if the new Cuba is to be understood at all, some attempt must be made to provide at least the outlines of the process by which an insurrection has developed into a revolution—how it happened, and why.

The primary fact to be grasped is simply this: the struggle against Batista was, whether consciously or not, a struggle against the economic and political domination of the United States, the smiling, ruthless Big Brother to the North. *The Cuban Revolution is, above all else, a declaration of independence from the United States.*

Does this come as a surprise to the American reader? Let him consider the pronouncement of a compatriot, uttered half a century ago:

At Theodore Roosevelt's command, the Cuban Republic rose in a night, on soil owned by others than its electors, swarming with a bureaucracy these foreigners and producing natives have had to support ever since. There it stands, tottering and pregnant with militant trouble as was the Trojan horse of old. When it finally collapses to its inevitable destruction, let Americans in hearing the crash recall distinctly that the Republic was not a creation of the *Cubans*—it was neither fashioned by them nor by them upheld—but on the contrary it was of all-American manufacture. Americans built it, Americans set it up when once it fell flat. American influence is all that sustains it at this moment. If they discover anything to criticize in it, or in its failure, let the Americans remember in so criticizing that they are dealing with *the work of their own hands*.

—Irene Wright, 1912.

Carleton Beals, writing about the Machado dictatorship (*The Crime of Cuba*) remarked that the warning above, which he quoted in his great book on Cuba, was "even truer today" (1933) than when it was written. The warning has even greater relevance to the Cuba of 1961.

Cuba has become a new front in the struggle that U.S. journalists like to describe as "the cold war," which now, at last, has reached the Western Hemisphere. The "traditional friendship" between the two countries, to use another politico-journalistic cliché, has been abandoned, if indeed it ever existed. Relations between the United States and Cuba verge on actual hostilities, as the result of a deadly clash both of interests and ideologies, which is no more than to say that a former colony resists colonialism, a satellite seeks to escape its planet, a tenant evicts a landlord, a worker dispossesses his employer; for it develops that what has been destroyed in Cuba is not merely the tyranny of Fulgencio Batista, venal steward of an American plantation, but the tyranny of the Yankee dollar, backed as always by the armed might of the United States of America.

How great, really, was the dominion of the dollar in Cuba? Once one knows the answer to that question, the events of the post-insurrectionary period, the rapid deterioration of U.S.-Cuban relations and the Cuban alliance with the socialist bloc cease to be surprising.

In 1958, fully forty per cent of Cuban sugar production, the mainstay of the economy, was in the hands of United States corporations. Some nine hundred corporations, foreign and Cuban, owned more than one-third of all of the crop land of the island; small farms of twenty-five acres or less occupied only a tenth of the amount of land given over to the great holdings, the *latifundios,* and seven of the ten largest *latifundios* were American, as were the largest and most efficient sugar mills. U.S. investors owned eighty per cent of Cuban public utilities, ninety per cent of the nation's mineral wealth, and, with the British, all of its oil and gasoline production.

Consider what it would be to have half of the U.S. steel industry, ninety per cent of the automotive industry, and most American railroads in the hands of, say, Germany, and Cuba's position will begin to be appreciated.

We have the word of former Ambassador Earl E. T. Smith for it that for all practical purposes the Batista regime, too, was owned by the United States, having scant volition of its own in matters affecting what Washington might consider to be the U.S. national interest. From Smith's own testimony of August 30, 1960, before the Senate Internal Security (Eastland) Sub-Committee:

Mr. Smith: Senator, let me explain to you that the United States, until the advent of Castro, was so overwhelmingly influential in Cuba that, as I said here a little while ago, the American Ambassador was the second most important man in Cuba, sometimes even more important than the President.

That is because of the reason of the position that the United States played in Cuba. Now, today his importance is not very great.

What were the social conditions engendered by the system under which the sugar barons grew richer, the Cuban *campesinos* poorer, and the American ambassador was the second most important man in Cuba, "sometimes even more important than the President"?

Seventy-five per cent of an agricultural country the size of England, with a population half again that of Ireland, was owned by eight per cent of the property holders, a few dozen rich Cuban families and the giant U.S. and Cuban sugar and cattle companies. Tens of thousands of rural Cubans lived in misery on marginal lands, in swamps and in the trackless mountains where their fathers and grandfathers had been driven by the ruthless expansion of the sugar monoculture, which produced sugar to rigid quotas and let millions of acres of land lie fallow to become overrun by brush and weeds.

Cuba's illiteracy rate was conservatively estimated at

thirty-seven and one-half per cent. In rural areas it was far higher than that; a third of the nation's school-age children never attended school at all, and one could go far in the mountains to find a *quajiro* able to write his name.

A million Cuban women and children had never worn shoes; ninety-five per cent of them suffered from the debilitating and often fatal scourge of intestinal parasites in consequence.

Half a million *campesinos* had never tasted milk since babyhood, nor meat in their lives, and five per cent of the total population suffered from tuberculosis.

Where was the sound economy, the prosperous nation, of which Batista's American public relations man and his friends in the U.S. Congress like to boast? The sugar corporations were prosperous. The great cattle ranches were prosperous. The oil interests fattened on their total monopoly, and the great Moa Bay Mining Company, tax exempt, planned to amortize its one-hundred-twenty-million-dollar investment in five years. But who was footing the bill?

Felipe Pazos, head of the Banco Cubano Continental, Cuba's largest private bank under the Batista administration, said that graft on public works alone during the seven years of Batista's rule came close to five hundred million pesos on a total public works budget of less than eight hundred millions. Cost estimates were customarily doubled, and the rake-off apportioned among the thieves. Such practices extended into every aspect of the nation's economic life. The officers of the general staff—Tabernilla and the rest—were notoriously Cuba's greatest smugglers of automobiles, refrigerators, cigarets, whiskey; the police fattened on the brothels and invested their illicit gains in apartment houses; Batista himself received a slice of everything, including the fantastic revenue of the great gambling casinos run by American gangsters—and "the second most important man in Cuba" was the honored friend of these rich and progressive friends of American Big Business.

A report written by Robert Alden in *The New York Times* of January 5, 1958, describes "the agent of the government, the man with the outstretched palm who is the key figure in the large-scale corruption in Cuba":

The owner of a small food store says: "I pay $2 to the 'collector' every time I pull the shutter of my shop up in the morning. I pay $2 when I pull it down at night."

The taxicab driver pays the "collector" $1 for the right to stay at his taxi stand for three hours, and, depending on their volume of business, a precise scale of payment is extracted from each of thousands of street vendors.

In February, 1958, it was estimated in the Report of the Cuban National Council of Economy that nearly twenty-seven thousand Cubans lived on the proceeds of gambling; eleven thousand five hundred on prostitution; five thousand were professional beggars.

The millions lost on the Havana gaming tables lined the pockets of Batista & Company and the mobsters of Las Vegas, Cleveland, and New York. Corporate taxes were low, to stimulate still more foreign investment, and the Cuban *latifundistas* paid more in bribes to the tax collectors than in actual taxes. The tax on an annual income of one million pesos (or dollars) never exceeded ten per cent, and even this was seldom paid. But the middle classes groaned under taxes both hidden and direct; and the urban working classes sweated to pay for imported rice, beans, and canned goods; while the United States enjoyed a trade with Cuba that showed a billion-dollar profit on the U.S. side of the ledger in less than ten years.

Of the total Cuban labor force of 2,204,000, some 361,000 persons were wholly unemployed throughout 1957; 150,000 were employed only part of that time, during the three- to four-month sugar *zafra;* 154,000 worked without pay (for example, as domestic servants earning only their board and lodging). Of the 1,539,000 Cubans who were gainfully employed during 1957, 954,000 earned less than seventy-five pesos a month, in a country where the peso was artificially kept at par with the dollar and had scarcely more purchasing power in Havana than it would have had in New York or Washington.

The nation's free gold and foreign exchange reserves, depleted by raids on the National Bank—i.e., treasury— and the unfavorable balance of trade with the United States, were down to one hundred ten thousand dollars by the end of December, 1958, when Batista fled. (How much he took with him, personally, may never be known.) The revolutionary government was faced with a current deficit of more than fifty million dollars and a national indebtedness of close to one and one-half *billions*.

This was the Cuban Republic, after half a century of United States stewardship. And this, it seems, was the wrong which the *fidelistas* had set out to right. Their task: to extirpate not merely the dictatorship nor the obvious social inequities engendered by a corrupt political order, but the very roots of these things, the twin evils of feudalism and foreign economic and political domination.

Here the trouble begins.

Social reforms might have been acceptable enough to the U.S. interests in Cuba; they would even have been welcomed, provided they did not interfere with profits and did assure political stability. And on the other hand, most Cuban businessmen would have welcomed limited economic reforms in their own favor—measures to curb foreign economic control, to provide greater equity in the trade with the United States, to protect domestic industry, to stem the flight of Cuban capital.

Unfortunately, neither the great Cuban landowners nor

the U.S. sugar and cattle corporations could begin to accept that without which the Cuban Revolution would not be a revolution: agrarian reform.

As previously indicated, considerable apprehension had been felt in Washington, long before Batista's fall, with respect to the radical tendencies of the *fidelistas*. If any hope was held for the preservation of the "cordial"—and profitable—relations that had hitherto prevailed between Washington and Havana, it was the hope that the young and politically inexperienced *barbudos* would find the task of running a government and a complex economy too much for them, and would relinquish the reins to older and more experienced hands—to men like Felipe Pazos, for instance.

For a very brief while, that is what seemed to be happening. The provisional government installed in the presidential palace in January of 1959 was headed by Dr. Manuel Urrutia Lleó, the Santiago jurist, as provisional president, and José Miró Cardona, head of the Havana Bar Association, as prime minister. Pazos returned to his one-time post as president of the National Bank.

The newcomers were inclined, with certain reservations, to give the business and financial interests of Cuba, both foreign and domestic, the cordial and cooperative kind of government, to quote *Fortune* magazine, to which they had been accustomed.

Unhappily for the peace of mind of the men in Washington and Wall Street, not to speak of the Cuban business community, there was still Fidel to be dealt with. Although he remained, for the moment, outside of the new government, he was clearly its master, by virtue of his own superior talents and of his overwhelming command of public opinion.

While the Council of Ministers deliberated, the "maximum leader" of the Revolution made decisions at the public forum, in vast public meetings and before millions of television viewers from one end of the island to the other, anticipating the popular will and subtly directing it into ever more revolutionary channels.

Those who had thought to use Fidel as a cat's-paw—and there were many Cuban businessmen and financiers in this category, whose interests aligned them with economic nationalism but who certainly did not endorse popular revolution—were keenly disappointed to find that he was extending and consolidating his popular support. Those who had thought that it would ultimately be possible to "do business" with the new leader were soon undeceived.

Almost before Fidel had reached Havana, the crash of revolutionary rifles sounded the fulfillment of the *barbudos'* first commitment to the people: the relentless execution of the *pistoleros,* the killers and torturers in and out of uniform who had kept Batista in power for so long. Swift justice overtook fifty such men in Santiago in a single day; bulldozers covered over their mass grave.

A great manhunt was in progress, combing the island for the *esbirros* responsible for the torture and murder of twenty thousand Cuban men, women, and children. One after another, they were brought in, confronted with their accusers, and taken to the *paredon,* the big wall from which no one returns.

The U.S. press, which had viewed the atrocities of Batista, and for that matter the holocaust of Hiroshima, with equanimity, was horrified. Few journalists troubled to inquire into the legal basis of the Cuban war crimes trials, the actual crimes of the accused, the justice of the executions. The fact that the trials were conducted in strict accordance with Cuban juridical forms, based on Roman law and the Code Napoleon, was completely ignored, as was the undeniable culpability of the prisoners, men who had boasted of their crimes rather than concealed them.

It had never occurred to the Cubans that there could be

any question of their moral right to rid the island of a plague. They had understood that they were destroying vermin, and even the Catholic clergy stood amazed by the flood of criticism and abuse that poured out on the news wires of the world.

Nevertheless, an effort was made to show the world that justice was being done. Provisions were made to try the war criminals being held in the fortress of La Cabaña, across the bay from Havana, in the full glare of publicity before the largest possible audience; and hundreds of journalists were flown in from the States and elsewhere, at Cuba's expense, to report the proceedings.

The plan was reasonable enough, but the site was ill chosen, and the motivations of the American press imperfectly understood. The hundreds of U.S. reporters who went to the Havana Sports Palace to attend the trial of Jesús Sosa Blanco, accused of one hundred and eight distinct assassinations and confronted by more than sixty witnesses, came away to write about the "carnival atmosphere" of the trial, with little or no reference to Sosa's crimes, his murderous record, or the victims of his atrocities.

An army of journalists ransacked the island for scandal, and torrents of sensational, adjective-packed prose, more in a few weeks than had been written about Cuba during two years of open civil war, told the Western world that the Republic was marching down the bloody road to totalitarianism.

Members of the United States Congress took up the cry. Senator Capehart of Indiana perceived the "spectacle of a bearded monster stalking through Cuba." Representative Wayne Hays, possibly better informed about the sugar beet industry of his own Ohio than about Cuban affairs, demanded to know what the State Department intended to *do* to "calm Castro down, before he *depopulates* Cuba." *Time* magazine informed its readers that the *fidelistas* were taking revenge on a conquered foe, and listed among the "typical victims" the name of Alejandro García Olayón, the naval officer who roasted six human beings alive in Pilón in 1956, and subsequently supervised the slaughter of three hundred persons in Cienfuegos after the uprising of September, 1957.

The Havana war crimes trials were removed to La Cabaña, and other trials were continued in the provincial district courts of the island. Gradually the press hysteria abated. There was a brief lull in the press campaign.

While it lasted, the provisional government launched a series of long overdue reforms.

Thousands of government sinecures, *"botelas,"* were eliminated, including the subsidies which had been paid, for obvious political reasons, to most Cuban newspapers and to many individual journalists.

A ministry for the recovery of illicitly acquired property was set to work to recover the millions of dollars in cash and more millions in real estate and other holdings stolen from the people during decades past—not merely under the Batista regime but under previous administrations. Hundreds of contractors who had enriched themselves by the "kick-back" system were forced to disgorge their illegal profits; and the vast estates of former government officials were confiscated.

Home and apartment rentals were reduced thirty to fifty per cent, to eliminate the rent gouging that had taken as much as one-third of the income of urban workers. Mortgage rates were reduced to provide relief for small landlords; owners of idle property in urban areas were compelled to build on their vacant lots or sell them to builders, stimulating employment and providing desperately needed space for home and industrial development; gambling, the national vice, was outlawed except in the big tourist hotels, and the national lottery was converted into an investment device to finance a massive home-building program, with each ticket having a small cash surrender value, win or lose.

The tax laws were revised to reduce the number of taxes by about two-thirds and to provide a more equitable distribution of the tax burden. Collections were rigorously enforced, and thousands of tax-dodgers now found themselves paying not only current but past taxes, which they had thought to evade. (Of thirty thousand members of Havana's twelve most exclusive clubs, it was discovered that only six thousand had ever so much as filed tax returns.)

Although there was some grumbling from affected sectors, mainly among landlords whose income had been reduced, the reaction to these first reforms was more or less favorable. The business classes had asked for honest government, and they found to their surprise that they were getting it, "for almost the first time," said Herbert Matthews, "since Columbus discovered the island."

So far, so good, at least on the surface. But this was only the beginning. The revolutionary government had as yet done nothing so revolutionary as to affect the billion-dollar U.S. private investments in Cuba. Now the Americans began to feel the stroke of the new broom, sweeping clean across the Cuban economy.

Government interventors were installed to oversee the affairs of the Compañia Cubana de Electricidad, a $300,-000,000 subsidiary of the American & Foreign Electric Power Corporation, supplying ninety per cent of Cuba's electrical power. After an inspection of the books, the Company was ordered to extend its neglected rural service and to reduce its rates by thirty per cent.

The books of the Cuban Telephone Company, a subsidiary of International Telephone & Telegraph, representing a $115,000,000 investment, were also examined. The rate increases which had been granted by Batista at Ambassador Gardner's behest in 1957 (Batista received a solid gold telephone from the company as a token of appreciation) were abolished; and the telephone company, too, was ordered to improve and extend its notoriously inefficient service.

The revolutionary government had already imposed controls on currency and imports, in an effort to conserve foreign exchange and to restore the lopsided balance of payments with the United States. Within the first few months of 1959, imports were slashed by more than thirty per cent, the restrictions being applied primarily to non-essentials like liquor and the general line of "soft" goods. The effect was, of course, to reduce substantially the profits of U.S. exporters trading in what had been the world's sixth largest market for U.S.-manufactured and agricultural products. Small wonder that *Business Week* and the *Wall Street Journal* believed that the *fidelistas* were taking Cuba down the road to economic disaster.

The worst fears of Washington and Wall Street were confirmed with the signing of the epochal Law of Agrarian Reform, May 17, 1959.

The law, to be administered by a newly created Institute of Agrarian Reform (INRA) with sweeping powers over virtually every aspect of the economy, invoked the provisions of the Constitution of 1940, forbidding the holding of *latifundios,* i.e., more than a thousand acres in a single property.

Holdings beyond the legal maximum were subject to expropriation, the land so acquired by INRA to be distributed among Cuba's seven hundred thousand landless rural workers, with priority to be given to any tenants, sharecroppers, or squatters who might be living on the expropriated property in question.

Each family was assured of a minimum of two *caballerias* (66⅔ acres) *gratis,* and the privilege of buying three additional *caballerias*. The law permitted the transmission through inheritance of such land grants, but forbade their sale, or any form of land speculation. The ownership of cane land by sugar mill owners was likewise forbidden, and so was the ownership of Cuban land by foreigners, this provision applying even to stock companies in which foreigners might hold shares.

Honest examination of the agrarian reform reveals nothing so very radical about it. The legal maximum holding permitted is generous by European standards; even in the United States a thousand-acre farm is a sizable estate.

The Cuban *latifundistas* and their American counterparts were, nevertheless, shocked by the new law, and even more shocked by the compensation which was offered: twenty-year 4½ % government bonds, payable in pesos and *not* convertible into dollars. (A useful comparison is the land reform imposed on Japan by General MacArthur, the compensation there being in twenty-five year, 3½ % government bonds, also non-convertible.)

Although the owners of the great Cuban sugar and cattle *latifundios* had for decades enjoyed extremely low taxation as the result of the minimal evaluations of their property set by themselves, they now were dismayed to learn that expropriation payments would be based on these same evaluations. Their choice: to accept payment at the tax assessment level, or to pay up the taxes which they had evaded through the years by under-evaluating their property.

The American press was prompt to denounce the agrarian reform as confiscatory and illegal. The complaints of the sugar cartel were translated into the language most familiar to the American newspaper-reading public: the land reform program was a Kremlin-inspired plot to destroy free enterprise. In Washington there was talk of reducing the Cuban sugar quota, an idea having particular appeal to the U.S. sugar Senators and the Congressmen of the sugar-beet belt.

The axe fell next on the American mining interests, and then on the foreign petroleum monopoly. A five per cent tax was imposed on all minerals extracted from the ground and a twenty-five per cent levy on all crude ore exported from the country. The oil deposits of the island were brought under the control of the industrial division of INRA, then turned over to a new Cuban Petroleum Institute.

On the political scene, meanwhile, the composition of the provisional government had radically altered. Miró Cardona, a figurehead of the "politically equidistant" government installed by Fidel at the beginning of 1959, had found himself completely ineffective in any real governing capacity as prime minister, thanks to Fidel's own unique way of settling public problems publicly (a procedure which one journalist aptly described as "government by television"). After several half-hearted attempts to resign, he finally stepped down for good in February, and Fidel became his own prime minister, assuming the title to go with the authority that was already his. To quote *The New York Times* of February 22nd:

> The action of Fidel Castro in personally taking over the office of the Premier of the Republic of Cuba reflects his recognition of the fact that the people accept him as their supreme leader. The truth is that they regard him as not only Premier in the Government of Dr. Manuel Urrutia, whom he proclaimed president, but as the very government itself.

Quite so. Nevertheless, the change was significant, reflecting an important consolidation of *fidelista* political leadership.

In mid-April, the new Prime Minister made a visit to the United States that seemed, briefly, to hold promise of improved relations with Washington, although the Eisenhower Administration was cool to the idea of receiving him at all. The crowds that turned out to welcome the Cuban revolutionary leader in Washington and New York demonstrated his popular appeal, and the effect of his various public appearances was generally favorable. But it required more than charm to melt the ice in official circles. President Eisenhower, vacationing in Georgia, did not trouble to see the Cuban Prime Minister, and Secretary of State Herter met him in his hotel rather than at the State Department, to emphasize that it was not an official visit.

Fidel, definitely snubbed, went on to the Council of Ministers of the Organization of American States in Buenos Aires and took the floor to hurl a direct challenge at the United States, calling on the Eisenhower government to live up to the long-forgotten promise of the Good Neighbor Policy by giving Latin America the sort of help that post-war Europe had enjoyed: specifically, direct government-to-government, ten-year loans totaling thirty billions of dollars for the rapid industrial development of the United States' hungry neighbors to the South.

The U.S. delegation shrugged off the proposal as demagogy. Two years later one sees the United States planking down $600,000,000 as the first installment on a considerably less generous but still expensive plan, hedged about with a hundred restrictions in the interest of private enterprise, in a desperate effort to stem the popular unrest born of the Cuban Revolution. (American newsmen describe it as a "Latin America Marshall Plan." South of the border— delicious irony!—it is known as "the Castro Plan.")

Perhaps the policy makers in Washington were deceived by their own propaganda and honestly saw no reason to treat with Fidel, believing that the economic "chaos" which American business insisted was the natural consequence of revolution would swiftly bring the Castro regime toppling down. Later developments suggest that there was, even then, some thought of assisting the toppling process.

As early as January of 1959, *U.S. News & World Report,* one of the most reactionary voices of American business opinion, was inquiring as to the possibility of a dictatorship taking shape in Cuba, and the Associated Press was speculating that the United States might have to intervene to save Cuba from "chaos."

In May, when the outlines of the agrarian reform program became known, there was renewed talk of intervention, to save Cuba not from chaos but from Communism. A vice president of United Press International, Lyle C. Wilson, said that the Communists would "probably" take control of the Castro government, and in such a circumstance he predicted that "the United States would promptly apply force to prevent the Reds from getting a foothold in the island Republic."

At about the same time, the Columbia Broadcasting System produced a half-hour television program entitled, rhetorically, "Is Cuba Going Red?" The answer: Cuba had already been converted into "a Communist beach-head in the Caribbean, only ninety miles off our shores, site of the American naval base that guards our southern defenses, anchor of our defense of the Panama Canal, and key to the future of Latin America . . ." The Hearst press quickly adopted the same line.

The interesting thing about the television broadcast is that it had the unofficial sponsorship of the U.S. Central Intelligence Agency. Whatever the inspiration of the program—and there is some question about this—it is certain that the script was reviewed in advance of its release by CIA chief Allen Dulles, who pronounced it "a service to the American people."

From the beginning, one can trace a rough correspondence between Washington's assessment of the revolutionary regime and the decible level of the anti-Castro campaign in the U.S. mass media. The journalistic image of Fidel Castro varied, even during the struggle against Batista, in direct ratio to the judgment made in American financial and diplomatic quarters of his intentions and capabilities. When he appeared relatively harmless, he was viewed with mild indulgence in the press as a modern-day Don Quixote, armed with a telescopic rifle instead of a lance.

The kidnapping of the U.S. naval personnel in the summer of 1958 came as a shock; the press began to see something sinister in the *fidelistas*. Fidel himself underwent a series of transformations, from the romantic bourgeois hero (supported by the "best elements" of Cuban society), to the potentially dangerous fanatic ("Burn the cane! After Batista we will have a *zafra* of liberty!"), to Senator Ellender's lead of "a bunch of bandits, burning sugar plantations." In 1959 Fidel is a prisoner of the Communists, or a madman, or both. In 1960 his sanity has been restored, but little doubt is left that, in the eyes of the popular press, he is for all practical purposes a Communist, whether with a large or a small "c" makes little difference.

Whatever else it has done, the Cuban Revolution has thrown a revealing light on the interlocking relationship of press, government, and business in the United States, and the subservience of the first two to the third.

Unfortunately, the business approach to foreign relations is often short-sighted. The invested dollar talks, screams when it is pinched; futures are sold short because there is no lobby for them.

Personally, I am inclined to believe that the long-range financial interests of the United States, as well as short-term considerations, would have put Washington at odds with Havana sooner or later; perhaps nothing short of a revolution in the United States itself could change that. The reason is that the Cuban Revolution is not, however much the State Department labors to isolate it, an isolated phenomenon; it is the beginning of a battle, the first manifestation of a movement that threatens the very foundations of American imperialism. Herbert Matthews reminds us of the stake:

About one-quarter of all our exports go to Latin America and one-third of our imports come from the area. United States private investments in Latin America now reach the amazing total of about $9.5 billion . . . At every point it has to be said: If we did not have Latin America on our side, our situation would be desperate. To be denied the products and markets of Latin America would reduce the United States to being a second-rate nation and cause a devastating reduction in our standard of living . . . Latin-American raw materials are essential to our existence as a world power. A friendly Latin America is necessary to our military security.

Having said that much, one must hasten to add that, even so, something might have been salvaged. Something might still be salvaged. The Cuban revolutionaries did not set out with any preconceived notion of establishing a new order in the Hemisphere. They were primarily concerned with their own country, its independence and well-being. Given a fairer shake, they would not have gone so far, so fast. If the United States is now alarmed by the "radicalization" of the Cuban Revolution, it has itself to thank; for most of the radical measures of the Castro regime have been taken in direct reaction to threats from Washington.

As "Che" Guevara put it, in an interview in *Look* magazine, November 8, 1960:

What lies ahead depends greatly on the United States. With the exception of our agrarian reform, which the people of Cuba desired and initiated themselves, all of our radical measures have been in direct response to direct aggressions by powerful monopolists, of which your country is the chief exponent. U.S. pressure on Cuba has made necessary the "radicalization" of the Revolution. To know how much farther Cuba will go, it will be easier to ask the U.S. government how far it plans to go.

How far, indeed?

Diplomatic relations with the Castro regime, reluctantly entered into after a desperate eleventh-hour search for an alternative solution, were rocky from the start. Ambassador Smith was conveniently recalled to Washington, at his own request, shortly before *Bohemia* published a feature article describing him as a "servant of the tyranny." He was spared some embarrassment in Havana by receiving word of the article in advance of its publication.

The hopes kindled by the appointment of Philip W. Bonsal to succeed Smith, Bonsal being a career diplomat and son of a famous journalist remembered in Cuba for his coverage of the Spanish-American War, did not survive his first weeks in the Embassy. Cuban Foreign Minister Raúl Roa privately explained why.

"The first question that he asked me at our initial meeting," according to Dr. Roa, "was: 'What do you intend to do to clean up Communism in Cuba?' "

Roa said he had tried to break the news to Bonsal, gently, that there had been a revolution in Cuba, and that it was now a free and sovereign nation. Bonsal was not representing a government that could accept such an idea. Future meetings were of coldly formal nature, occurring chiefly when the Ambassador visited the Foreign Ministry to present the various notes by means of which the Eisenhower Administration continued to dispute the right of the Cubans to conduct their own affairs. For a time, the notes followed so thick and fast that "Here comes Bonsal to deliver the mail!" became a standard joke in the Foreign Ministry.

The principal demand of the Eisenhower government was for a voice in determining the compensation to be made to U.S. stockholders for the sugar and cattle land to be expropriated under the agrarian reform. (Seizure of the cattle ranches began almost immediately; expropriation of the sugar plantations was postponed, in most cases, until after the 1959-1960 winter *zafra,* so as not to interfere with production.)

Some 17,000,000 acres of Cuba's best land were in the hands of the cattle and sugar companies, foreign and domestic. Much of it had been acquired for virtually nothing; for example, the Bay of Nipe Company, forerunner of United Fruit in Cuba, acquired 122,000 acres in Oriente in 1905 for just one hundred dollars. "Investments" of this sort had paid handsomely. The net profits of the eight largest sugar companies over a seven-year study period came to an average of twenty-three per cent after taxes, and most of the profit was sent abroad, leaving little for Cuba but the miserable wages of a starving army of part-time workers who were fortunate to have employment three or four months of the year.

Washington did not concern itself with this aspect of the matter. It took a dim view of the bonds which the Cuban government offered as compensation, and continued to press for negotiations.

"Notes from the State Department rained on Cuba," said Fidel at a later date.* "They never asked us about our problems, not even out of a desire to express condolence or commiseration, or because of the hand that they had had in causing the problems. They never asked us how many died of starvation in our country, how many were suffering from tuberculosis, how many were unemployed. * * * They demanded three things: speedy, efficient, and just payment. Do you understand that language? Speedy, efficient, and just payment? That means, 'Pay right now, in dollars, and whatever we ask for our lands.' "

Fidel ignored the clamor. He had other problems to solve. The revolutionary reforms quite naturally produced a

* Fidel Castro in the United Nations General Assembly, September 26, 1960.

build-up of potential counter-revolutionary sentiment inside the country; it would be too much to expect to make
a revolution without meeting opposition from affected sectors of the population, the landlords whose income had
been halved, the *latifundistas* whose empires were marked
for expropriation, the outlawed speculators, the disgruntled
bankers and businessmen whose profits had been nipped
by credit and import restrictions, the professional and civic
"leaders" who no longer led, and for whom the Revolution
had as yet found no suitable role.

The first major task of the Revolution, carried out swiftly
and thoroughly, had been to demobilize the entire professional army. A few officers who, although hardly revolutionaries, had helped in the struggle to overthrow the dictatorship, were posted to embassies abroad, as military
attachés, or put to work in military schools. There was no
such easy solution for thousands of non-commissioned
officers and enlisted men, who now joined the army of the
unemployed, and became, in many cases, prospective recruits to the counter-revolution.

Abroad there were the fugitive *batistianos* and *masferristas* in Santo Domingo and in the United States, already
plotting a come-back. And even in the ranks of the Revolution there were malcontents, who had hoped to have a more
important part than the one to which they now found themselves assigned.

There were a number of defections, among them that of
Pedro Luís Díaz Lanz, an airline pilot who had briefly
commanded the Revolutionary Air Force, and who fled
from Cuba in a small boat on finding himself under investigation for alleged peculations involving Air Force
funds. Shortly thereafter Díaz turned up as the star witness
at a televised Washington hearing of the Senate Internal
Security Sub-Committee, presided over by James O. East-

land of Mississippi, who had apparently decided that the Cuban Revolution was a threat to the internal security of the United States.

The substance of Díaz Lanz' testimony was that the Cuban government had been taken over by Communists, from Fidel Castro on down.

The Cubans were infuriated by the hearings, and the slander publicized thus officially by the United States Congress. "Anti-communism" was rapidly becoming a synonym for counter-revolution. The rift between Cuba and the United States continued to widen.

In July, President Urrutia, who had never pretended to be a revolutionary, however much he had opposed Batista (and he must certainly be given credit for the integrity of his stand at the trial of the *Granma* survivors) made the mistake of joining the "anti-Communist" chorus. Urrutia had been dragging his feet on the question of the agrarian reform, allowing dust to gather on decrees that required his signature. When he took occasion to issue a gratuitous declaration that had the effect of reviving the false issue of communism-in-government, the long-pending crisis broke. Fidel met the problem in his own fashion, by taking the dispute to the popular forum. In a three-hour television appearance, he accused Urrutia of "near treason" and announced his own resignation. Before he had finished speaking, Urrutia had resigned. Huge demonstrations called for Fidel's return, and after some slight delay, he resumed his post. Dr. Osvaldo Dorticós Torrado, former president of the Cuban Bar Association, was designated provisional president to succeed Urrutia.

In the interior provinces, the cattlemen were resisting the agrarian reform and, unexpectedly, finding some support in revolutionary quarters. Huber Matos, the *commandante* in command of Camagüey Province, was inclined to go along with those who argued that the Revolution was attempting too much, too soon. In actual fact, Matos was fretting at the relative obscurity of his position: he had considered himself to be a rightful leader of the Revolution, and wished to have a voice in policy making.

In what seems to have been a maneuver to force Fidel to treat with him publicly, he issued a statement offering his resignation and denouncing the "communist influences" in the government, which he said had prompted his decision. He took pains to send copies of his statement to the newspapers, and then settled down in his headquarters in Camagüey to await developments, surrounded by a group of young officers who had, according to report, pledged themselves to resist any effort to oust him.

Fidel flew to the provincial capital to make a personal appearance, and, as usual, his personal authority was sufficient. The threatened resistance evaporated. Matos and thirty of his officers were put under arrest and hustled off to La Cabaña. Matos was subsequently tried for treason, and sentenced to thirty years' imprisonment on the Isle of Pines.

There was a tragic sequel to the plot. Camilo Cienfuegos, temporarily relieving Matos in Camagüey, vanished in a light plane while flying back to Havana in mid-October. Weeks of intensive search failed to find even a trace of wreckage. Presumably the plane had been blown out to sea by a sudden squall.

The *esbirros* in Miami were beginning to spend some money to stir up trouble for the Castro government. During the early autumn there were several air incursions from the North, light planes attempting to bomb sugar mills in Pinar del Río and Camagüey. In October, with an international convention of tourist agents coming to a close in Havana, a twin-motor bomber piloted by the defector Díaz Lanz appeared over the capital to drop anti-Castro pamphlets and a more deadly cargo of anti-personnel grenades. The Havana anti-aircraft batteries opened up. Some of the explosive projectiles, missing their mark, began to burst in the crowded streets of the city. Two Cubans were killed, more than forty wounded. The ailing Cuban tourist industry, which had formerly brought some fifty million dollars annually into the country, was completely killed. Within two weeks a dozen shipping companies had cancelled their scheduled winter cruise stops in Havana. The airlines reduced service. Tourism slowed to a trickle and the great luxury hotels echoed hollowly to the steps of idle employes with no one to serve.

The air raids continued. Millions of *arrobas* of cane burned during the late fall and early winter as the light planes from Florida landing fields made their almost daily incendiary raids on the canefields. The Washington government at first denied that the raiders came from the United States, then blandly explained, after an American pilot had blown himself to pieces while trying to bomb a sugar mill, that with hundreds of small airfields in Florida to police it was very difficult to prevent such flights.

The Eisenhower government was insisting, during this period, that it intended to persevere in a policy of "patience and forbearance" in the face of the "insults" hurled against it by Fidel Castro. Patiently, too, the Administration was doing what it could to make life difficult for the revolutionary government. Cuba was refused normal credits for the purchase of agricultural machinery and other imports of a similar sort, a matter which the State Department could have mended merely by dropping in a discreet word in the right quarter. The sale to Cuba of helicopters and light planes for crop-dusting was banned, on the pretext that they would be used for military purposes. Cuban efforts to obtain European credits and to float a bond issue in western Europe were discreetly blocked by the State Department. The miniscule amount of U.S. technical assistance which the Cubans had been receiving was cut off;

the agricultural inspectors who had facilitated the shipment of fruit and vegetables to the United States were withdrawn. A serious threat to the Cuban economy was posed by increasing talk of a "punitive" cut in the Cuban sugar quota.

Diplomatic relations were strained to the breaking point in early March, 1960, by a disaster in Havana which made the October air raid on the capital seem trivial by comparison. The revolutionary government had blocked the threat of a counter-revolutionary invasion of mercenary and *batistiano* forces from Santo Domingo the previous summer, when two Cuban double agents, Elroy Gutiérrez Menoyo and the American *comandante* William Morgan, lured a planeload of arms sent by Trujillo into a trap in Las Villas, after betraying a group of prominent Cubans who had been privy to the plot. But the situation was still dangerous and Fidel was making strenuous efforts to buy arms and build up a powerful popular militia. U.S. influence prevented Cuba from buying arms in Britain, France, Italy, but the Cuban purchasing mission ultimately succeeded in buying a large quantity of automatic rifles and rifle and mortar grenades from Belgium.

On March 4, the French freighter *Le Coubre,* laden with munitions, was being unloaded on the Havana waterfront when a powerful explosion occurred. Fire broke out aboard the ship, setting off a series of further disastrous explosions. More than one hundred longshoremen, soldiers and rescue workers—the destruction was such that the exact number will never be known—were killed by the blasts.

Fidel indignantly denounced the disaster as sabotage, leaving no doubt as to where, in his opinion, the guilt lay. An airplane was sent aloft to drop some of the unfused rifle grenades on a highway, to prove his argument that the *Le Coubre* disaster could not have been an accident.

As to the perpetrators of the sabotage, he said that it was only reasonable to suppose that those who had tried to induce Belgium not to sell the arms—that is, the United States—would have taken more extreme measures, if necessary, to see that they were not delivered.

Another sharp note from Washington, and another Cuban rejection.

The Cuban response to the State Department's unavowed policy of economic attrition was to apply new and more drastic foreign exchange and import restrictions under a stringent austerity imposed by "Che" Guevara, who had replaced Felipe Pazos as head of the National Bank the previous November. In the end, failing to satisfy their urgent economic and defensive needs in the United States, the Cubans turned "elsewhere"—as Fidel had said would be the case. It is difficult to account for the apparent amazement with which Washington viewed the Havana visit, in February, 1960, of Soviet First Deputy Premier Anastas Mikoyan and the signing of a trade treaty with the Soviet Union.

If there was no reason for surprise, Cuba having no visible alternative in the circumstances, there was some reason for concern. The initial agreement with Moscow committed the Russians to purchase one million tons of Cuban sugar annually for five years, with payment to be partly in cash, partly in credit for things which the Cubans desperately needed—machinery and replacement parts, trucks, tractors, a variety of manufactured products and whole factories, along with the technical assistance to get them running, for the rapid industrialization of a lopsided economy. Among the essentials—petroleum.

One of the key factors in assuring the success of the CIA-directed *coup d'état* against the socialist-oriented Arbenz regime in Guatemala in 1954 had been the threat to cut off the country's gasoline supply. Fuelless Cuba, equally dependent on imported petroleum for the oil and gasoline to operate its transport, power plants, and sugar mills, would have been in the same perilous position without Soviet oil. With it, the danger was removed.

Fidel's original intention had been to diversify the island's petroleum sources, and this is consistent with the effort made with regard to import and export markets for all sorts of other materials. There was no intention of becoming dependent on any one nation for anything.

The three big oil companies which monopolized the Cuban oil market, Esso, Texaco, and Shell, forced the issue in June of 1960 by refusing to refine the Soviet petroleum just then beginning to arrive. The refusal was in outright defiance of a 1938 statute that required the refineries to process all government-owned oil, from whatever source. The Havana government responded by intervening the refineries and forcing them to accept the Soviet crude. The oil companies, motivated by financial as well as political considerations, their profit coming from control of the entire production, from oil field to gasoline station, halted further imports from their Venezuelan oil fields, and the logical consequence was an arrangement by which the Cubans then proceeded to obtain their *entire* supply from the Soviet Union, instead of merely twenty-five per cent, as had been planned.

President Eisenhower, enraged by this development, retaliated almost immediately by jamming a bill through Congress giving him authority to revise sugar import quotas for the rest of the year, "in the national interest." The House Agriculture Committee had already approved (June 1) legislation that would simply have extended the current sugar program for another year. The White House, on learning of the outcome of the oil crisis in Cuba, sent word to Congress that the President was "furious" and "insistent that he have a weapon with which to deal with the [Cuban] situation before Congress goes home." The outcome was a bill giving the President what he asked.

Three days later he cancelled the Cuban sugar quota for the rest of the year, some seven hundred thousand tons, in a cut-off-your-nose-to-spite-your-face decision that only had the effect of driving the Cubans into a closer alliance with the Soviet bloc. Soviet Premier Nikita Khrushchev announced immediately that the Russians would buy the surplus, and, for that matter, as much more sugar as the Cubans might have need to sell. China signed an agreement to buy half a million tons annually for five years. Washington was left to consider the serious problem of how to supply the U.S. eastern seaboard refineries, which were equipped to process cane sugar, but not the beet sugar produced in the West.

Fidel had warned that he would respond to every act of economic aggression with a counter-blow, *"golpe por golpe,"* against what remained of the U.S. investment in Cuba, taking everything, he said, "down to the nails in their shoes."

It was not idle talk. On August 6 he announced the nationalization of the electric power and telephone companies, the oil refineries, and all of the sugar mills in Cuba, save those that had already been taken by the Ministry for the Recovery of Stolen Property. His terms for compensation could be taken as a bitter joke: payment would come from a percentage of the proceeds of all Cuban sugar that might be sold in the United States in the future, *above* the three million tons a year which had been roughly the amount of the Cuban quota.

Washington retaliated October 19 by banning all exports to Cuba with the exception of medicines and foodstuffs, President Eisenhower piously letting it be known that he did not want the Cuban people to suffer. Vice President Richard Nixon's election campaign managers, hoping to capitalize on anti-Cuban sentiment, spread the word that it had been Nixon who had masterminded the export ban. Havana reacted in the manner to be expected and by the end of October nearly two hundred other U.S.-owned enterprises had been nationalized, including the Cuban branches of the American banks, by a series of decrees which, according to *The New York Times* of October 26, "virtually eliminated major investments of United States citizens in Cuba."

The end of 1960 found practically all Cuban industry, whatever its former ownership, in the hands of the Revolution. Small business remained, and the owners had the assurance of the government that they had nothing to fear: the purpose of the Revolution was to eliminate exploitation, not to set itself up in the grocery business.

As it was, the revolutionary leaders had their hands full. The state, acting largely through INRA, had branched out into scores of new industries, manufacturing everything from toilet bowls to frogskin shoes, in the effort to make the island more nearly self-sustaining and to relieve the still critical unemployment problem.

By the end of the year, some two hundred thousand Cubans had been added to the employment rolls. More than six hundred agricultural and fishing cooperatives were flourishing, providing year-round work and permanent homes for the chronically underprivileged rural proletariat. Thousands of former share-croppers, squatters, and tenant farms now held title to their own plots. Sugar production was up, despite a reduction of the sugar acreage in favor of food crops. The Revolution had constructed ten thousand new schools, twenty-five thousand homes, hundreds of miles of new roads. Rural electrification and sanitary projects were proceeding apace. Camp Columbia had been converted into Ciudad Libertad, a vast educational complex, and Ciudad Escolar Camilo Cienfuegos, named after the revolutionary hero, rose in the Sierra Maestra, a tremendous school city designed to house twenty thousand children, as a monument to Fidel's pledge that 1961, Year of Education, would see the end of illiteracy in Cuba.

It was the impression of Columbia University sociologist C. Wright Mills, with whom the author toured Oriente Province in August, 1960, while the former was researching a book on Cuba,* that the Revolution was "over the hump" economically, thanks to the trade treaties with China, the Soviet Union, and other countries both inside and outside of the socialist camp.

To say that it was over the political "hump" would be an exaggeration. Counter-revolution is the other face of revolution; it arises from the social conflict that occurs when one class displaces another in leadership and prestige if not in privilege. The old guard does not surrender easily, and the middle class often suffers from what a Cuban psychologist, Dr. Hans Stettmeier of the University of Oriente, calls "the anticipation of loss," the fear of losing status or the advantage that one had hoped to give one's children.

When the counter-revolution is incited and abetted by powerful forces outside of the country, close to its borders, it is all the more dangerous.

The policy of the United States (it was the policy of the Eisenhower Administration and has been adopted more aggressively by the Kennedy Administration) has been, consistently, to back the counter-revolution, to encourage dissension within Cuba and to seek to alienate her from her neighbors.

Such a policy obviously requires some semblance of popular support within the United States itself. Hence the fury of the press campaign, the alacrity of the Washington government in feeding it, the refusal of the newspapers, on

* C. Wright Mills, "Listen Yankee," McGraw-Hill, 1960.

the one hand, to recognize the existence of any popular sympathy with the Cuban position, and, on the other hand, the determination of the right wing to brand any such sympathy as "Communism."

"Are Red Russian military technicians helping the anti-American Castro Cuban government to build a missile base?" This is an example of the scare technique employed by the Hearst press as early as November, 1959, and references to imaginary "Red" missile bases continue to be heard, although the only foreign base in Cuba is, as anyone can see, the huge U.S. naval base at Guantánamo Bay, which U.S. spokesmen continually threaten to "defend" against hypothetical attacks.

The patent failure of the Eisenhower policy of economic attrition *vis-à-vis* Cuba leaves Washington with the obvious alternatives of accepting the fact of the Cuban Revolution and learning to live with it, or falling back on outright military aggression. As of this writing, there has been nothing to indicate that the moral and intelligent choice has been made. On the contrary, the signs all point in the other direction.

The real danger of the threatened invasion from Santo Domingo in the summer of 1959 was not that expeditionaries could have prevailed against the revolutionary regime, with its overwhelming popular support, but that even the *appearance* of insurrection and disorder might have served as a pretext for intervention.

The same applied to a small-scale landing, led by two Americans, in Pinar del Río in 1959, similar landings on a somewhat larger scale in Oriente and in Las Villas in September of 1960, and a long-drawn guerrilla campaign, strongly supported by air drops of U.S. arms—the list includes hundreds of rifles, scores of machine guns, bazookas, mortars, hundreds of grenades and thousands of rounds of ammunition, even a couple of 57-millimeter recoilless rifles, all factory fresh and of the latest models, obviously drawn directly from military stores—that was finally brought to a successful conclusion by the popular militia in March of 1961.

The guise under which intervention might be made acceptable was first suggested by Hearst columnist David Sentner in the fall of 1959.

The United States must immediately lead a movement by the Organization of American States and the U.N. for the replacement of the Communist-dominated Castro regime in Cuba. Otherwise within six to eight months, many other Latin-American nations will follow the Castro pattern and confiscate all American property.

So predicts Dr. Emilio Nuñez Portuondo, former U.N. Security Council President and distinguished Cuban diplomat . . .

Fortunately, the OAS, while pliable enough under most circumstances, showed no willingness to sanction any aggression against Cuba. An effort by the State Department to obtain OAS "condemnation" of the Cuba revolutionary regime in 1960 was rejected by the Latin-American delegates, who were well aware of the likely popular reaction in their respective countries to such a resolution—and the political peril of it.

The best the United States delegation could obtain at the OAS meeting in Costa Rica was a resolution condemning "extra-continental" (i.e., Soviet) interference in the affairs of the Hemisphere. The action was based on Soviet Premier Nikita Khrushchev's warning that any armed attack on Cuba would be met by Soviet military might and if need be, "figuratively speaking," Russian rockets. It was a sufficiently disturbing threat, whatever Khrushchev might have meant by the phrase "figuratively speaking."

Even so, the OAS resolution was too much for the Venezuelan foreign minister, who walked out of the conference, warning against attempting "to limit democratic liberties under the pretext of fighting Communism." The Peruvian minister also refused to sign. Mexico issued an apologetic disavowal of any intention to single out any specific country or government. The State Department insisted on its own version, maintaining that the "Declaration of San José" was effectively a condemnation of the Castro regime.

The intentions of the Washington government remained to all appearances unchanged. The fact that Cuban counter-revolutionaries, mercenaries for the most part, were being recruited in Miami and trained in half a dozen camps in Florida was an open secret. Reports on the subject, complete with photographic evidence, were carried by the *Miami Herald*, the *New York Daily News*, and other newspapers more as boast than exposé.

Dr. Ronald Hilton, director of the Institute of Hispano-American Studies at Stanford University, published a report based on the well-documented investigations of a reputable Guatemalan journalist, telling in detail of a base in Guatemala to which mercenary forces were being flown aboard American aircraft and trained by U.S. military instructors. The report was subsequently published by *The Nation* and several other periodicals; and correspondents of *The New York Times* and the *St. Louis Post-Dispatch* confirmed these reports, but none of it made much of an impression in the United States. The attitude was, generally speaking, that the Cubans were getting what they deserved, and even Senator John F. Kennedy, the "liberal" Democratic candidate for president, found it politically expedient to propose that the United States do, formally and officially, what it was already doing under the table—lend material aid to the Cuban counter-revolutionaries.

In December new invasion threats, the continued air drops of arms in the mountains of Las Villas, and a wave of incendiarism and small bomb explosions in the Cuban cities caused a marked worsening of relations with the United States. The Cubans were of the opinion, based on intelligence reports and the arrest of several accused U.S. agents, that the material for the sabotage, as well as its inspiration, was coming directly from the U.S. Embassy in Havana.

The Guatemalan government was having its problems, partly as a result of the disclosures concerning the training base for which the American CIA was said to have paid a million dollars. When small-scale popular revolts broke out in Guatemala and Nicaragua, President Eisenhower promptly dispatched an aircraft carrier and six destroyers to patrol the Central American coastline. The show of force was intended to serve warning that popular revolution would not be tolerated in the Hemisphere and that those governments that opted for the "American way" could depend on the armed support of Uncle Sam. A border dispute between Peru and Ecuador brought the blunt warning from Washington that the United States would intervene with troops, unilaterally if need be, to "keep the peace." In December the Peruvian government cynically paid its debt to Washington by abruptly breaking relations with Cuba.

The rupture came simultaneously with a Cuban intelligence report that the Eisenhower government had circulated a message to *all* Latin-American governments, urging that they, too, break with Havana. The report was seen in Cuba as the prelude to outright U.S. military aggression, and the island's entire military establishment, including a civilian militia now more than six hundred thousand strong, was put on emergency alert.

The arms which Fidel had gone "elsewhere" to get now came into view. Soviet anti-aircraft guns appeared on the rooftops and in emplacements throughout Havana. Soviet 105-millimeter cannon were wheeled into defensive positions along the Malecón. The Isle of Pines, a likely invasion target, became an armed fortress. Armed guards appeared before all public buildings throughout the island, and militiamen began digging trenches outside the luxurious Hotel Habana Riviera, where three hundred forty American members of The Fair Play for Cuba Committee were sojourning.

Year's end brought the inevitable rupture. On January 2nd, following a daylong parade of thousands of militiamen bearing Czech submachine guns and Chinese bazookas, following long lines of Russian tanks, armored cars, and six-wheeled Russian military trucks, Fidel announced a crucial decision. All but eleven of the Americans employed in the U.S. Embassy in Havana—precisely corresponding to the number of Cubans allowed in the Cuban Embassy in Washington—were ordered to leave the island within forty-eight hours.

It had already been rumored that Washington was going to break relations. Within twenty-four hours, President Eisenhower responded to the Cuban challenge by severing all relations, diplomatic and consular, and recalling all U.S. personnel. The big Embassy building on the Malecón, employing some four hundred Cubans and Americans, was locked up. A U.S. ban on travel to Cuba, making exception of certain businessmen and "qualified" journalists, soon followed. The last of the thousands of Americans who had once made Havana their home and luxurious playground in the richest of all American colonies packed their bags and prepared to go home. Their going marked the end of an era.

What is Cuba today, and what are the prospects for the future?

Economically, Cuba is a socialist country, the only one in the Western Hemisphere, still undergoing transition, retaining some of the better aspects of private enterprise, gradually modifying others, flourishing and with no major economic problems in sight, despite the U.S. boycott, the expense and distraction of mobilization and military preparations, and the difficulties of diversifying and industrializing what was essentially a one-crop agrarian economy.

To discuss whether Cuba has, in the process of socializing, "gone Communist," is to indulge in a pointless semantic exercise. The Czech submachine guns in the hands of the popular militia and the Soviet tankers docked on the Havana waterfront are the symbols of resistance to the only enemy the Cubans have known: the rich and aggressive "colossus of the North" that made Cuba an American colony and kept it one for half a century. This does not necessarily imply any further political commitment. The Cuban Communists, a numerically small party, are part of the Revolution; they take part in it and share its goals. They do not direct it. Cuba is not in any sense a "Red base." The Revolution is a Cuban Revolution. In a larger sense, it is part of the American Revolution.

A revolution necessarily assumes total power. If it did not, it would not be a revolution; the revolution would not be permitted to occur. Thus the question whether Cuba is a dictatorship is also academic. It is, for the moment, a *popular* dictatorship, and this, too, defines revolution. The important question to be asked must be with respect to the political future of Cuba rather than the present.

A legitimate line of inquiry has to do with what C. Wright Mills speaks of as the orderly transmission of power. Who is to determine what the economy needs, how the nation is to be fed, how it shall educate its children, and a multitude of similar questions? For the present, the Revolution decides these questions. In Cuba, Fidel and the members of his provisional government are the Revolution, subject only to their own integrity and their own interpretation of the popular response to what is said and done in the name of the Cuban people.

No one who has honestly studied present-day Cuba can question that the Revolution is doing what the overwhelming majority of Cubans need and wish to have done. But the truth is that as yet no political forms have emerged through which the authority now vested in the revolutionary leadership shall be transmitted to others. Cuba has been living in a permanent state of emergency—and of social and economic transition—since the first day of 1959. It is too soon to demand clearly defined political forms. They must arise from the needs of the country and develop naturally in a manner consistent with their social and economic base; they cannot be artificially or arbitrarily imposed. The whole experience of the Cuban Republic, an unsuccessful American graft on a foreign culture, demonstrates that.

What forms will evolve remains to be seen. The best assurance for the future comes from the observation that the base is being constructed solidly. The economic democracy, the social justice, the equality before the law which any notion of democracy demands have been established beyond all question in Cuba. One sees no reason to doubt that the political forms of the future will be equally democratic and just. To ask whether they will be "Communist" is at this point meaningless cant.

The better question to ask might well be—what is the future of the United States? The unreasoning commitment to the profit motive to the detriment of all other objectives is and should be cause for grave concern. There is no sign that it has given way to any more enlightened policy—as far as one can judge from the Cuban case—since the business government of President Eisenhower was succeeded by the "liberal" Democratic government of John F. Kennedy.

On the contrary and sadly, Kennedy has adopted the

Eisenhower policy as his own. U.S. planes from U.S. bases continue to drop U.S. arms into the mountains of Cuba. American P-T boats from American ports deliver counter-revolutionary cargos to Cuban shores and shell the Cuban oil refinery at Santiago. Kennedy himself says that there is no thought of restoring relations with Cuba, and offers massive bribes to those Latin-American countries which do not follow the Cuban path. The great liberal leader, Adlai Stevenson, heading the U.S. delegation in the United Nations, says that he will not speak with the Cuban delegation. And Chester Bowles, now a member of the Kennedy foreign policy team, discreetly forgets the warning that he voiced in 1959:

> Above all, let us not lose sight of the essential issue. The real choice in Latin America, as in Asia and Africa, is citizenship or serfdom, hope or despair, orderly political growth or bloody upheaval. Our failure to understand this choice, or to support the vital new elements which are striving to assert leadership, would be catastrophic.

To end on this note would be to leave the reader with a sense of hopelessness and futility, feeling that—well, here is a new outcropping of the dismal old "cold war," and what can *I* do about it, after all? One sometimes has that sense of despair on reading the cold facts of international politics, stripped of their human content.

But there is, after all, some hope. It lies precisely in the *human* quality of the Cuban Revolution, in the fact that the Revolution has been made not by parties or movements but by individual human beings, in all their living, breathing variety. The Revolution retains what the Cubans call *"pachanga,"* their own special kind of gaiety which is heard in their music and seen in the way they smile and talk and walk, in the pride of their accomplishment and the pleasure they find in being alive.

The huge mass meetings, which the foreign press describes as "hate" rallies, are anything but grim. The people laugh and clap and invent new slogans to go with old rhythms—at Christmas there was one sung to the tune of "Jingle Bells" that went, "With Fidel, with Fidel, always with Fidel . . ." Vendors sell tiny paper cupfuls of black, sweet Cuban coffee in the crowd, mothers bring their babies, and the atmosphere is one of fiesta. One sees a ferocious-looking *rebelde* with a magpie's nest of a beard, carrying a submachine gun and armed with a tremendous revolver as well. From the pocket of his shirt protrudes a huge harmonica. His companion, equally hairy and ferocious, is eating an ice-cream on a stick, and grinning cheerfully while Fidel, with the same good humor, lectures an old man in the crowd who complains that he has not yet been given a cow, although the latest voluntary program promises a cow for every *campesino* family.

Despite the problems that still confront the Revolution, the very grave danger that threatens not only Cuba but all of us, should the friction between Havana and Washington ignite the spark of a shooting war, and all of the fears and doubts relating to an unforeseeable future these are the impressions that the visitor to Cuba takes home with him: a bearded soldier grinning and eating ice cream, young girls self-conscious and proud in their militia uniforms, marching, families that lived last week in palm-thatched one-room *bohios,* unable to believe that the shining new tile-floor homes that they now live in are really theirs, and an old man who wants to know about his cow.

It is a Revolution with *pachanga.* The people like it. They are prepared to defend it. One feels that it is here to stay, and more, that it represents the future for the people of what Mills calls "the hungry-nation bloc," all over the world.

The Cubans were hungry. Now they are feeding themselves. They were degraded; now they are proud. They were exploited, now they are free, and they burst with pride about that.

As Camilo told me at Camp Columbia, long ago: "We did it!"

Index